# DON'T DROP THE COFFIN!

# DON'T DROP THE COFFIN!

Lifting the lid on Britain's most
remarkable undertaker

Barry Albin-Dyer
with Greg Watts

Hodder & Stoughton
LONDON SYDNEY AUCKLAND

First published in Great Britain in 2002

10 9 8 7 6 5 4 3

British Library Cataloguing in Publication Data
A record for this book is available from the British Library

ISBN 0 340 78664 7

Typeset by Avon Dataset Ltd, Bidford-on-Avon, Warks

Printed and bound in Great Britain by
Clays Ltd, St Ives plc

Hodder & Stoughton
A Division of Hodder Headline Ltd
338 Euston Road
London NW1 3BH

To my sons Simon and Jonathan. As you pick up the historical mantle of F. A. Albin, guard well its honour but enjoy its gifts. Rule it – don't let it rule you. Together you will be invincible.

To my beautiful granddaughter, Olivia, and all my future grandchildren. My wish is for you to be happy.

# CONTENTS

# PREFACE

For many years I have wanted to write a book about my life as a funeral director. It finally came about with the help of journalist Greg Watts, who, over many hours of interviews in my office, managed to draw out my memories and thoughts. At times it was exhausting but I can honestly say that it has all been worth it. In order to protect confidentiality, some names and places have been changed.

There have been many people who have helped to shape and influence my life and, unfortunately, there isn't space to list them all. But I would like to particularly acknowledge my family, friends, staff, past and present, at F. A. Albin & Sons, The Wednesday Society, the polytechnic football club, all the wonderful people of Bermondsey and those inspiring people I have met on my travels around the world.

*Barry Albin-Dyer*

# FOREWORD

Barry Albin-Dyer is a great friend of mine and his family are, and have been for years, one of the great Bermondsey families. I am privileged to have been their Member of Parliament for nearly two decades. And a long time ago I decided that when I, like the rest of us, come to the end of my time on this earth, nobody would do the necessary formalities better than Albin's. Book early to avoid disappointment.

Just as a good wedding can make even the most awful relationship seem blessed and full of potential, so decent and dignified dealing with death, disposal and public commemoration of the departed can bring to a wonderful end not just the saintly life but the lives of the rest of us sinners as well.

As I think back over many local tragedies – the death of the penniless alcoholic, or the fourteen-year-old footballer full of promise, or the murdered father of six – the overwhelming memory is of the incredible love, care and attention given by Barry and his family firm. Every last moment of every last day and last journey have made every funeral an event to remember with comfort, hope and pride. Literally, in death all human life and decency are there. Albin's have given after-care a whole new meaning.

If contracts for funerals were awarded on merit and quality, Albin's would be funeral directors all over the world. As it is, we are proud to have them based in Bermondsey and Rotherhithe, but now doing funerals for the richest and poorest at home and abroad.

This book will help to explain why many of us love our tumultuous corner of south-east London so much, and why it is a place of such character and such commitment. It is families like the Albins and the Dyers who have made it so. And if ever you needed persuading of the merit of the small family firm, or of a career in the funeral industry, this book should do it.

Barry Albin-Dyer has told his life and death story. It is a story wonderfully worth telling. Even those without faith in a god should finish this book with greater faith in at least some of our fellow human beings. Countless people will be grateful for this great book – and never see the prospect of death in the same way again.

*Simon Hughes*
*MP for North Southwark and Bermondsey*

# INTRODUCTION

When my three-and-a-half-year-old daughter Rachel was
dying of leukaemia, my parish priest, Fr Alan McLean,
wisely suggested to Rachel's mother and I that we think
about making plans for her funeral. And that was when I
first met Barry Albin-Dyer, although, like everyone in
Bermondsey and Rotherhithe, I knew of him and had seen
him, in his top hat and carrying his wand, walking funerals
through the streets of south-east London. 'Barry will help
you through all of this,' said Fr Alan.

Rachel breathed her last one Saturday afternoon, in
Chatham, Kent, where she lived with her mother. She had
defied the doctors and nurses who had predicted that she
wouldn't last until Christmas. However, eventually her frail
body packed up. I phoned Barry with the news and within
the hour he was at the house, accompanied by Jackie, his
office manager. Sitting in the back of Barry's car, I cradled
Rachel in my arms during the journey to Albin's funeral
home in Bermondsey.

Barry and his team provided wonderful care, advice and support both in the weeks before the funeral, during it and after it. What stands out for me is that Barry wanted the funeral to be in accordance with the wishes of Rachel's mother and I. The Requiem Mass at the Church of the Most Holy Trinity, Dockhead, was a celebration of Rachel's short life. Afterwards, in a tiny white coffin, with some of her toys, Rachel was taken from the church to the cemetery, not in a hearse but in a limousine. Barry sat in the front, Rachel's mother and I in the back, with the coffin across our knees.

That was in January 1996. Over the next few years, I saw Barry occasionally, either at church or on one of the estates in Bermondsey conducting a funeral. Then, after Mass one morning in 2000 I got chatting to him about writing. He told me he wanted to write a book about his life as a funeral director. The following week we met for lunch at a restaurant beside the Thames and, after discussing what kind of book he might write, I agreed to help him pull together his memories and stories.

Neither of us at that stage knew how successful our working relationship would be. When I began to turn up at Barry's funeral home each week armed with my tape recorder and A4 pad I, like most people, knew very little about the life of a funeral director and, if I'm honest, I wondered how anyone could enjoy such seemingly gloomy work. After a few sessions with Barry I found myself thinking what an extraordinary man he was. He had done so much in his life, and not just in the funeral industry. There was his involvement in football, his other business ventures and his travels around the world. Over a period of time, a book began to take shape, not as an autobiography, which was the original plan, but as memoirs.

Soon, I was looking forward to my meetings with Barry. He had such a fund of stories, was so passionate about his work and his corner of south-east London, knew everything there was to know about funerals, and also was never short of humorous observations and classic one-liners. For a writer, he was a gold mine of material. During these many interviews I wondered at times if I was taxing him too much with my questions and search for the small details. Why do exhumations always take place so early in the morning? Why are caskets so popular in America? Why did the cortege stop outside that pub on the Old Kent Road? Which cemetery was the fight at?

I also witnessed the high standards F. A. Albin & Sons operate. A confessed perfectionist, Barry says in the book that perfection is all about getting the small details right. Indeed, I would say that if anyone wanted to know how to run a business that was both successful and maintained the highest ethical standards, then they should pop along to the funeral home at Culling Road. The secret of Barry's success is not only how he treats the families who come to him at their most vulnerable moment but also how he treats and motivates his staff. His firm, with its daily staff breakfasts in the kitchen, really does feel like a family.

So, here is *Don't Drop the Coffin!* It will, I hope, provide a glimpse into the workings of the funeral industry and into the world of a long-established south-east London undertaker and provoke thoughts about not just death, and the rituals and practices that surround it within different cultures and belief systems, but also, just as importantly, how we live our lives.

*Greg Watts*

# 1

# DOWN AMONGST THE COFFINS

I did my first removal at the age of eight, that of an elderly gentleman, with a thin moustache and wearing grey socks and long johns, in St James' Road. My dad told me that carrying a coffin had to be done in a certain, dignified way, explaining that the bearers were split into 'footmen, headmen and those who will fit anywhere'. One of the first golden rules he drilled into me was, 'Whatever you do, DON'T DROP THE COFFIN. You can hit the floor but the coffin must never.' On one occasion, at a house in Hamilton Square, when he was coming down the stairs the coffin slipped and he put his hands out to stop it hitting the wall, damaging his fingers in the process. Despite the pain and the blood dripping from his glove, he still drove the hearse to the cemetery. He protected that coffin. I've never forgotten that.

F. A. Albin's have been involved in funerals in Bermondsey, south-east London, since the late eighteenth century when, I believe, they were wardens of a cemetery.

They are one of Britain's oldest independent firms of funeral directors. When I was very young, Albin's had four funeral shops, as they were known then, in Bermondsey, first in Snowsfield and then Jamaica Road, Lewisham, Downham and Leytonstone. My dad was the senior manager. Fred, Ernie and Arthur Albin were the joint owners.

I often say to people that I was conceived a funeral director. I was born at Guy's Hospital, next to London Bridge Station, on 2 February 1951. Even though my family name was Dyer, at school I was always known as 'Barry from Albin's' and, later, when I began to do work for the Iranian Embassy they called me at various times 'Albin', 'Barry Albin' or 'Mr Barry'. Many people assumed my dad was Fred Albin's brother and consequently I was the young Albin.

When I purchased F. A. Albin & Sons in 1986 I decided to use the name Albin as a way of maintaining a continuity with the Albin family. Fred was like a father to me anyway. It's not that I'm not proud of being a Dyer. I am. Dyer, though, isn't perhaps, the best name for a funeral director. My sons Simon and Jonathan, who have followed me into the business, call themselves Albin-Dyer because people have also called them Albin. Calling myself Barry Albin is only a bit like using a stage name. Increasingly nowadays I call myself Barry Albin-Dyer. But I consider myself a blood line funeral director because the Dyers, distant members of my dad's family, were funeral directors in east London.

During my childhood, Bermondsey and its neighbour Rotherhithe were a bustling docks area, recovering from being severely bombed during the Second World War. Ships from all over the world would sail up the Thames, bringing wood, sugar, spices, bananas, ivory and all manner of products, which would then be unloaded, stored in the wharves and eventually transported across Britain. Many of the families had some sort of connection with the docks, as did my grandad.

In those days, Bermondsey was home to some of the country's leading manufacturers and almost every street seemed to have its own smell: custard (Pierce Duff), vinegar (Sarsons), jam (Hartley's), chocolate (Lindt), shortcake (Peek Freans) and tea from the warehouses alongside the river. These were pleasant aromas, but the smell from a perfume factory in Grange Road was absolutely awful and I had to hold my nose each time I walked past. Bermondsey was a mainly poor, hard-working, tight-knit community where people looked after each other. 'We was all one' is the local saying.

I have lived most of my life in Bermondsey and Rotherhithe. My first home was in Weston Street, a few doors from Albin's garage. When I was five we moved to Tranton Road, where we lived above the chapels of rest in a former dairy. Later, we lived above the F. A. Albin & Sons shop at 62 Jamaica Road. Then, after I was married, I lived with my wife and sons in the flat above our present Culling Road funeral home. Today, I live in a house by the river in Rotherhithe.

My most vivid memories of the funeral business are derived from the shop on Jamaica Road. On the wall at the rear of the shop, facing the London Bridge to Kent railway line, were the words, 'F. A. Albin & Sons. Funeral Directors. Burials and Cremations. Embalming Available' written in black letters on a white background. I was frightened of death in those early days and my friends at school wouldn't come around to play with me because I lived in a funeral home. I admit there were times when I was very lonely, especially as I was an only child.

When I went to see my nan at her flat by the Bricklayers Arms, she would pull a face and say, 'Barry, give me your clothes – I can smell death on you.' This, I have learnt since, was due to the smell of timber and French polish on my clothes. On the other hand, there is also a taste of death. This happens when you inhale a lot of the gas of a deceased person.

Back then, F. A. Albin's work was carried out on four sites: the shop on Jamaica Road, the chapels of rest in Tranton Road, and the garage, where we kept our hearses and limousines, in some railway arches on Southwark Park Road. Embalming was carried out by the mortician at Guy's Hospital. This is a long way from our modern, all-in-one, two-storey funeral home, complete with state of the art mortuary, at the end of Culling Road, a cul-de-sac close to the entrance to the Rotherhithe Tunnel. Southwark Council once erected a 'Dead End' sign, but when they realised what they had done, they replaced it with 'No Through Road' (whichever, there's no way out!).

At the age of nine I was given a summer holiday job at Albin's. I'd clean the cars, learn how to make stillborn baby coffins in the workshop, put the mouldings on adult coffins, and French polish them with linseed oil. The final polishing was done in the front of the shop in full view of the customers. I'd be there in my apron, polishing away. There was a magical old glove that must have been with the firm from the earliest days. It was rock hard. French polishing was very difficult. If I made a mistake with the final brushing, I would have to wait for it to dry, then sand it off and start again.

As a teenager, I had toyed with the idea of being a photographer, policeman and professional footballer (I played for Crystal Palace schoolboys and later went on to play at non-league level), but I don't think there was ever any doubt that I would end up working for Albin's. The moment when I knew I wanted to be a funeral director came when, in the middle of the night, I went with my dad to the mortuary at Guy's Hospital to collect a deceased man and take him to Moorfields Eye Hospital. His eyes were to be used to help give someone else sight. We were given a police escort from Guy's. It was incredibly exciting and dramatic, speeding through the traffic, and it felt like we were on a life and death mission. And this was when I discovered my vocation.

Since then, sitting in the hearse on a cold, wet day in a cemetery, with the rain trickling down the windows and windscreen wipers going da-da-da-da da-da-da-da, I have often reflected that this is where I belong. It's a melancholic feeling, and one that goes to the core of who I am.

When I left school and started working full-time for Albin's, my first job in the morning was to polish the brass on the front of the shop door. I would also make buttons, small round pieces of oak wood that covered the screws in the side of the coffin. As a child, I used to sit down on a board and put little nails into the buttons, which were then polished before being tapped into the coffin. Because of the tedious nature of the work, I used to pretend they were soldiers and have battles with them. There would always be a smell of linseed oil from the coffins. I used to hate having to carry the timber that we used to make the coffins; not because of the heavy lifting involved but because of the stag beetles that I would often find. They were awful looking insects and I used to constantly put my hand down the back of my shirt to make sure there was none of them there. My dad and Ernie Albin used to give me one and six pence a week for these jobs.

A plumber used to come in to seal the metal coffins for deceased persons who were going to be shipped abroad. I was standing beside him one day watching as he sealed the coffin of a man who was being sent to Israel. I was fascinated, both by the thought that this coffin would never ever be opened and also by the fact that it was bound for the land of Christ. When he sealed the coffin, I realised that my tie had become trapped. I panicked and for one brief moment I thought that I was going to have to go to Israel as well. 'Dad! I'm trapped,' I cried. 'Don't worry, son,' he replied calmly and, taking a pair of scissors, snipped off the end of my tie. 'You're going nowhere.'

From an early age I had developed a knack for laying deceased people out. I learnt how to apply make-up and do their hair. I also learnt that the round wrappers from inside a box of chocolates could be used to support the eyes of a deceased person and prevent them from sinking. I used to cut out the round holes from the inside of the Maltesers boxes and do the same with them. And when, in the early 1970s, Albin's bought Knox's, another Bermondsey funeral firm, Mrs Knox, who like me was known by the name of the funeral directors she worked for, always insisted that I lay the bodies out.

When a client came in to book a funeral it would be done in the tiny office. On the floor of the office was a rug. After the family had left, I would be called in, the rug pulled back, a little trap door lifted up and I would be lowered down into the dark cellar below, where the coffins that were three-quarters finished were standing. I would have to take one of the coffins and push it up through the hole for it to be French polished. If someone came in while I was down below, the trap door would be closed and the rug would be pulled back over the hole and I would have to wait for the family to go. But sometimes Dad and Fred would forget I was down there. When this happened I had to find my way through the darkness of the cellar and up the stairs to a locked door, which had coffins stacked in front of it. I would then bang loudly on it until someone heard me.

The name plates for the coffins were done by hand on a little wriggling board. We used to use Windowlene over the top of the plates and then draw lines with a ruler. I wasn't very good at this but people like Fred Albin, my dad and especially Stanley Albin were amazing. We would write the name in old English across the Windowlene and then take a little chisel making little grooves. Then that plate would be cleaned and put in the window so that people could see who had died recently. Alongside that was a board on to which were pinned letters of thanks from families whose funerals we had carried out. In the window there was also a blue clock lit by an ultra-violet light. Passers-by would use this to make sure they were on time.

I used to enjoy accompanying Fred Albin when he went out to sell memorial stones. Trailing around after him in my suit and carrying a bag, I was a bit like a miniature Fred. He had his own sales patter with families. Sitting down and opening his case, he would begin, 'Now, there are two types of stone you can have. You can have Italian Carrara marble, from the quarries of Carrara. It's the only true marble and it has a grey vein in it. It's a bit softer than granite, but it will last a long time. The other is Scottish granite, highly polished. It cleans itself and will last forever. The letters are gold leaf. Now, you cannot carve granite. It is sandblasted.' At this point he would always produce a photo of boxer Freddy Mills' headstone, before continuing. 'There are two parts to an inscription. There's a factual inscription, which always starts with a heading: in loving memory of, in cherished memory of, in devoted memory of. Then you say who the person was: a dear wife, or father. After that comes the name and a prefix: who died, fell asleep, departed this life, passed away. Then come the date and their age. This is a factual inscription. Now underneath this . . .' He would pause here, 'but not taking up too much space, you can have a verse, a prayer or some words with a special meaning.'

When I was nineteen I conducted my first funeral, that of a little girl, in Brixton. Having acted as a bearer and a driver on numerous funerals, Fred felt I was now ready to take the lead role. I was thrilled.

In those days, Fred and Ernie Albin set the rules for a funeral. When people used to come into the shop and say 'We've lost mum,' they would be told, 'The funeral will be next Wednesday. We'll meet at 8 a.m. at your house and the service will be at so and so church at 9 a.m.' The families were grateful and would reply, 'Thank you, Mr Albin.' They just accepted that the funeral director, like the doctor and the priest, knew best. And Fred and Ernie were just following the tradition of taking charge. Of course, today people have more choice when they book a funeral.

When Tuesday morning came, my excitement was tinged with nervousness. Fred went over the various tasks that I had to do as a conductor; not that he needed to though, as

I had watched him brilliantly conducting funerals on countless occasions. He took out his well-thumbed A–Z and ran his finger over the route. We carried the small coffin out of the chapel of rest and placed it in the hearse. Just as I was about to leave, Fred said, 'If you have any problems phone your dad in the office. Oh, and by the way, the family are West Indian.'

This was 1970 and Bermondsey was quite a closed community with many people living and dying there without ever having left its boundaries. I had little experience of other cultures, apart from an Indian man in a turban, who used to come round selling ties out of a suitcase. The only West Indians I had met had been bus conductors, hospital porters and nurses. Brixton, like neighbouring Peckham, had a large West Indian community, but Bermondsey was still mainly white, with a well-established Irish population. I wasn't sure what to expect. Little did I know that I was about to be taught one of the most important lessons I was ever to learn as a funeral director – and as a human being.

We arrived at the house, in a smart street of semis off Brixton Hill, at 12.55 p.m., five minutes early. We had been booked into the chapel at Streatham Park Cemetery at 1.45 p.m. I noticed a phone box across the street, but I didn't think I would need to phone Dad. Getting out of the car and walking up the path, I felt very proud to be the person in charge of the funeral. My nan had given my shirt an extra iron that morning, washed my white baby funeral gloves and spent half an hour brushing my suit. Dad told me that when I arrived at the house I was to go in and take the family straight to the cemetery for the service, bury the child and then return to the funeral home.

9

'Hello, I'm Barry from Albin's,' I said to the well-built man who answered the door. 'Are you Sophie's father?'

He nodded.

'Do you have any floral tributes before we leave for the cemetery?' I asked. From inside of the house I could hear the sound of mournful gospel music and a smell of food filled the air.

'I have just one flower,' he replied. 'Bring my daughter in, please.'

'I'm sorry I can't,' I told him apologetically. 'My dad says we are not allowed to.'

'Bring the child in. We're waiting,' said the father, pointing to the hearse.

'I'll have to phone my dad and see what he says. That's not part of the arrangement. Excuse me a moment.' I walked briskly down the path and hurried across the street. The men with me were wondering what the problem was. I waved my hands to signal that everything was fine.

I fumbled for some change and dialled the office. I heard my dad's voice at the end of the phone.

'Dad, the family want me to bring the child in. What do I do?'

'Never mind that, son. You just tell them that you have to go straight to the cemetery. They'll be fine.'

'Okay, Dad,' I said, not entirely convinced, having seen the determination on the father's face.

'My dad says that we have to go to the cemetery.' I explained when I returned to the house.

'No. Bring our child in the house. We're not going to the cemetery until you do that,' said the father emphatically.

'I'm sorry, but I can't. My dad says . . .'

'Bring the child in.' He was starting to look angry.

I stood there, not knowing what to do and feeling a little bit frightened of the responsibility on my shoulders. There was no way I was going to fail at conducting my first funeral. Fred and Dad had put their faith in me. Yet the family were grieving and I didn't want to make matters worse for them. But how could I resolve the situation?

'I'm sorry. I'll have to phone my dad again.'

He didn't look pleased and went back inside the house. I explained to the men what the delay was and ran across the road to the phone box. 'Dad, the family won't have it. They say I have to take the child in, or they won't leave for the cemetery.'

My dad paused and then said, 'Very well. Take the child in.'

Relieved, I ran back to the house. The father brightened when I told him that my dad agreed. 'Good, I'll bring the coffin in then.'

'Oh no, you can't do that. We have to do that.'

He scowled at me and repeated, 'I'll bring the coffin in.'

I didn't want to get into another argument with him, nor did I want to go and phone my dad again, so I told him I would help him carry the coffin into the house. I was anxious about being late at the cemetery. It was now 1.20 p.m.

The father placed the coffin on a table in the front room, which was full of mourners, eating and drinking. Then he told me he wanted to undo the lid and that they wouldn't leave for the cemetery unless they could see the child's face. I didn't know what to do. It seemed a reasonable request. So I went back to the phone box.

This time Fred picked up the phone. 'Alright, son. Calm down. Let them take the lid off then. But on no account are they to touch the child. That's unheard of.'

I went to the hearse and took the old wooden screwdriver out of the glove compartment and returned to the house. As I unfastened the lid and took it off the family backed away, screaming. Then, to my amazement, they came back over to the coffin and began singing to the child. I stood there, taking it all in and thinking that this was marvellous. The father placed some toys, an apple and a coconut into the coffin and then motioned me to screw the lid back on and said they were all ready to leave. The mourners filed out of the house and then I led the bearers down the path. That strange, deep silence you get at funerals descended as we slid the coffin into the hearse.

I checked my watch as we drove through the cemetery gates. It was just after 1.45 p.m. Hopefully, the cemetery superintendent wouldn't be awkward and tell us that we had to wait. He came out of his office, making tut tut sounds and pointing to his watch.

'Are we okay?' I asked.

'Are you conducting, young man?' he asked in a serious, patronising tone.

'Yes. It's my first time.'

'I see. Well, Fred and your dad will have told you never to be late at a cemetery, I'm sure of that.'

'They have. It's just that we had a few problems at the family's house.'

'Alright. Off you go.'

Following the short service in the chapel, we drove over to the grave at the far end of the cemetery. As we were lowering in the coffin and the minister was reciting the prayers, the father said that he and his family were going to fill in the grave.

'You can't do that. That's our job,' I said.

After some negotiation, two men picked up the shovels and began filling in the grave. By now I realised it was futile to say anything. This was the way they wanted the funeral to be. What right had I to tell them they were wrong? I could see that while Fred and dad were excellent in the way they conducted a funeral – professional, dignified, caring, they were doing it in accordance with their tradition. I saw for the first time that in the future some traditions would need to be changed and that a funeral director had to be more flexible.

When I arrived back at the shop and told my dad and Fred about the funeral and how I felt it was right that the family's wishes should take precedence, Fred shook his head. 'You're making a rod for your own back, Barry. Believe me.' But as I went upstairs I heard Fred say to my dad, 'George, he's learnt a lot today. And we should be proud of him.'

Fred was right, in one way. Allowing the family to have a say in the way a funeral is conducted does make life more difficult. But I could see that by inviting the family to make decisions over the kind of funeral they wanted for their loved one, the day would be that extra bit special and those present would remember it for many years to come. From that point on, the way Albin's conducted funerals began to change, because times were changing, and my philosophy as a funeral director was formed.

## 2

## IT'S YOUR FUNERAL

Driving into a Bermondsey council estate in the hearse one
Monday morning I could tell something wasn't quite right.
A woman in her late twenties was leaning over the balcony
of a fourth floor flat, shouting and screaming at some of
my mourners in the flat below. As I got out of the hearse, a
bottle smashed a few feet away in front of me. I didn't
know what was going on, but whatever it was it was serious,
I concluded, as I headed quickly for the bereaved family's
flat.

'What's happened?' I asked one of the sons when I
reached their flat.

'She's a nut case!' he retorted, leading me into the living
room, where a number of the family were sitting. 'Her
brother let off some fireworks in the chute and I went and
had a go at 'im,' continued the son angrily, pacing up and
down. 'And then she starts. She's asking for it. What does
she expect if he doesn't show respect? This is our funeral.'

'Yeah, if she doesn't shut it I'm going to throw her off

that bleedin' balcony,' threatened a burly bloke sitting in an armchair. And I could see from the look on his face that he meant it.

Foreseeing trouble ahead, I said, 'Look, let's keep calm. This is your dad's funeral. We want to make sure the day passes as peacefully as possible and that you don't have anything to worry about. Let me go up and have a word with her.'

As I left the flat, a neighbour came out, leaned over the balcony, and released a volley of insults at the woman above. She screamed back in kind. This was getting nasty.

Halfway up the stairs the burly bloke barged past me, furiously cursing under his breath. I hurried after him, hoping to prevent him inflaming the situation even more. Rounding the corner to the fourth floor balcony I saw the bloke up against the wall and a gangly youth with cropped hair holding a carving knife to his throat. The big bloke backed away slowly then fled back down the stairs, leaving me alone on the balcony with the teenager, his sister and a knife pointing at me.

'Do you want some of this then?' he asked menacingly, narrowing his eyes and taking a step towards me.

'Let's not make this situation any worse than it is,' I said, thinking that I had literally backed myself into a corner this time. I have always followed the example of my dad and Uncle Fred in never backing down where a funeral was concerned.

As I was trying to calm the woman, all the time assuring her that I understood what she was saying, the youth came at me again, still brandishing the knife. He had a crazy look in his eyes and waved the knife in front of me. 'I ain't messing about, you know.'

'I'm not scared of you and I'm not going to run away,' I said slowly, taking a step back, without taking my eye off him. 'I'm not standing here threatening you. But I'm telling you to put that knife away. Your life is on the line here.'

He looked hard at me for a moment, then at the knife. Only a few days before, I had been to the mortuary at Guy's Hospital to collect the body of a young man stabbed to death in a fight.

'It's not worth it, believe me. Come on, go inside,' I urged delicately. My heart was pounding and, rigged out in my mourning suit, and with the sun beating down, I could feel the sweat under my armpits and my inside was taut. I just hoped my softly-softly approach would work.

It was unnerving the way the youth continued to stare at me. I could hear one of the crowd gathered below shouting something and in the distance the sound of a train.

'Come on,' I repeated, even more slowly, 'Go inside. Is it worth it?'

He glanced furtively along the balcony, first one way then the other. He seemed unsure what to do. Then he seemed to relax. 'I like you, man. You speak sense and you're respectful.'

'Come on, go inside.' Tensely, I waited to see what he would do.

He lowered the knife to his side and then turned and went back into the flat.

I heaved an inner sigh of relief and went back down to the family and told them the problem had been sorted out and we could now leave for the cemetery. A police van arrived as we were preparing to move off. When I explained what had happened the officers congratulated me on how I had handled the situation.

It was only on the way to the Camberwell New Cemetery that the reality of the incident hit me. I had been inches from having a knife plunged into me. Over the years, I've dealt with enough grieving families of people who have been stabbed to death to know how, in an instant, life can disappear. But I've always seen my role as a funeral director as that of the protector, both of the dead and the bereaved. And I will not let anyone – even if they are waving a knife around – interfere with the conducting of a funeral.

The one thousand or so families who each year book Albin's to conduct their funerals are offered what you might call a comprehensive menu of services. Funerals today are about consumer choice.

We provide five types of funeral: disposal, which is exactly what it says and doesn't include limousines or a religious service; practical, where we make all the arrangements; ecological, with a cardboard coffin; budget, with a hearse and one car and covered by the DSS; and tailor-made, where you can have as many cars and additional services as you want.

The services we provide include different types of embalming; the dressing of the deceased; chapels of rest; a wide variety of coffins and caskets, headstones and urns; cryonics; Daimler, Rolls Royce or horse-drawn hearses; floral tributes made to order; memorial cards; photographs; our own cremation cemetery; newspaper entries; and even catering. You can even have an Internet funeral. We will assist in planning both religious services and secular services. We also offer pre-need funerals, help in claiming DSS benefits, and I provide a free legal service, i.e. I will advise people in court, and help draft wills and act as an executor.

Today, for example, you can be buried in one of a selection of graves at your local cemetery, buy a vault or mausoleum, have a woodland burial, or have your ashes scattered in our cremation cemetery, at sea, in the Thames, at a football ground, in your back garden or in outer space. You can also have them made into a coral reef. And if you don't believe in the resurrection, then you can even be frozen and stored in a capsule in Michigan in the hope of being brought back to life at some point in the future. And whether I am conducting a funeral for a president, a gangster, a murderer, a priest, a group of bikers, a down and out, or a foetus, I want that funeral to be the best ever. In my eyes, all are equal in death.

As a funeral director my job has many dimensions: I'm part counsellor, priest, doctor, lawyer, social worker, police-man, financial consultant, master of ceremonies, actor, chauffeur, travel agent, make-up artist, mechanic, removal man, diplomat, courier, flower arranger, salesman, ex-hibitor, choreographer, DJ, private investigator, linguist, photographer, fashion consultant, historian, navigator, excavator, clairvoyant and, occasionally, bouncer.

What's more, caring for a deceased person and planning a funeral with their family is a very complex and personal business, with little room for error, and one that has to operate within a legal framework. The funeral director is at the centre of a network of professional relationships that might include doctors, nurses, morticians, coroners, pathologists, police, social workers, bereavement coun-sellors, the fire brigade, customs and excise, airlines, registrars, solicitors, bank managers, priests, vicars, mini-sters, pastors, imams and other religious figures, cemetery superintendents and grave diggers; not forgetting the

companies that supply everything from embalming fluid
to coffin handles.

How far consumer choice has affected the funeral
industry can be gleaned from an unexpected phone call I
took one evening. Please forgive the language, but the caller
was a rather colourful character.

'Ello. Albin?' said the voice at the other end of the
phone.

'Yes,' I answered.

'Bal?' asked the voice.

'That's right.'

'Lovely. No, you don't know me, but Hatsie's told me to
ring you.'

'What, Mickey the Hat?'

'That's 'im. 'E said you buried his brother who got
murdered a few months back. And 'e said you're the dog's
bollocks, mate.'

'Oh, that's nice,' I said, recalling how Micky the Hat's
brother had died after being savagely attacked outside a
south London restaurant one night. 'So what's up?'

'Now, my old man was the guvnor, an eytie, and he's just
died. Now I want the 'orses. Have you got the 'orses, Bal?'

'Yes, I've got my own horses,' I replied, 'named George
and Fred, after my dad and uncle.'

'Ow, fackin' 'ansome. And the carriage?'

'Yes. It was built in 1864 and used for the funeral of the
first president of Ireland.'

'Fackin' 'ell! Perfic. Right. Now I want six cars. I've
bought a big mausoleum for the old man, me, mum and the
old woman. It's down at Streatham. I want a zinc-lined
coffin . . .'

'I'll have to stop you there. He'll need a lead shell and

oak case, just like I've made for the Royal family. It will have to be two inches thick, dove-tailed and jointed, because you don't want it coming apart,' I explained.

'Wot, you mean like the Queen? Fackin' 'ell! You're the fackin' guvnor. Now, 'ow much?'

'I'll need a few minutes to work it out. Do you want Dad embalmed? I think you should.'

Unlike some funeral directors I know, I always give people the choice whether or not to have a deceased person embalmed.

'Yeah.'

'And you want a Mass?'

'Yeah. Spot on.'

'Where are we going? The Italian church in Stockwell?'

'Wot! Do you know it?'

'Course I do. This is my game.'

'So that's what I want. Now, the old woman, she's got to do all the running around. So, how much?'

After a quick calculation, I said, 'About £4,100.'

'Four one? Fackin' 'ansome. But can the old woman see the coffin, so that she's happy?'

I told him the coffins we used for mausoleums were imported from Italy. 'Where does your dad come from?'

'Er, 'e comes from . . . er . . . not far from Milan.'

'Well, that's funny because our coffins are made in Peschiera del Garda, which is about a hundred kilometres north-east of Milan.'

There was a pause. 'Your fackin' 'aving me on! Fackin' 'ell!' Then he called to someone in the background, 'The fackin' bloke 'ere, 'e's got it dead right. You wouldn't believe it.' Then the phone suddenly cut out. After a few seconds it rang again.

'Sorry, Bal. I shouldn't be using this,' he said apologetically.

'Well, phone me on the land line,' I replied, thinking he was possibly on a mobile phone.

'I can't.'

'Why?'

'I'm in the fackin' nick, ain't I!'

This was a first. I don't think I had ever had a funeral booking from inside a prison. 'I see,' I said.

'They'll let me out for the funeral but only for six hours.'

'Well, in that case I'll write a letter to the governor and I'll explain that you're genuinely going to the funeral and that I'm a magistrate and will be responsible for you . . .'

'Wot! You're a magistrate!'

I smiled to myself. 'Yes.'

'Fackin' 'ell. And you're one of us?'

'Not exactly,' I replied, thinking I wasn't sure what 'one of us' was. 'But you've got to be straight,' I warned. 'Don't go and drop me in it by doing a runner. This is your dad's funeral and you have to show respect.' A prisoner did once do a runner at a cemetery, and his family blamed me because I hadn't locked the doors of the limousine. I told them I was a funeral director, not a jailer.

'Don't worry, Bal. 'Ere, you're a fackin' diamond. A fackin' diamond geezer. So when we 'aving it, then?'

'Why don't you have it on a Saturday morning,' I suggested.

'Wot. I can 'ave it on a Saturday morning?'

'Yes, and then maybe you can get the weekend pass, maybe, and be with mum.'

'Ah, I didn't fackin' think of that,' he said excitedly and

then called to someone, 'Ere, ere, 'e's gonna do me a fackin' Saturday funeral for my old man.'

An hour later his wife telephoned me, worried about all the running around she would have to do. 'My husband said he'll give you five grand if you'll come over to me. He said he wants the best funeral ever.'

I told her that it would be the best ever funeral at £4,100 and I would still come and see her anyway.

'No,' she insisted, 'he says that you have to take five grand. And he won't hear otherwise.' I didn't argue, deciding that I would give the extra money to the Albin-Dyer Bermondsey and Rotherhithe Foundation, a charity I set up for local people in need.

This story illustrates perfectly what I have strived to achieve in my forty years as a funeral director: to offer people the kind of funeral they want and one that will live on in the memory of those present for years to come. In other words, I want to give a bereaved family the best funeral they could imagine, however small or large.

During and immediately after the Second World War funerals were, by and large, small affairs. This was still a time of tightening your belt and low expectations. But the rise in the standard of living in the 1960s, when people started to have central heating, bathrooms, inside toilets, cars, TVs etc, changed the way people thought about life and broadened their expectations. They found excuses to celebrate family occasions again: engagement parties, Mother's Day, Father's Day and so on. And, of course, the death of someone is a major family event. The bigger the funeral, the longer the memory. That is the usual thinking.

Some of the more unusual funerals I have conducted have included one for a biker, with a flotilla of Harley

Davidsons, and one for an Italian ice cream salesman, the Tonibell man, with about fifty ice cream vans (though they weren't playing their jingles, let me add). I've conducted several for firemen, where the coffin was carried on a fire engine and I've done gypsy funerals where the mourners have been in carriages pulled by shire horses. After the funeral everyone has gone back to the caravan where the person lived and set light to it. When a young woman died after taking Ecstasy tablets I conducted a Gothic style funeral. The coffin was black, hand painted and adorned with gold braid. The woman's face had white make-up on it and she had long painted nails. At the funeral of Daisy, the Pearly Queen, all the Pearly Kings and Queens sang and danced around the grave, with the smell of Woodbines hanging in the air. The funeral of a Bermondsey woman named Dolly was another jolly affair. The family asked for white horses and booked a jazz band. Mourners were tapping their feet and singing 'When the Saints Go Marching In' and 'Hello Dolly'.

On the other hand, the funeral at St James' Palace of the Queen Mother's butler was a much more solemn occasion. When the twelfth Duke of Argyll died in a London hospital in 2001 we were asked to transport his remains to Inveraray Castle, Argyllshire, and, working with Jonathan Harvey, a highly respected Glasgow funeral director, organise the funeral. After a service in the parish church, attended by bagpipers and soldiers in full regalia, the duke was taken on a boat to a small island for a private burial.

One of the most fitting funerals I have ever been involved in was that of Big Albert, a local breakdown man. On the way to Camberwell New Cemetery the Rolls hearse broke down on New Cross Road. After walking the length of the cortege to explain the delay to the mourners, I opened the bonnet to try and discover what the problem was. Just then, Paul, like Big Albert, a local breakdown man, pulled up alongside me in his black Rolls Royce Corniche and asked if he could help. When I told him it appeared the electrics had gone, he told me not to worry and positioned his car in front of the hearse. Then he went to the boot, whipped out a tow bar and hooked up the hearse to his Roller and towed it all the way to the cemetery. Paul saved the day, as breaking down on a funeral is one of my worst nightmares. And Big Albert would, I know, have been proud to be going to his grave in a Rolls towed by another breakdown man in a Rolls.

Before the introduction of cars, conducting a funeral could be very physically tiring, as Fred Albin used to tell me. At one time, the funeral cortege would walk to the cemetery with the undertaker supplying the bearers as the cortege moved away from a house to begin the journey. The bearers would carry a pair of trestles on their back. After about twenty minutes they would get tired and stop at the nearest pub and then men supplied by the family would take over carrying the coffin. Everyone would then go into the pub for about a quarter of an hour for refreshment. Afterwards the new set of men would pick up the coffin, place the trestles on their back and off they would go. This happened all the way along the route. To complete the walk could take up to four hours. So you can imagine the state everybody was in by the time they got to the cemetery!

I remember Arthur Albin - known fondly as 'the old man' - telling me about the funeral of a leading trades union man many years ago. It left Bermondsey at about 9 a.m. and arrived at St Patrick's Cemetery, Leytonstone, about eight miles away across the river in east London, at 1 p.m. Many of the mourners, as was common before the advent of motorised funerals, walked the entire journey. Six horses drew the hearse, which was covered with ten black ostrich plumes, which stood approximately four feet six inches high. Behind came ten coaches, each drawn by four horses. Leading the funeral were eight gold union banners, which were about sixteen feet wide and ten feet high. Around 200 men followed the cortege. The service and the burial in the cemetery took between an hour and an hour and a half. But it was about 10 p.m. before everyone arrived back in Bermondsey, because after leaving the cemetery they all adjourned to a pub nearby. After two hours there they went to another pub, the Thatched House, which was a renowned halt of funerals. Arthur Albin once spoke of seeing thirty coaches from different funerals parked outside. From the Thatched House the cortege would make its way through Stratford and then down the Mile End Road. When they reached the Minories, near Tower Hill, they stopped at another pub before crossing Tower Bridge and arriving back in Bermondsey.

So what's the biggest funeral I have ever conducted? Well, while I have conducted the funeral of a former prime minister of Pakistan, which included forty seven Rolls Royces in the cortege, and was accompanied by police outriders, and I have led several thousand mourners through central London to the mosque in Penzance Gardens, the answer has to be that of the son of Mr Jafari, a wealthy Iranian, in 1974. He had died of a drug overdose.

The Iranian Embassy gave me the phone number of a Mr Sabbar, who was representing the family. When I phoned the number I discovered it was the Carlton Towers Hotel, a very expensive place in Knightsbridge. Eventually, a terse-sounding voice came on the line.

'Mr Sabbar? It's Barry Albin from F. A. Albin. I'm phoning about the funeral arrangements,' I said.

'Yes. Meet me in the lobby at the Carlton Towers Hotel at 11 a.m. sharp tomorrow.' And with that, he put the phone down. An extremely wealthy man, Mr Jafari, I learned, flitted between the Carlton Towers Hotel, where he rented a suite, and houses in Chelsea, Germany and Iran.

When I arrived at the Carlton Towers – dressed in my best suit – I went up to the receptionist and introduced myself. She picked up the phone to tell Mr Sabbar I was here. A few minutes later, an immaculately dressed man with a moustache appeared.

He shook my hand firmly and led me to the bar. As we sat down, he explained matter of factly that he was making the arrangements for the funeral as he was Mr Jafari's personal assistant. Studying me closely, he then asked me if I was good at my job.

'You tell me why you are here,' he said sharply, non-chalantly lighting a cigarette and leaning back in his seat. 'Why?' he repeated.

'Why am I here?' I replied, wondering what sort of question that was and feeling slightly intimidated by Mr Sabbar. I was, after all, only twenty-four, and I still had much to learn about planning and conducting funerals.

'I'm here because everybody's told you that I am the only person who can do this funeral.' I felt I needed to be bold and confident with Mr Sabbar, even though I felt nervous in his presence. Yet I reminded myself that a few weeks before I had conducted the funeral of Mr Khazem, the UK managing director of the National Iranian Oil Company. I had taken his body all the way from his home in Surrey to Brookwood Cemetery, and then afterwards taken the mourners to an Iranian restaurant in the West End for a reception.

'You are right,' Mr Sabbar said with a nod.

'Well I must be good in that case. My time is yours. Until the funeral is over you will own me.' Little did I know how true these words were to turn out to be.

He smiled thinly. 'I hope so, Mr Albin, because this is going to be one of the most difficult times of your professional life.' He instructed me to return to the hotel with two cars at 9 a.m. in the morning to take Mr Jafari, his wife and himself to Westminster Coroner's Court for the opening of the inquest. The full inquest wouldn't take place until a few weeks later. 'Don't be late,' were the parting words of Mr Sabbar as he swivelled round and walked off towards the lift.

The next morning Freddy Collins and I took two matching black Ford Granadas to the hotel, arriving fifteen minutes early. I have always been a very punctual person anyway but, given Mr Sabbar's attitude, I wanted to make doubly certain that I arrived on time.

We pulled up in the forecourt of the hotel and waited. Shortly, Mr Sabbar and another well-dressed man emerged, followed by a stocky man with a moustache, and an elegantly dressed lady. After Mr Sabbar made the introductions, Mr Jafari and his wife got in the back of my car and Mr Sabbar and the other man got in Freddy's car, and we drove to Westminster Coroner's Court.

The coroner, after ruling that Mr Jafari's son had died

28

from a drug overdose, gave permission for the body to be removed from the mortuary and for burial to take place. Saddened by the cause of death, Mr Jafari then instructed me to take him around some cemeteries to find a suitable burial place for his son. 'I'm never going to return to Iran. That's why I would like my son buried here,' he said. 'And one day I will be with him.'

We spent the whole day visiting cemeteries. I drove him to Kensal Green, then over to Richmond, then on to Putney and Roehampton, then down to Woking and then up to Grove Park. Each time, I would point out which plots were available and which, if any, sections were Muslim. Mr Jafari would pace around silently for a while and then get back in the car and say, 'No, not this one. Drive on to the next cemetery, please.' I was now beginning to see what Mr Sabbar had meant when he had said that these were going to be some of the most difficult days of my life. Mr Jafari was a man who knew exactly what he wanted, and he wouldn't be satisfied until he got it.

Finally, he chose Charlton. I was surprised at this as the cemetery is very ordinary and it's in the lower reaches of south-east London. I had thought that Mr Jafari would opt for somewhere a bit more ornate, such as Kensal Green. He then announced that he wanted to buy twenty graves so that all his family could be buried in one place.

'Well, Mr Jafari, the problem is that in London there is a shortage of burial space,' I replied. 'So families are restricted from buying large numbers of graves at public cemeteries. But because Brookwood, for example, is a private cemetery you could do that there.'

He reluctantly accepted the restrictions and asked me to buy as many graves as I could at Charlton Cemetery.

The following morning, I collected him again at the hotel and drove over to our funeral home, where his son now was. I had embalmed him the night before. This is unusual in Muslim funerals, unless a deceased person is being shipped to another country. But Mr Jafari was quite Westernised in many ways.

'I want to dress my son. And I want him standing up,' said Mr Jafari. This was a very unusual request. With tears in his eyes, he helped us to dress his son in a blue Versace suit and tie and we then stood the coffin up at an angle. I left Mr Jafari alone in the chapel, thinking that it was very touching for a father to want to help to dress his son.

While Mr Jafari was in the chapel, Mr Sabbar gave me precise instructions about the funeral. He told me Mr Jafari wanted photographs taken of all the principal mourners and that people were to phone me to order flowers and I was to keep a detailed record.

'And how many cars would you like?' I asked.

Opening his briefcase, he pulled out a file and ran his eye down a sheet of paper. 'By my calculation, seventy-one limousines. And matching, please.'

'Pardon!'

'Seventy-one limousines,' he repeated. 'We will have nearly three hundred mourners. Is that a problem, Mr Albin?'

'Er, no, of course not,' I spluttered, thinking to myself, yes, this was one hell of a problem. In those days, our entire fleet only consisted of three limousines and the average number of limousines for a funeral was two. Trying to find this number of cars at such short notice was, I knew, going to be a nightmare.

When I returned to the funeral home, Fred Albin and

Dad were stunned by Mr Sabbar's request. 'Well, I hope we can get hold of them. You're going to have to do a lot of ringing around, Barry.' Fred had great confidence in me, but I think even he thought I might have bitten off more than I could chew. Nevertheless, he was happy to leave the planning of the funeral to me, while he handled the other funerals.

The cars had to be all black and also of a suitable make for a funeral. You couldn't have Ford Escorts or something like that for such a high profile funeral. They would look out of place. Mr Jafari was expecting the best, as Mr Sabbar had reminded me, and he was prepared to pay for it. His mourners had to travel in style.

That night, I lay awake in bed worrying about the funeral. It was in two days' time. What would I do if I couldn't find the right kind of cars? What would Mr Sabbar say if I had to hire Ford Escorts? I didn't dare contemplate this scenario. My reputation was on the line here.

But I needn't have worried. Freddy Collins, who ran a local car hire company, came to my rescue. Using his contacts at Godfrey Davis and Green's car hire, he tracked down seventy-one matching limousines. I learnt, not for the first time, that in business so often it's not what you know, it's who you know.

I booked a local photographer, Arthur Wood, to take photos of the funeral and Green's, a florist on St James' Road, to provide the flowers and floral tributes. Over the weekend the phone never stopped ringing. Iranians from America, Canada and other parts of the world had flown into London for the funeral and they all wanted me to go over to the Carlton Towers Hotel to show them the floral tribute brochure. Each order had to be listed. Green's had never seen anything like it and had to rent a railway arch to store the tributes in until the day of the funeral.

The day of the funeral finally arrived. It was grey, cold and wet, a typical London day. I had met with the police and received permission to park all the cars along the bottom of Hyde Park, as there was no way we could park in front of the Carlton Towers. Each car had to display a numbered card on the windscreen so that the mourners knew which car they were travelling in.

I took up position at the entrance to the hotel and using a two-way radio called each car down to the forecourt individually as the mourners came out of the hotel. This took about an hour. Mr Sabbar seemed very impressed by my organisational skills and, for the first time, gave me a genuine smile. 'Very good, Mr Albin.' When we were ready to depart I had to have the last car run me down to the hearse – which was in Victoria – because the cortege was so long.

Unsurprisingly, many people stopped to stare as the cortege snaked its way across London to our chapel of rest in Bermondsey, where I had arranged refreshments for the principal mourners who wanted to pay their last respects to Mr Jafari's son. Because there were so many cars I had to ask permission from the Evangelical church next door to use their car park. The mass of flowers and floral tributes was unbelievable. There must have been at least a thousand.

After the ceremonial carrying of the coffin on to the Rolls hearse, we set off for Greenwich. I remember stopping in the middle of Blackheath and looking back. It was an unforgettable sight: in the afternoon sunshine, a row of black cars stretched as far as the eye could see. The multitude of floral wreaths and flowers on top of the cars added to the spectacular image.

When we reached the grave, which was in the middle of the cemetery, the last car was still out on the main road. The men formed a semi-circle and the women stood behind them, as is traditional at Muslim funerals. Water from Abraham's well was sprinkled, soil from Mecca was scattered at the graveside and the body was placed into the grave facing south-east. Behrouz, an elderly imam, then read a special prayer, asked if anyone was owed anything by the deceased and then placed soil into the paper on which the prayer was written and then dropped it into the grave. Mr and Mrs Jafari then dropped soil into the grave and then other mourners were invited to do the same. After this, a wooden stake and a photo of the deceased was placed on top of the grave.

It took my team some time to place all the flowers on top of the grave, which is the usual practice. And again, as is our standard practice, they then gathered all the cards from the floral tributes for Mr Jafari and his wife to keep. Before people left the graveside they all bent down to touch the grave and leave behind a personal thought.

The cortege travelled back to the Carlton Towers Hotel, where I had arranged a champagne reception in the main ballroom for 1,000 people. Mr Sabbar came up to me towards the end of the evening and said, 'Mr Albin, I need 170 albums with photos of the funeral.'

I had to do a double take. '170!'

'Yes. 170,' he repeated matter of factly. 'Is that a problem?'

'No . . . No, not at all, Mr Sabbar.'

'And I need them delivered to the hotel by 5 p.m. the

day after tomorrow.' He paused. 'Mr Albin, I did tell you this would be one of the most difficult times of you life,' he said, sensing my disbelief. And with that, he was gone.

When I went to Arthur Wood's house to ask him if he could provide the albums, he was flabbergasted.

'You're joking, Barry. But I don't stock that many,' he said, pointing to a dozen or so burgundy albums on a shelf.

'Well, can't you try some of your contacts? I'm sure they will have some albums.'

'I suppose I can,' replied Arthur, looking thoughtful. 'But I'll need the money to buy them. I don't keep much cash here.'

'Here,' I said, handing him a roll of notes. 'But get your skates on. There's not much time, Arthur.'

'I'll do my best, Barry.'

Arthur did do his best, but, even with the help of some of his friends, only managed to complete about eighty albums. It was another week before I delivered the rest of the albums to Mr Jafari. But he understood the reasons for the delay.

But my work wasn't done yet. Seven days later, I took Mr Jafari, his wife and a large number of the mourners back to Greenwich Cemetery for the erection of the memorial, which was three feet high by two feet wide with a small base for a vase, and made of white Italian marble with a Farsi inscription in black lead lettering. Forty days after the funeral we returned to the cemetery for a memorial service and again on the first anniversary of the funeral. Mr Sabbar's final request was that I arrange for fresh flowers to be placed on the grave every week for the next five years.

Despite this funeral being so demanding and exhausting, it really made my reputation within the Iranian community.

I learned from it that to be a successful funeral director you needed to be very well organised and have contingency plans in case things didn't go according to plan. And the funeral also underlined how much a funeral director relies upon the help of other funeral directors and businesses, be they car hire companies, florists or photographers.

Five years later, Mr Jafari's other son died in similar circumstances in Ireland and I flew out and brought him back to London. I had to go through the process once again, although the funeral was only half as big this time. Ten years later I conducted Mr Jafari's funeral and in 2000 that of his wife. And when Behrouz, the imam, died I arranged for his body to be returned to Iran.

Yet, despite all the best laid plans, funerals sometimes go wrong. Over the years as a funeral director I have had to deal with everything from punch-ups at cemeteries to drunken mourners and collapsing graves. But nothing had prepared me for the bizarre train of events that happened one dreary Friday in November 1995. You might call it an Ealing comedy.

I had been asked to conduct the funeral of an Iranian man in Ealing. We had to drive to west London to collect the mourners and then back across London to the Central Mosque beside Regent's Park. From there we would drive to Hampstead Cemetery and then to a hotel near Ealing for a reception. Five limousines and a Daimler hearse had been booked. I had told my team to be ready to leave at 8 a.m.

Arriving at the funeral home at 5 a.m., I discovered that one of the limousines wouldn't start. I put my overalls on and tried to find out what the problem was. I'm no mechanic, but I make it my business to understand something about the cars I drive. After about an hour with my head under the bonnet I managed to start the car. I then had a wash and changed back into my mourning suit and joined the staff for breakfast in the kitchen.

Our hearses are equipped for every eventuality, bar a nuclear war. We carry magnetic flags, straps to keep the flowers down, hooks in case we have to hang them, tape in case we have to secure them, a sort of blue tack which is used to hold wreaths in place on the coffins. Each hearse has two ladders, so that we can place flowers on the roof. We also carry a built-in tape recorder and CD player, a video camera, 35 mm camera, first aid kits, smelling salts, London A-Z, and bottled water. One of my hearses used to be equipped with a portable organ which, if there was no electricity at a crematorium chapel, we could connect to a car battery. In addition, all our limousines have sets of arm bands in case someone turns up and wants to wear something as a mark of respect, a red carpet, which we roll out for the family, and a set of steps for those who might find it difficult to get in, as well as a wheelchair. We even often carry a buggy, baby blanket, sterile bottle and distilled water and colouring books for children. I think we are unique in carrying such a range of equipment. But I have always been prepared to go the extra mile in order to provide the best service possible.

With all my team assigned to a specific vehicle, just after 8 a.m. the cortege left the yard to begin the journey across London. I was travelling with Blind Bill in the hearse, while Mick, Tom and Lee were driving the three limousines. Bill wasn't blind but his eyesight was a bit dodgy.

On the north side of Lambeth Bridge I realised that Lee's car was missing. Where had he gone? He'd been there at the Imperial War Museum. Glancing in my wing mirror I saw his car approaching the bridge and pulled up and waited. After a few minutes, I saw him behind us, flashing his lights to continue along Millbank. I still didn't know what had delayed Lee, but we had to push on.

Fortunately, the traffic in Chelsea, Hammersmith and Chiswick was light and we were soon turning off the A4 and heading along Gunnersbury Avenue into Ealing. We've all heard the saying, 'He'd be late for his own funeral.' But to be unreasonably late for a funeral is, in my opinion, one of the biggest sins for a funeral director. Arriving late can cause major problems, and frayed tempers, at a busy cemetery or crematorium.

We easily found the street, consisting of typical post-war semis, and we drove slowly along it looking for number 38. Strange, I thought. Where's number 38? So we turned around and drove even more slowly back down the street. Number 34, number 36 . . . a playing field! Did we have the right number?

I stopped the car and took the daily sheet out of the glove compartment. No, it definitely said number 38. I got out of the car and paced quickly up and down the street.

'What's up Barry?' called Freddy Collins.

'Don't know,' I replied, puzzled. 'There doesn't seem to be a number 38. I'd better phone the office.' This was unusual, as we operate thorough checks on every aspect of a funeral, from the possessions of the deceased, which we store in a safe until after the funeral, to the address where we are to go to rendezvous with the mourners.

I grabbed my mobile phone. 'Rose, can you check the address for me? We can't find number 38 anywhere.' Glancing at my watch, I waited impatiently while she found the file. 'It is number 38? But that's a playing field. Are you sure?' She double-checked and told me the address was definitely correct.

'Here, Barry, guess what?' shouted Freddy, waving an A–Z. 'There's another street of the same name about a mile away.'

I couldn't believe it. 'Right, come on, let's get going,' I said getting back in the hearse. 'We're late.'

As we drove off to the other side of Ealing, I made a mental note to tell the staff at our team breakfast on Friday that we should double-check all addresses to avoid a repeat of this. It turned out we had been given the wrong postal code. We were now fifteen minutes late. As we waited at a set of traffic lights I heard a tap on the window. I looked up to see the face of a policeman, leaning down from his motorbike.

'Put your seat belt on,' he said officiously.

This was the last thing I needed. 'I'm really sorry, officer, but you wouldn't believe my luck today, so don't make it worse for me,' I said angrily, winding the window down. Here I was sitting in a hearse, wearing a top hat and with a deceased person in the back, and he's going on about a seat belt.

'You're not wearing a seat belt, sir,' he repeated in a monotone voice.

'Look, never mind my seat belt. If you really want to be helpful, give me an escort. We're late!' He clearly didn't want to get into an argument with an extremely irate funeral director, so he rode off, muttering under his breath.

When we arrived in the correct street I apologised to the family for being late and explained that there were two streets of the same name in different postal codes.

The husband, a large bearded man, brushed aside my apology with a smile, saying he was sorry, as he had given Rose the wrong directions. I told him to ask all the mourners to get into the cars for the journey to central London, and assured him that all would be well.

I opened the door of one of the cars for three girls to get into, but to my amazement, they got out again the other side. What was going on? Then a man cried out loud and began shaking his fist in the air.

'What's happened?' I asked the husband.

'He's left all the special sweets in the house, along with his key. What are we going to do?' he replied.

'Whereabouts are the sweets?' I asked.

'In the kitchen.'

I signalled Lee and we went up the path to the house. I lifted him up to an open window and he clambered through. He emerged with three trays of sweets and placed them, along with the keys, in one of the cars. At last, we were ready to leave. As we pulled away, a girl in one of the cars opened the door to get out and smashed it against a lamp post.

'What's the matter?' I asked, alarmed, getting out of the car which was still moving.

'I need to go to the toilet.'

'Please, can't you wait?' I replied, doing my best to stay calm.

'No, I can't' she replied and ran to one of the other cars to get the keys to the house. While she was in the house, I inspected the damage to the door. It could have been worse, I consoled myself, but it's going to cost a few quid to get it mended. I stood by the car waiting for her to emerge from the house. What was she doing in there? Eventually, she came out of the house, shot me an embarrassed glance, and got back into the car.

Finally, we were on our way. As we neared Hammersmith, the traffic became thicker. Then we got stuck in a jam. I got out of the car and walked up to the lorry in front to ask the driver what the delay was. He told me there had been a security alert at Hammersmith Bridge.

There was only one thing for it, I decided: we would have to use the bus lane. Picking up my wand, I got out of the car and took up position in front of it. The tradition of a funeral director carrying a wand dates back to Victorian times when the theft of corpses was common, as was the belief in evil spirits. I then began to walk the cortege along the bus route. The *Mirror* once said in a story that if you are stuck in a traffic jam, then it's probably because of Barry Albin and one of his funeral processions.

Unsurprisingly, the bus drivers were not too happy, but I have always believed that desperate situations require desperate measures. When we reached Hammersmith Broadway I got back into the limousine. We were over the worst bit of the jam now. Once through Hammersmith, we picked up speed and half an hour later the golden dome of the Central Mosque with its 141 ft minaret came into view. But we were an hour late.

As soon as we arrived, some of the mourners got into an argument with our imam and a group of Iraqi men. At the time Iran and Iraq were still locked into a bitter war, which was claiming thousands of casualties on both sides. I went over to the group. Their voices were becoming louder and angrier.

'Look, we're here to do a funeral,' I said to the imam, who was standing in the middle. 'Please, let's all have some respect. Put your disagreements aside and let's proceed.'

He studied me for a moment and then muttered something in Arabic before walking off towards the entrance to the mosque, beckoning me to follow him. Relieved, I signalled to all the mourners to follow. Then a bossy little man with a moustache came up to me, waving frantically, and announced that the women wouldn't be allowed in because they were wearing skirts instead of the traditional Muslim choudah. He was clearly an official of some sort.

'Look, there's going to be a riot here in a minute,' I replied with exasperation. 'Is that what you want? Just let the women go up into the gallery. Let God be the judge.' But he insisted that they were not allowed in. I told him I understood and respected his view but it was equally important that the funeral went ahead. Eventually he agreed to allow the women in.

We all took our shoes off and entered the mosque. Then suddenly, lo and behold, a woman had an epileptic fit and began kicking and screaming. We put her in a recovery position and after a few minutes the fit passed. Finally, the imam began the service. I looked at my team standing at the back of the hall and we all breathed a collective sigh of relief.

On the way out of the mosque after the short service, a very large lady next to me let out a cry and started to fall backwards. With the kind of reflexes that were worthy of David Seaman, I just managed to catch her before she hit the floor. Supporting her with my knees, and bouncing her along the floor, I tried to get her over to one of the cars. I told Mick to phone for an ambulance. What made this feat even more difficult was that I had no shoes on and it had begun to rain. By the time I reached the car her face had gone blue. It was clear that she had suffered a heart attack. Once she was in the car, I managed to roll her on to her side into a safe position, checking that she hadn't swallowed her tongue. The ambulance arrived after a few minutes and the paramedics gave her oxygen and then took her off to hospital.

'Where's everyone going?' I asked Mick. For some inexplicable reason, the mourners were all rushing out of the mosque. 'What's going on?'

He began to laugh. 'You won't believe this, Barry, but the Iraqis nicked all their shoes while they were in the mosque.'

I hurried to the mosque entrance. I have never seen such a hilarious sight. For strewn across Park Road were about fifty pairs of shoes. The mourners were holding up the traffic as they all hobbled around trying to find their shoes. But then I looked down at my own stockinged feet. Hang on, where were my shoes?

'Barry!'

I turned around to see a grinning Mick holding up my shoes.

After all the shoes had been retrieved I asked the family if they wanted to cancel the funeral and have it on another day. No, they said. But before we left, I had to clean up the sick in the back of the car from the woman who had had a heart attack. As I was doing this, a police van swung into the courtyard and half a dozen officers piled out.

'Are you the undertaker? Are you in charge of this funeral?' a stern looking inspector asked as he came towards me.

'That's right.' I answered, thinking that you didn't need

this many police officers to arrest someone for not wearing a seat belt.

'Well, sir, I suggest that you leave as quickly as possible before there is serious trouble.' Over his shoulder I could see a crowd of men milling around outside the entrance to the mosque. They began to taunt the Iranians.

'Yes, we're going now, officer,' I replied.

'Well,' I said to Reg, as we set off for the cemetery in Hampstead, 'things can only get better, as they say.'

'You reckon, boss,' he replied, obviously unconvinced.

Eventually we reached Hampstead Cemetery. Standing by the graveside, I felt something trickling down my nose. It was the dye from my top hat. I'd had it re-dyed the day before and it hadn't dried properly. No wonder I was getting strange looks from some of the mourners.

The rain was pouring down now and the grave had begun to fill with water. This was disastrous. I asked one of the lads to get the rope from the hearse and a bucket from the cemetery office. With the mourners sheltering under umbrellas, we then began to bale out the water, but with only one bucket it was a tedious process. What's more, it was now 4 p.m. and getting dark. After about half an hour, we got rid of most of the water and the imam then said the prayers.

I told my drivers to switch on their headlights and position their cars around the grave. We then began to fill it in. It wasn't long before we were all soaked to the skin and caked with mud. We hadn't eaten all day and we all just wanted to get home, have a meal and a bath and get into some clean clothes. But before we could do this we had to take all the mourners back to Ealing.

Believe it or not, on the way to Ealing one of the cars

developed a puncture, which we had to repair. The family had booked a hotel to have a reception. I said my goodbyes to the family, secretly relieved it was all over. As I was walking back across the car park with Freddy to where the limo was parked, I heard a shout, but continued walking.

'Hey, where do you two think you are going? Come back here and get a tray. We've got a funeral party in. Or didn't you know?'

I turned around to see the man who I took to be the manager advancing towards me with a serious expression.

'Hurry up. The guests are here. We need some glasses. What are you playing at?' he continued.

I had to smile. Because I was wearing a mourning suit he had assumed I was a waiter. Obviously, he must have drafted in agency staff for the reception. 'We're the funeral directors. And I'll tell you what, after the day we've had, we're not going to stand there giving out drinks.'

He stopped in his tracks, stood for a moment, as if unsure whether to believe me, and then did an about turn and headed back to the hotel.

We arrived back at the shop at about 9 p.m. Talk about it being good to be home. I was cold, wet, tired and hungry.

'Barry, I've not been able to tell you all day, but you remember when you lost me just before Lambeth Bridge,' said Lee hesitantly, as I was about to close the garage doors.

'Yes. What happened?'

'Well, a bloke in a white van was trying to cut in between the cars. And when you went over the bridge he did it. Then he got out of the car with a hammer and started smashing the car. I locked the door. I was so stunned I never even managed to get his registration number. I think you'd better have a look at the damage.'

I went over to the limousine to discover a scratch mark about an inch wide from the front to the back.

I was speechless and didn't know whether to laugh or cry. The day had been a catalogue of disaster from start to finish. Nevertheless, despite this comedy of errors, we had successfully carried out the funeral. I defy any funeral director to beat that story.

Another occasion when things didn't go to plan was when I went to a flat in Waterloo to take a deceased man to St George's Catholic cathedral for a requiem Mass. The man had hung himself. I don't know why, but it may have been because he was facing a prison sentence for various offences. I arrived with my team and they took up positions at each end of the coffin, which was on a trestle in the living room.

'Right, boys,' I instructed, 'set together and up,' and they all lifted together.

My son, Simon, let out a scream. 'No! No!'

'Hold it, hold it,' I said, wondering what the matter was. Looking around I saw that Simon had caught the top of his coat on one of the wreath holders on the coffin and he was standing on tip toe, with an agonised expression on his face. Realising that the coat was tightening around his neck, I ordered the team to lower the coffin back down. Given that the man had hung himself, there was something a little chilling about this incident. True to form, Simon did not drop the coffin.

Once we got outside, we began our usual slow walk to the horse-drawn hearse. A number of family and neighbours had gathered in the street to pay their last respects. Then I felt something under my shoe. I had caught a nut and bolt under my shoe. I tried to shake it off, but it wouldn't budge.

The faces of those watching took on bemused expressions. John could see what was happening and, knowing that funerals are an extremely serious event, was struggling hard not to break into laughter. When we reached the hearse, I moved to one side, only to find that my foot was in the dip of a drain, which meant that I was now leaning at a forty five degree angle, like a gymnast, and on the verge of keeling over. It was as if I was hanging from a cliff, but, of course, the coffin wasn't.

Like most people, you have probably never given a second thought to your own funeral or that of anyone in your family. Death is still the great taboo in Britain. While sex is discussed ad infinitum in the media, and advertisements assault our senses with sexual images, death and funerals are rarely talked about. And, unlike in the United States, you won't see roadside hoardings advertising the services offered by your local funeral director. It seems that as a society we prefer not to think about the only certainty in life, namely death.

A funeral is, I believe, the most important event in a person's life. You become a stigma of everybody's thoughts; the dread of everybody's imagination. The ceremony is about your life. It is solely and selfishly devoted to you. All of a sudden a very ordinary man in the street dies and he is a celebrity, for a brief moment. He may even ride for the first time in a Rolls Royce or a Daimler, albeit a hearse and albeit on a one-way journey.

And the funeral director, or, as he is sometimes known, the undertaker, is often seen as a slightly creepy, dour figure. Think of the undertaker in the film *Oliver!* or Private Fraser, the undertaker in *Dad's Army*. Our world, it is thought, is one made up of dead bodies, chapels of rest, mortuaries,

coffins and caskets, hearses, and cemeteries and crematoriums. What's more we are associated with the colour black,
traditionally the colour of death in Britain, and dressed in
our mourning suits and top hats there appears to be
something almost Victorian about us, something Dickensian
even.

Some people even feel uneasy being in the presence of a
funeral director. It's as if they think that by being around
him, death might rub off on to them. On one occasion,
after a reception held in a social club in Surrey Docks, I
stuck my head around the door of the bar downstairs where
a group of old dockers were drinking and, whipping out a
tape measure (which had been presented to me as a joke),
shouted, 'Look, anyone want me to stay?' I won't tell you
what they replied.

People wonder how anyone could make death their
profession. It must be such a gloomy and depressing job,
they say, being surrounded by death. Wouldn't you rather
be a doctor, a lawyer or a teacher? Wouldn't you rather be in
a job where you could have a bit of a laugh? And this is what
people don't realise: that the role of the funeral director is
primarily to work with the living, not the dead. True, I care
for and protect the dead, but I can't restore them to life –
although, as you will read later, cryonicists in the United
States think that they might be able to do this, one day –
but I can do a great deal for the family and friends a
deceased person leaves behind. I can help them to carry on
living. And, as for having a laugh, well, let me tell you that,
despite the solemnity and dignity of my work, humour is
never far away. Without a doubt, being a funeral director
has to be the best job in the world. But, in my opinion, it is
also probably the hardest. I said to my sons that I would be

very proud if they chose to follow me into the business because they wanted to but if they did it to please me then it would be the worst job in the world for them.

At the back of St Peter's Catholic Church in Paradise Street, Rotherhithe, there is a list of phone numbers for crisis situations. With a touch of his characteristic humour, Fr Jack has written at the bottom, 'As a last resort, Barry Albin, undertaker.' I like that.

## 3

# BRINGING OUT THE DEAD

'Thank God you're 'ere, mate,' said the caretaker, as I got out of the private ambulance outside a low-rise block of flats on Tower Bridge Road. 'I'll tell you what. I ain't going in there. Bleedin 'ell, not likely.'

'Why. What's the matter?' I asked, opening the back doors to take out the collapsible Washington stretcher.

He pulled a face and stubbed out his cigarette on the wall. 'You'll find out soon enough.' Then, with admiration in his voice, he added with a shake of his head, 'I'll tell you what, I don't envy you mate with what you 'ave to do. I wouldn't do it for all the tea in China.' He silently handed me the key to the flat, reminding me to drop it into the estate office the next day, and he was gone.

I didn't know what he was referring to. When the coroner's office had phoned to ask if we would remove a deceased man, they hadn't said that there was anything unusual to be aware of. As my dad was unwell, I had decided to come on my own. I was seventeen and eager to gain experience. Doing a removal is easier with two of you, but it's not that difficult to do alone with a Washington stretcher (which I had imported from the USA – an easy mover with a sheet of plastic that slides under the deceased), when a flat is on the ground floor and there are no steps.

Carrying the stretcher, I walked into the entrance hall of the flats. The door of the flat was ajar and the lights were off. I gingerly pushed it open and flicked the light on the wall, but nothing happened. Switching on my torch I entered the flat, leaving the stretcher in the hall. The flat felt cold and spooky. I shone the torch around and then peered into the bathroom. No. Nothing.

But I could smell death; a smell like bad lard, due to the body having been in the flat for a few days. At times like this, when it is hot, I follow this smell in order to locate the body. There will often be flies and maggots around the body. When the maggots hatch and leave the body they wriggle under lino. If it's hot, they will bake, making a crunching sound when you step on them.

Any minute now, I am going to fall over the body, I thought, as I checked the toilet. This was scary. And what was the caretaker on about? Why wouldn't he go into the flat? After double-checking all the rooms, including behind the doors, I was puzzled, and also apprehensive. I was definitely in the right flat, so where was the body?

I decided I would have to ring the coroner's office and explain that there was no body there. Before I did though I thought I would try to find the mains for the electric. I spotted a cupboard in the hall and opened the door. As I did so, I leapt back in shock. Staring out at me was the terrified, contorted face of a man. His eyes were almost out of their sockets and his tongue was protruding. He was hanging by the belt of his trousers from the hook on the back of the door, like something out of a Freddy Kruger film. His trousers were around his ankles. My God! How on earth could the police doctor have just left him hanging there. Why didn't they cut him down? It was scandalous. When I recovered, I took out my knife, cut the belt and lifted the deceased. As I placed my arms around him, vomit spewed out of his mouth and all down my back. It was awful. It was with much relief that I wheeled the stretcher to the ambulance.

That has to be the most terrifying removal I have ever done. But another particularly gruesome removal occurred when Fred Albin and I were asked to go to Guy's Hospital mortuary one day. When we arrived, we discovered that the deceased person was, in fact, just a head. It turned out that the police had stopped a car one evening and, upon opening the boot, discovered various human remains in a bag and the head in a pressure cooker. I later learnt that a couple of people had killed the man, chopped him up and eaten part of him. Even now, it makes my stomach churn just thinking about it.

Some of the sexual interests of people are astonishing. I remember one man who died in the toilets of Peak Frean's biscuit factory in Bermondsey after placing a plastic bag over his head while he was masturbating. Apparently, the reason for this was that just before you pass out you ejaculate and obtain a sexual thrill. You could say, as a coarse but humorous mortician at Tennis Street mortuary remarked, 'Instead of coming, he went.' But I think it's very sad.

Another time, I was called to remove a body from a flat on the Silwood Estate in Rotherhithe. When I entered the room where the deceased was I was confronted by a strange looking contraption that looked like a rocking horse. A man wearing suspenders and with a plastic bag over his head and a noose around his neck lay on the floor. He had been rocking himself backwards and forwards with his penis inside a velvet ring, which was attached to the contraption. However his attempt at sexual thrills had gone tragically wrong when he slipped off the saddle and hung himself.

In cases such as these the coroner will always be called in. A coroner must be a barrister, solicitor or doctor of not less than five years' standing. Their duty is to investigate the cause of death of a person if there is reason to believe that the death was due to violence or was unnatural, sudden or of an unknown cause. Where appropriate, the coroner will order a postmortem and an inquest.

One of the most extraordinary coroners I have ever worked with was an elderly man who used to sit at Southwark Coroner's Court, which today covers the boroughs of Southwark, Lewisham, Greenwich and Lambeth. A flamboyant and eccentric man with a handlebar moustache, he always wore a bow tie and had a flower in his lapel. To make himself look taller he had wedges under his shoes. He was also a GP in Kennington and used to drive around in a Daimler.

I remember another coroner, who shall also remain nameless, who was once presiding over the death of a woman who had had an enema. When the midwife was called to give evidence he asked her how long she had been in the profession. Thirty years, she told him proudly. Then he asked her how many enemas she had done.

'Over a thousand,' she replied.

'A thousand!' he exclaimed and then asked to see her enema equipment.

The clerk passed the tube to him. 'Is this yours?' asked the coroner, holding the implement aloft.

The midwife said it was and that she had had it ever since she first qualified. The coroner asked her to describe what she did with the tube. And as she did, he lost his concentration, held it up in the air and then absentmindedly put it in his mouth, as if it were a pen. Everyone in the court looked on in horror, all thinking the same thing: that's been up a thousand backsides!

Pathologists value the experience and observational powers of a funeral director. Ian West, the renowned former Home Office pathologist, would often ask me if I had noticed anything in particular about the body when I found it. Sometimes I might notice one little thing that would make a difference. I remember once going to remove a body from a block of flats in Coopers Row. The CID officer had conceitedly concluded it was probably a suicide, not a murder. But when we came to lift the body I saw that the man's penis had been cut off and stuck up his backside. It turned out to have been a homosexual murder. I don't know how the detective could have missed this.

Over the years, I have been called to remove numerous bodies from the banks of the Thames. My dad told me that at one time the Wapping police used to push the body towards Rotherhithe on the opposite side of the river and the Rotherhithe police used to push the body back towards Wapping. Neither wanted the responsibility for it. In most cases, the body has been washed up or fished out of the river by police divers after a murder or a suicide. I remember one body we took away from the riverbank. There was a lump in the back pocket. When we cut it away we found £5,000 in soggy notes.

Late one overcast afternoon I received a phone call from the coroner's office, asking me to go to the riverbank at Greenwich to remove a deceased person. The only information I was given was that the deceased was to be found near the power station. So I set off in one of my private ambulances with Mick, one of our best men.

We parked up near the power station, took the fibreglass shell out of the back of the ambulance, put on our protective suits and wellingtons, grabbed our torches and walked towards the river path. To my surprise, the police had left the scene. Usually they wait for the funeral director to arrive. We walked up and down the river path but there was no body to be seen anywhere. We were both puzzled. The coroner's office had definitely said that it was near the power station.

I went in search of a phone box (thank God we have mobile phones today) and rang the coroner's office. 'Well, we've been up and down the river bank and we can't see the body anywhere,' I said, feeling slightly foolish, but also angry that the police hadn't waited for us. There either was a body or there wasn't.

The coroner's officer said with resignation in his voice that he would come out to locate the body for us. By the time he arrived, it was dark and the tide was coming in. What's more we were both freezing. 'Follow me,' he said tersely and headed off in the direction we had already come from. Like us, he too walked up and down, unable to spot the body. After a while, he exclaimed, 'There it is.' True enough, lying on in the mud down below was a dark shape that resembled a body.

Mick then climbed down the ladder on the wall and I passed him the shell. I followed and as soon as my feet hit the ground I was knee deep in mud. We walked towards the shape, shining our torches in front of us, but the deep mud made it very difficult. I nearly fell backwards on a couple of occasions. The shape turned out to be that of a middle-aged man in a long coat. There was no telling how long he had been in the river for. The smell from the body was awful and, as is common, it had become twice its normal size because of the gases. To deflate the body, I took out my Swiss army knife and pricked the man's testicles – which were the size of balloons – and, making a whoosh sound, the air left the body and it went back to its natural size.

The police would probably be able to identify this man, I concluded, as, unlike some deceased persons I have removed, he hadn't been decapitated. Where no one comes forward to identify a body, fingerprints and dental records will often provide the answer. Or DNA.

Squelching through the mud, with the tide lapping around you, to collect a deceased person on a cold November evening is not an experience I would recommend to anyone. The most difficult thing we had to do was climb back up the ladder on the wall, while holding on to the shell at the same time. But, after a number of struggles, we managed it – just. We then took the deceased to the public mortuary in Ladywell where a postmortem was later carried out. It transpired that the deceased was a Norwegian sailor who had got drunk and had fallen overboard. A week later, I conducted his funeral at St Olave's Norwegian church, which was built originally as a seamen's mission, across the road from the funeral home.

I've met some strange doctors over the years, but Dr Jones, a GP who used to have a surgery on Jamaica Road, probably wins the prize for the most bizarre behaviour. One morning I went with my dad to move a body at Blackfriars Pier. The police had pulled it up out of the water – as should be the case – and then put it on the side of the pier to await the arrival of Dr Jones.

'Where's the body?' asked Dr Jones briskly when he arrived.

Taken aback, I looked at the policeman and he looked at me. 'It's there, Dr Jones.' I said, pointing to the side of the pier.

Dr Jones gave a little snort and then walked over to the body, knelt down and took his stethoscope out of his bag and placed it on the man's chest. What on earth was he doing? Judging by the horrendous smell from the body and the condition of the skin, it had probably been there for about two weeks. Then Dr Jones took out a thermometer. Now what was he doing? I couldn't believe it. He pulled down the man's trousers and then put the thermometer up the behind of the man to take his temperature. Then he pulled it out, licked his fingers and pulled them across the thermometer.

'Yes, he's dead,' concluded Dr Jones, putting his stethoscope and thermometer back in his bag. Then he saw that the police officers, my dad and I were all smiling. 'What's the matter?' he asked, looking slightly miffed. 'Did I say something funny?'

While Bermondsey people pride themselves on cleanliness, some of the flats I have been into in south London have been indescribably filthy. You come outside fighting back the vomit and wondering how on earth anyone could live in such conditions. One of the worst was at the Elephant and Castle. Arriving on the fourth floor of a run-down council block to remove the body of an elderly man, we couldn't get through the door until we had cleared a mountain of bundled newspapers. Once inside, the squalor was unbelievable. On a table in the middle of the living room was a pile of empty baked bean tins, rotten food was everywhere, while the blackened kitchen was full of piles of dirty plates and saucepans and insects crawling around. Yet what was extraordinary was that a few days later the police discovered hidden under the newspapers that covered the floor of the flat £50,000, laid out neatly in £10 notes.

I was once called by Social Services to arrange the removal of a deceased man from a flat in Peckham. There was nothing remarkable about this – except that when Dad and I arrived there we realised that one vital piece of information was missing: the man, who was sitting with his elbow on the table, must have been at least thirty-six stone. There was no way Dad and I could carry him out. In situations like this there is only one thing you can do: call the fire brigade.

Within minutes I could hear a siren in the distance. There were a lot of smiles on the faces of the firemen when they came into the flat. When we moved the table away the man remained in exactly the same position because rigor mortis had set in. We strapped the man to a ladder and, using a winch, the firemen managed to hoist him through one of the windows. Dad and I, assisted by several firemen, then heaved the deceased into the back of the private ambulance.

Because of the size of the man, a coffin had to be specially made and the cemetery notified. There have been cases when a very large deceased person has arrived at a cemetery or crematorium and the coffin has been too big to go into the grave or cremator. The following week, when the cortege made its way up Rye Lane with the man's coffin, which was the size of a grand piano, lying on an open top hearse, there were plenty of bemused looks from shoppers.

My men have, like me, all been trained to carry the coffin in the correct way, whether they are carrying it out of the chapel of rest and into the hearse or up the aisle of a church. They do it slowly and in unison, always placing their left foot first. And they always bow respectfully before moving away. I suppose you could say the moves – 'hold', 'centre', 'under', 'side' – are carefully choreographed, a bit like a ballet. As a mark of respect to the deceased, I always take my top hat off every time the coffin passes me.

I have my own coffin finishing and supply company, Barry Albin & Sons Ltd, located near Millwall football ground and producing, on average, around 4,000 coffins a year, for F. A. Albin & Sons or other funeral directors and coffin manufacturers, such as Vales, one of the largest in Britain. Coffins come in various sizes and finishes, and we even make tiny ones for foetuses.

The wood we use comes from trees that are properly forested in places such as South Africa and Austria. In other words, for every tree that is cut two more are planted. We also supply coffin panels featuring, for example, Our Lady, The Last Supper (a Rastafarian family once asked for the panel to be removed – because Jesus and the apostles were depicted as white) and the Sacred Heart. For families who want to have the deceased at home before the funeral we offer chapel sets, consisting of a crucifix and four large candle stands, all made out of pine or a similar wood. In addition, we import coffins from a factory in Peschiera del Garda, Italy. Fully automated, and with a fleet of articulated lorries that travel across Europe, the factory is an enormous place and the largest local employer.

Some years ago we were asked by Kenyon's to make a batch of coffins for the Royal Family. Although Kenyon's still had the Royal contract, they had ceased coffin manu-facturing. After our premises were inspected by a Royal aide, we received a delivery of oak from the Royal forest at Windsor. Royal coffins are based on the design used to bury Henry VIII and are all handmade and with a lead shell inside. Instead of nails and screws we used Oakdales 'elephant glue' and bitumen. The coffins were taken to a vault at Kensal Green Cemetery for storage. I don't know when and how many of them have been used, but it's quite possible that Princess Diana was buried in one. The reason I can't be sure of this is because Diana's coffin was draped in a flag throughout her funeral.

I also have a very unique claim to fame in having supplied coffins for both the Shah of Iran and Ayatollah Khomeini. It's quite ironic that while they were divided by their sharp political differences in life, they both ended up being placed in coffins made by a small company in Bermondsey, bringing home the point that we are all equal in death. You could say that on this occasion I was *The Equaliser*.

One of the most unusual requests I had came from the Greenwich Maritime Museum who were planning an exhibition on the life of Peter the Great, the former tsar of Russia, who worked in the Greenwich shipyards. I was asked to make a replica of the lead and leather encased solid oak coffin that Peter the Great took back to Russia. During his time in Greenwich, studying how the timber was used to make the ships, he realised that the practice in Russia of chopping down a whole tree and scooping the middle out to make one coffin was wasteful. The highlight of the exhibition for me was meeting the Duke of Kent, who showed a keen interest in how the coffin was made.

The design of coffins and caskets hasn't changed much over the years. Coffins are still shaped at the shoulders and rectangular, which gives them that distinctive Gothic look. But the variety has increased. Today, you can opt for a biodegradable, veneer, solid wood, wicker, steel or even gold-plated coffin. Coffins used for transportation of the deceased overseas are always zinc-lined, so that there is no risk of body fluids leaking. In America caskets are more popular than coffins. Unlike coffins, the top of a casket opens in the manner of a chest. We import caskets from Marsellus Caskets and Batesville Caskets in the USA. One of the first American caskets I supplied was for the landlord of the Justice pub (which featured in the Paul McCartney film *Give My Regards to Broad Street*) in Bermondsey. The casket was left open and placed in the bar overnight, amidst all the regulars. From then on caskets started to become popular in the area.

Removing the body of a king is, I imagine, an honour few funeral directors have had. This happened to me when we were asked to remove the body of King Freddie of Buganda, a province in Uganda. He had died in Rotherhithe, where he had been living after being toppled from power.

So my dad and I went up to the house. Two muscular African guards wearing ceremonial dress and holding spears were standing outside the house. Inside were gathered a number of African men in suits and a UK diplomat. We were ushered upstairs, where King Freddie was lying on his bed. In his open-neck shirt and trousers he looked very ordinary and not at all how I imagined a king would look. When we began to carry the shell down the stairs I felt a sharp jab in my back from the spear of one of the guards. Once again my dad's words came back to me: DON'T DROP THE COFFIN. The guards accompanied us to the coroner's mortuary in Tennis Street and when King Freddie was taken into our chapel of rest they stayed with him two days.

As it wasn't possible for the body of King Freddie to be sent back to Uganda he was embalmed, put into a lead-lined casket and then taken to Kensal Green Cemetery where he was placed into an underground vault until there was a change in the government. This didn't happen until around twenty years later.

The journalist John Simpson, who had interviewed King Freddie the day before his death, suggests that if he did die from alcohol poisoning, which was the coroner's verdict, then it had been forced upon him by supporters of the new regime in Buganda. Whether or not he was murdered, we will probably never know.

During the writing of this section about King Freddie a very strange thing happened. I hadn't thought or spoken about King Freddie for twenty years, but at the point of writing this chapter a woman came to the funeral home one day to ask me to send a deceased member of her family home to Uganda. As we began to discuss the arrangements, it emerged that she was King Freddie's daughter, a princess, and the family member would be given a state funeral. She said her family had remembered the help we gave to the king.

Over the years there have been cases of funeral directors

removing the wrong body. I remember the time when one leading funeral director in south London was sued for burying the wrong body and one of the country's biggest firms was sued for cremating the wrong body. Things had got so slack with one well-known funeral director that they used to place a bolt and chain on every coffin in the chapel, while the key was attached to the deceased's documents in the office.

Thank God, I have never removed the wrong body, but there have, I admit, been a few close calls in the past. One such time was when I went to Welsh House old people's home in Bermondsey. I and one of the team went there to remove the body of a woman who had died in the flu epidemic that had swept through the home. A care assistant led us down a corridor, pointed to a room and said, 'It's the lady there behind the blinds.' We went into the room with the shell and placed it on the floor. I went over to the bed, pulled the sheets back and the woman opened her eyes and shrieked, 'Ah! It's not me, love. It's the lady over there.' Sadly, just two weeks later that lady also died of flu.

Today, before we set off for a funeral we carry out a rigorous check to make sure that we are carrying the right body. We check that the name on the coffin matches the name of the deceased on the documentation and then check the name tags on the wrist and ankle. After this, the coffin is fastened down and carried in a dignified manner out of the chapel of rest to the hearse. Jackie, the office manager, then checks her documentation to confirm all the details of the deceased and the time of the funeral. Finally, I ask the hearse driver the name of the deceased.

Apart from these checks, we make doubly sure that all jewellery has been removed, unless the family have requested otherwise. After a cremation once, the deceased's family turned up at the funeral home claiming that a ring hadn't been removed from the body. Fred Albin believed, and I think correctly, that there wasn't a ring on the deceased person in the first place. Being a true professional, he gave them what they said the value of the ring was. This incident taught me a lesson not to get myself into that position in the first place.

My sons, Simon and Jonathan, have followed me into the Albin business and, like me, they started learning about funerals at a very early age. But I never forced them into the work. I can still remember the first time they both came with me to do a removal, that of an elderly man who had died in Blackheath. It was Christmas Eve 1985. Simon was nine and Jonathan was five. Not wanting them to experience the same fear of death that I had as a boy, I made sure that they were able to go anywhere in the funeral home.

I had phoned the daughter, who I knew, to ask if she minded if I brought my two sons. Not at all, she said, and expressed amazement that we were coming as a family.

Upon entering the bedroom, I held the head of the man, and I instructed Simon to hold his feet and Jonathan his middle. Both boys were very strong for their age and used to seeing and touching deceased persons at the funeral home.

When Jonathan placed his hands around the middle of the man, he squeaked, 'Oh, Dad, the man's pooed himself!'

'Never mind, son, just hold him tight,' I said. 'We'll clean the gentleman when we get back.' Collecting a deceased person can, at times, be very messy and unpleasant but you learn how to prepare yourself for it.

When we arrived back at the funeral home, we laid out

the deceased on the mortuary table and then removed his clothing and placed it in a marked bag, at the same time checking for jewellery and other valuables. All valuables are recorded in a book before being placed in a safe and then returned to the family. I was amazed that the boys helped me to clean the deceased. I reflected that even at such a young age they were doing what seemed to come naturally to them. Their mother and I have always been incredibly proud of the boys.

One of the specialities of F. A. Albin & Sons is repatriation – returning deceased persons to their homeland. I was first introduced to the international dimension of funeral directing when, as a young boy, I used to accompany Ernie Albin and my dad to Nuffield House, a private wing of Guy's Hospital. Back then, many overseas patients, mainly from the Middle East, came for treatment at Nuffield House, and unfortunately some died there and when that happened they would often be transported back to their homeland.

We once turned up at Nuffield House to collect a middle-aged Iraqi woman. Having parked the ambulance at the back entrance, we took out a shell and made our way to the second floor. When we arrived on the ward a nurse directed us to the bed where the lady was. Nuffield was the only place where we would take a deceased person from the ward. In other hospitals, the person would be taken to the mortuary. The reason for this, I think, was that at Nuffield they never wanted to admit that those who paid for their medical treatment ever died.

As we were lifting her on to the stretcher, all of a sudden out of her mouth gushed a mass of worms. They were as long as your arm and the nurse told me afterwards that they had come out of her intestines. A young nurse who had witnessed this incredible sight while the lady was still alive had fled from the ward screaming and never returned to nursing. I stood there transfixed, both repulsed and fascinated by what I was seeing. With admiration I watched as my dad and Fred, like the true professionals they were, calmly cleaned the lady up and deposited the worms in a plastic bag to take to the hospital waste incinerator. I can tell you something: it was a long time before I ate spaghetti again!

Another introduction to the international world of funerals occurred when my dad woke me late one night and told me we had to go out to remove a body from a Russian ship in the Thames estuary. Excited and fascinated by the prospect of a trip up the Thames in the dark, and going on board, of all things, a Russian ship, I hurriedly got dressed and jumped in the ambulance with my dad for the short journey to Cherry Garden Pier. A police launch was waiting for us when we arrived. Sailing up the Thames in the middle of the night was thrilling. Apart from the throbbing engine of the launch and a gentle wind blowing across the river, London was bathed in silence.

After about an hour, near Tilbury, the lights of a ship came into view. The launch circled the ship and then positioned itself alongside it and we clambered up a rope ladder. At the top we were hauled on board by Customs officers, who were surprised to see a young boy. They led us along the deck to where the body of the captain lay. He had shot himself in the head. Looking down at him, for the first time I glimpsed my own mortality. I could see myself there in that pool of blood. One day, I reflected, someone is going to be removing my body and taking it to the mortuary. I am going to die.

The Russian crew, all big, ferocious-looking men with beards, were very angry, and full of vodka, and wouldn't let us remove the deceased because they wanted to take him back to Russia. But the Port of London pilot and customs officers wouldn't let them, as they were inside the three-mile limit and under British jurisdiction. My dad told me to go back to the police boat and get the fold-up stretcher.

This was around the same time as the Cuban missile crisis. A few weeks before we had been called for a special service at school because the general feeling was that the world was on the brink of a nuclear war between America and Russia. Russians were seen as incredibly sinister. Walking across the deck of the Russian ship fear gripped me. Like any young boy, I had a vivid imagination. What if I was attacked or captured? I might never be seen again. As we took the body off the ship the Russian sailors clamoured around us, protesting, but customs officers stepped in and cleared a path for us. We got back home at 5 a.m. Four hours later I was sitting behind my desk at school.

Although I had helped Dad remove the body of that Russian sailor, the first funeral I was involved in with an international element was when a young man who was about the same age as me, sixteen, was killed in a car accident in France and his distraught parents asked us to go to there and collect him. This was the first time I came across Pompes Funebres Generales, France's biggest funeral directors. Only they were allowed to ship a body out of the country. In other words, they had a monopoly.

So early one sunny morning, my dad and I got in the black Bedford van and drove across to Cargo Village at Heathrow Airport to collect the young man. Sitting in the ambulance on the apron of the airport, watching planes landing and taking off, I wondered to myself what his body would look like. I had never seen anyone who had died abroad before. There was something mysterious about it. I can still remember hearing the song 'God Only Knows' on the little transistor radio I had.

When we arrived back at the funeral shop I was tingling with a strange sort of excitement as I helped Fred unfasten the lid of the huge coffin. I have never forgotten the sight of that young man. He had auburn hair and was wearing a houndstooth jacket. Due to the method of embalming that had been used, his skin was rock hard.

The young man's family wanted to have his body at home until the funeral two days later. But we couldn't get his coffin in through the door of the flat because the coffin was so big, so we had to lower it in through the window. He was buried at Camberwell New Cemetery and I remember that his parents had a table tennis bat and ball engraved on a black granite headstone, as John had been a keen player.

His parents were not well to do and were unable to pay for the funeral, so Fred Albin paid Pompes Funebres and allowed the family to pay in weekly instalments. I was deeply impressed by this; by the fact that a funeral firm wasn't simply out to make money. Today, at least once or twice a year, I wander over to that young man's grave and spend a few moments silently reflecting on his death and my own life.

I once travelled with my dad in an old hearse to Southampton to collect the body of an American lady who had died while on board the Queen Mary. Standing there on the quayside watching the crane swing the crate containing the deceased lady off the ship was fascinating.

The family requested that the coffin be covered in a grey cloth. We bought this from a man called Bertioli, a very suave character who wore a flower in the lapel of his checked jacket and drove a Rolls Royce. He supplied funeral directors with everything from coffin handles to urns and was, because of his way of conducting business, known as 'the bandit'. He also sold us plaster crucifixes which were made by a small Italian man, Weegle Leone, who had a shop in Shoreditch.

The American woman was kept at the funeral home for a month because the family decided to continue with the month-long cruise. It was my job to check each day that she was alright. Her body had been smothered in Vaseline to stop mould growing.

It was when I began doing work for Turner's Air Agency in the 1970s that I really learned about moving human remains between different countries. Through working with Iran Air, who had a cargo office behind the Chelsea Hotel, I had learnt how to do ticketing, shipping orders and various other tasks involved in transporting human remains overseas. The Iranian Embassy would often phone me to ask if I could get so and so on a flight to Iran and I used to have regular business lunches with Iranians at The Great American Disaster and Parrs, two west London restaurants.

I am someone who has always looked to improve things and try out new ideas. When Iran Air announced they were closing their cargo office and just going to keep their Piccadilly office open, Barry Groves and Brian Ratcliffe, who ran a freight agency called Turners, located in Goodge Street, asked me to be a consultant for their Iranian business. They knew King Hussein of Jordan very well –

and they used to send him a supply of Walls ice cream on the daily flight to Amman.

I devised a simple scheme to increase business for Turner's. It worked like this. I persuaded Iran Air to allow us to display Turner's leaflets on the front desk of their Piccadilly office. The idea was that Iranians would pick up a leaflet, get a taxi to Goodge Street, leave their baggage with Turner's and receive £2, the cost of the taxi. It was a resounding success. I remember walking into Turner's on one occasion to find about 100 Iranians milling around there in the middle of a mountain of suitcases and boxes. It was an amazing sight. I later went on to become a director of Turner's. Today, I have a consultancy with them and count Barry and Brian amongst my good friends.

Shipping human remains between different countries is a complex business and also very lucrative for airlines, who always say 'freight pays for the fuel'. What makes this work difficult is that each country and airline has different rules. That was why I wrote a small booklet on the subject for the UK funeral industry.

For example, while shipping human remains to America is relatively straightforward and can normally be done within a day, Italy requires that a coffin is dovetailed, two inches thick, has twenty screws in it and is wrapped in three steel bands. A funeral director has to contact the Italian Embassy and the mayor of the town or village where the deceased is to be laid to rest. The mayor has to certify that he is giving permission for the burial or cremation. On top of this, umpteen forms – all written in Italian – have to be filled in. Apart from the usual 'free from infection' declaration required from a doctor, the Italians also insist on an area 'free from infection' declaration.

With so much cargo passing through airports, it is not uncommon for bodies to get lost or even sent to the wrong countries. Not many people know that deceased persons are not allowed to be stored with animals during a flight because animals have an adverse reaction to dead people, it seems.

Because of the risk of fluid leaking from human remains, most countries insist, quite correctly, that coffins are metal-lined and hermetically sealed. They are carried only in a hold, or cargo section, designated for human remains. A coffin has to be weighed, both by the funeral director and the airline. The heavier it is the more expensive it is. Under no circumstances will any airline ship a coffin on the same aircraft as either food or animals. A coffin usually has to receive the embassy seal and be checked to make sure it doesn't contain drugs, guns or explosives. Because airlines were receiving claims for damaged coffins, wooden air trays were introduced. These help to secure the coffin during a flight.

Transporting human remains around the world can lead to problems, it has to be said. One night I received a phone call from the manager of a warehouse at Cargo Village, Heathrow Airport. Although British Airways and Aer Lingus have their own chapels of rest at Heathrow, most airlines place human remains in a section in one of the warehouses. The manager explained that he had received a coffin from Morocco and it was due to be shipped to the Middle East but the remains inside were leaking. As a result he had been forced to close off the area of the warehouse where the deceased person was, causing massive disruption and delaying flights. The reason for this is the risk to public health that a spillage could cause. Something like

TB or hepatitis could be contracted by the staff.

I knew the manager well as a result of previously transporting remains back to Iran and agreed to help him out. Surprisingly, there is no legal requirement for bodies to be embalmed before transportation to another country, although many countries request it. The problem is that in some countries, such as Kenya, there might only be one international funeral director and only a handful of embalmers available. And when I ran my business in Iran I was the only funeral director with the ability to transport human remains.

When I walked into the huge warehouse, located on the edge of the airport, the manager's face lit up. 'Barry, I don't know what I would have done without you.' Leading me through the stacks of crates, he took me to the far side of the warehouse and gestured to a table, where, he said, I could carry out the embalming. The warehouse was icy cold. No wonder the manager had a woolly hat and a heavy coat and gloves on. A forklift truck brought the coffin over and lowered it on to the table.

'Phew, what a stench,' squirmed the manager, turning his head away, as I unfastened the coffin lid with my screwdriver and cutters.

'I've smelt worse,' I replied with a chuckle as I put on my face mask before carefully lifting the remains out of the coffin and on to a table.

Whoever had embalmed this gentleman had done a very poor job. A considerable amount of body fluid had already drained out of the deceased, an elderly Moroccan man. I opened my case and took out my spatula, athesium hook, vein drains, trochar, forceps and arterial clamps and then prepared the fluids.

# Don't Drop the Coffin!

It was a difficult and messy job, made more difficult by not having the full facilities of our mortuary available and also by the cold conditions. I always talk to the deceased person while I embalm. It might sound weird but it helps me to remember that the body on the table in front of me is a person. As long as deceased persons are in my care, I treat them as if they were still alive.

After several hours, I succeeded in making the man look presentable, placed him in the zinc-lined coffin I had brought with me and sealed it. Before leaving, I checked the gentleman's name tag, made a note of it in my book, signed a declaration to the effect that the body had been embalmed according to the correct international procedures and the coffin didn't contain guns, drugs or anything else apart from the deceased, and then, as usual, washed my hands with anti-bacterial soap.

The film *Avanti*, starring Jack Lemmon and Juliet Mills, shows what a bureaucratic nightmare shipping human remains between countries can be. It tells the story of an American man and an English woman who shared a summer romance on an Italian island each year for twenty years without their family knowing. Eventually, they both die there. When the son comes to Italy to claim the body of his father and the daughter comes to claim the body of her mother, they too fall in love. But the struggle they have with the mayor to have the bodies released for transportation back home is as funny as it is true. In the end, both the father and the mother are buried on a cliff overlooking the sea.

Language barriers pose another problem. When customs and other officials are unable to read a document because they don't understand it, this can lead to delays in laying the deceased to rest.

In my capacity as the UK delegate on Federation International des Associations de Thanatologues/ International Federation of Thanatologists Associations (FIAT/IFTA), the international funeral directors' body which represents 500 members in 50 countries, I have had my proposal for a travel document for the dead or, if you like, a passport for the dead, accepted. This happened at the meeting in Majorca in 2001.

Written in over twenty languages, the 'passport' will contain information such as the name and address of the person, age, place of death and cause of death. The idea is that you complete the section in your own language and when you go to a country where another language is spoken, officials there can understand the details by simply looking at the page in their language. In other words, you will not need to get a translator when a document is sent from a country with a different language. Transporting human remains around the world will now be a lot easier for all concerned. This is indeed progress and much needed unification.

Over the years, I have also arranged for a large number of deceased British people to be brought back home, including several celebrities. Through my consultancy work with Pompes Funebres Generales, I had a reputation as someone who knew how the French funeral industry worked. One day in 1995 I received a phone call from a theatrical agent asking me if I would go to Nice to bring back human remains.

'Yes. What's the person's name?' I asked, curious.

'Donald Pleasance,' came the reply.

Donald Pleasance was one of the best-known actors of his generation. Although he had appeared in classic films such as *All Quiet on the Western Front*, *The Great Escape* and *The Eagle Has Landed*, he built up a reputation for playing sinister roles in films such as *You Only Live Twice* and *Halloween*. He was also a great classical actor. Shortly before his death, he had appeared on stage in *King Lear* with his three actress daughters.

When I told my son Jonathan that we were doing Donald Pleasance's funeral, he said, 'He won't look very nice because he's got that scar down his face.' He was remembering him for his role as the Bond villain in *You Only Live Twice*.

After Donald's remains were flown into Heathrow we took him to the funeral home, and a few days later he was cremated at Putney Vale Crematorium. Afterwards, his wife invited me back to the spacious house in Putney for a reception. She was a lovely woman, and the two of them had enjoyed what you might call a champagne lifestyle. I spent an absolutely fascinating few hours mingling with people I had only ever seen on TV. Amongst them were Ian McShane, Bill Wyman, Sir Richard Attenborough, Sir John Gielgud and Alan Bates, who booked me for his funeral, although whether that was him or the champagne talking, I don't know. That night, BBC TV news carried a report of the funeral and a couple of weeks later I found myself appearing in *OK* magazine, which had covered the funeral.

A very different repatriation was that of Scottish rock star Alex Harvey, who died in Bruges. Norman Dugdale, his agent, who I played football with at the Polytechnic of Central London, phoned me up and asked me if I would go and bring Alex's body back to London.

Many people will remember Alex's *Sensational Alex Harvey Band* for 'Delilah', their huge hit in 1975. After they split up two years later, Alex formed the short-lived Alex

Harvey Band. At the time of his death he was about to relaunch his career with a new album and a European tour.

When I went to see Norman at his Maida Vale flat-cum-office to make arrangements for Alex's wife to provide me with the power of attorney, he asked me to go to a meeting with him as his 'lawyer'. I thought it sounded fun so I agreed. The meeting was with an Austrian, who had the tape of the last show that Alex Harvey ever did, in a night club the night before he died. The two of them haggled over the price. Enjoying my role as a lawyer I talked about contracts, indemnities and so on, even though I didn't really know what I was on about. In the end, Norman didn't buy the tape, but the episode was great fun.

I went over on the ferry to Bruges with Fr Frank Carter, who taught me much about bereavement. Frank, who was seriously ill with cancer at the time, was very gregarious and a fan of trivia. I always remember him telling me on the way there that classical music was used on TV commercials because, if it was over fifty years old, no rights had to be paid.

Arriving at the mortuary, tucked away in a small street in one of the suburbs, I was amazed to discover that Belgian law did not require the coroner to disclose the cause of death to the family. I was absolutely shocked by the state of Alex's body. I learned that the autopsy hadn't been completed. Back then in Belgium after autopsies, remains were placed in a coffin, which was sealed and never opened again. Families were prohibited from viewing their loved one. To me, this was blatant disrespect, and ever since I have campaigned to put an end to such practices.

When we got Alex's remains to the funeral home, I had to spend many hours practically rebuilding him before his wife could see him. She wouldn't have recognised him otherwise.

As you might expect, the funeral at Golders Green Crematorium was a star-studded affair. Amongst the mourners were two of the Rolling Stones, Ian Dury and Kid Jensen. During the service, Alex's music was played. Because Norman's business went bust and Alex's wife had no money it took me five years to get paid. That happened when Capital Radio decided to start playing Alex's records, which provided royalties for his wife.

Another time, a Bermondsey man, an epileptic, died while breaking into a chemist's in Barcelona to get some medication. His family came to see me and they said they had been told it would be three weeks before he could be returned to London. I told them I could get him back in a few days and what it would cost. So they asked me to go to Barcelona. I booked my ticket, flew out the next day and booked into a hotel overlooking Barcelona FC's superb stadium.

At the British Consulate, I met an official who took me to the headquarters of the Barcelona funeral industry. Located in the dungeon of an old military hospital, it was also a funeral museum with carriages, vintage coffins and military uniforms. When I was shown the body of the man from Bermondsey, I was astonished to see that he had been laid out on bricks. What's more, the body was bloated and foul smelling because it hadn't been embalmed. The mortuary had no refrigerators. I am glad to say that facilities there today have improved vastly.

The mortician, a surly man with a thick moustache, refused to let me take the body, even though I had a letter of authorisation from the family and the consulate official to vouch for me. After a lot of arguing, I could see that he wasn't going to budge. On the advice of the consulate official, I offered the mortician a 'cash incentive', which, given that his wages were very low, he eagerly accepted. The next day, after registering the death at the consulate, I flew the remains back to London (along with a suitcase full of bread, as there was a bread strike in Britain at the time).

Funeral directors, I believe, can provide valuable assistance not just when a manager of an airport warehouse is in a crisis because of a leaking coffin, but also at major disasters.

The first major incident I was directly involved in was the Moorgate train crash in 1975. We received a call that morning from the police informing us that there had been a serious train crash and asking if we could urgently come and help to remove some of the bodies and take them to the mortuary at Golden Lane in the City. It transpired that at around 8.40 a.m. a train packed with commuters sped past platform nine at twice its usual speed of 15 mph and then ran out of track and rammed into a dead end tunnel.

We hurriedly loaded some fibreglass shells into the private ambulance and immediately set off for Moorgate, about two miles away in the heart of the City. I had never attended an incident like this before and didn't know what to expect. Fred Albin warned me to prepare myself for what I might see. Over the years, he had attended several train crashes, such as that at Hither Green.

There were chaotic scenes when we pulled up outside at the station, which served both Underground and British rail services. Ambulances and police cars were parked everywhere and nurses and doctors were running around in a panic. Accompanied by two police officers and carrying the shells we were led through the station and down the stairs to the platform. The first thing that really hit me was the smell of death, in this case it was the smell of burning electricity. This smell is something I have become very familiar with over the years. It's very hard to describe, but it's a terrible smell and it makes you want to vomit. This, I think, is your body's way of protecting you.

I was shocked by what I saw when we reached the platform. The first three of the six coaches had telescoped at the end of the eighty-yard tunnel after crashing through sand piles and over the buffers. We picked our way through the carriages towards the front of the train. It was eerie. A couple of hours before these carriages were full of people on their way to another day at the office. Many were now lying in hospitals or dead.

We made several trips to remove deceased persons from Moorgate during the next two days. When Golden Lane mortuary filled up we were forced to use Guy's. I remember when we neared the front of the train, we discovered that the first fifteen feet of it had been compressed into two feet and embedded in the wall. Reaching the cab, I found the driver sitting there with his hand on the accelerator lever. He was squashed up to about six inches wide. I later discovered that a teenage police woman was carried out of the wreckage after twelve hours. One of her feet had been pinned down by the tangle of metal and she had to be amputated on at the scene. The final death toll was thirty-five, with many more injured, making it one of the capital's worst rail disasters for many years.

Some years ago, Des Hindley, the chief embalmer at Kenyon's and a brilliant man, invited me to be a member of an international air disaster team set up by Kenyon's funeral directors and British Airways. I was approached because I had built up a reputation for embalming, transporting human remains abroad and, I think, having a good constitution. My job would be to assist in the identification and autopsy, clean and embalm bodies, put the bodies into containers, seal them and ship them home.

After attending a number of training days at Kenyon's Notting Hill headquarters and with British Airways at Heathrow Airport, I was given special ID, which would enable me to be admitted to the restricted zones of most airports in the world. There were two teams, home and away. I was part of both. Members of the team, which could be hired by a country who didn't have the expertise to deal with a major disaster, included dentists, doctors, nurses, embalmers, RAF pathologists, fingerprint experts, bereavement counsellors, pilots and engineers.

When I first began this work I was amazed at the amount of technical ability and team work required. I learned that each body at a scene has to be identified before an autopsy can be carried out. After this, the body is embalmed, the coffin sealed and then returned to their home country. Emergency mortuaries are often set up, sometimes with floodlighting and canteen facilities, and often in airline hangers. Also, family viewings are arranged. And after every air crash every piece of jewellery, clothing and personal effects are collected, then cleaned and returned to the families.

I helped out at Kenyon's emergency centre when the *Herald of Free Enterprise* capsized off Zeebrugge, with around 200 people drowned, and when an Air India Boeing 747 plunged into the sea off the Irish coast, killing 325 people. (Coincidentally, I had been on board another 747, flying back from the US, at the time the bomb went off.) And I supplied zinc-lined coffins when a Yugoslav Airlines plane crashed at Heathrow after a door blew off; also 100 matching American caskets after the Pan Am jumbo was blown out of the air over Lockerbie, killing its 259 passengers.

On one occasion I flew out to the scene of an air crash in the mountains around Barcelona. One image I will never forget amongst the carnage was the sight of a mother and father with their baby between them, still sitting in their seats. Their legs had been severed and they had died instantaneously of shock. The image that has stayed in my mind is of the three of them holding hands.

Over the years, F. A. Albin & Sons have carried out repatriations for Greeks, Portuguese, Spaniards, Iraqis, Nigerians and many other nationalities, but the company has built up a particularly close relationship with Britain's Iranian community ever since we repatriated the nephew of the Shah of Iran. We have repatriated thousands of Iranians and also buried many more in Britain. Today, there are still around 200 deceased Iranians buried in steel coffins in special sandy graves at Brookwood Cemetery. Their families are waiting patiently for things to change before repatriating their loved ones. I was very honoured to receive the official seal of approval from the Shah of Iran when I met him after a dinner at a West End hotel in the late 1970s.

In 2001, I received a phone call asking me to collect the body of Princess Leila Pahlavi, the Shah's youngest daughter. Aged thirty-one, she had died in a London hotel after taking an overdose. We took her remains to RAF Brize Norton and she was flown out to Paris for the funeral.

Our relations with the Iranian Embassy at Princes Gate, under both regimes, have always been excellent. I put this down to the fact that I have no political agenda and that Iranians are kind and loyal people. Furthermore, the staff have never mocked my attempts at speaking Farsi (well not often, anyway). However, there was one occasion when it looked as if we might lose our Iranian work.

My dad and I were summoned for an urgent meeting with senior diplomats. After the usual chit chat and cup of tea, one of the diplomats said, 'Are you Jewish?' Dad and I were surprised at the question, but, given the volatile situation in the Middle East, we were also worried about any implications for our business. It turned out that old Mr Taslim Ali, who ran a funeral home in Whitechapel, had, in an attempt to win our Iranian work, said that Albin was a Jewish name. Dad and I explained that we were not Jewish, but they didn't seem convinced. Only when I returned the next day with my baptismal certificate did they accept that we were Christians.

I am happy to say that Taslim and I didn't fall out over that incident but instead went on to become close colleagues and good friends. For a number of years, I used to do Taslim's embalming. I would go over to his then makeshift mortuary, near the East London Mosque, at 4 a.m. and, wearing a miner's hat with a lamp because the light was so poor, embalm on a table in a shed. His son, also called Taslim, has now taken over the business, called Haji Taslim Funerals, and he too has become a good friend and business colleague and made a wonderful success of the business.

In 1977 I opened a funeral agency in Iran. I had signed a contract with Balfour Beatty and BICC, two of the major contractors working there. The arrangement was that I would take charge of their deceased employees. Because of the dangerous nature of the work, there had been a number of fatalities.

I took the lease on an apartment in Abadan owned by Balfour Beatty, bought a Mercedes ambulance and employed Dr Fazal, a pleasant American-trained local doctor to carry out embalming for me, live in the apartment and run the business. The money I paid to Dr Fazal for one embalming was more than he earned from a month's work with his patients. I taught Dr Fazal all he needed to know about embalming and repatriation and sent him a supply of international shipping coffins and embalming equipment and fluids.

The work went very well. We shipped a number of human remains to various countries, including Italy, Germany and America. But when politics and religion clashed in 1979 and revolution swept through the country my business closed. Incidentally, I still have my Bank Meli chequebook and also a bottle of Iranian vodka (unopened and, I imagine, very rare).

When the British Government banned all flights to and from Iran during the revolution our mortuary in Culling Road rapidly filled up. When I explained my predicament to the Iranian Embassy the military attaché told me that he had a solution: I could fly human remains out from RAF bases. I was astonished to discover that despite an unfair embargo behind the scenes the British Government were flying in medical supplies and other essential items. And when Ayatollah Khomeini came to power, a top Harley Street heart specialist was quietly flown out on several occasions to treat him.

Each time I drove to an RAF base and transferred human remains on to one of the large RAF transport planes I found myself thinking that when it comes to politics nothing is ever the way it seems. Politicians will tell you one thing while the opposite is true.

I was leaving the Iranian Embassy one morning in April 1980, after a meeting with one of the diplomats about my funeral account in Iran. It still contained a significant sum. On my way out Mr Ali, the receptionist, invited me to join him for a cup of tea, something he did often. I shook my head. 'No, I've got a funeral to do, Mr Ali. By the way', I said, pulling one of the new fifty pence pieces out of my pocket and handing it to him, 'Have you seen this?'

He examined it closely in the palm of his hand. I told him that I had heard that some of the 50ps had been minted with eleven hands instead of ten. 'If you found a fifty pence piece with eleven hands it would be worth a lot of money.'

'Really, Albin,' he replied brightly, handing the coin back to me.

'No, keep it. For luck,' I replied dropping it into his top pocket. This insignificant exchange, I was to learn later, would be one that Mr Ali would never forget.

I said goodbye to the policeman, who was standing between the inner and outer doors. As I was walking down the road to my car, I can recall a group of three rough-looking men of Middle Eastern appearance deliberately brushing past me. I was annoyed by their rudeness but thought no more of it until half an hour later when, on the car radio, I heard that the embassy had been stormed immediately after I had left.

What became known as the siege of the Iranian Embassy lasted for six days, until, captured live on TV, the SAS dramatically stormed the building amidst gunfire and explosions. And as Albin's were known to be the official funeral directors for the Iranian Embassy, we had been put on red alert by the coroner's office.

The first call to attend the embassy came on Monday afternoon. The embassy press officer, Abbas, had been shot dead and his body dumped on the pavement outside. Dad and I headed over to Kensington in a private ambulance, placed the deceased in a shell and took him to St Stephen's Hospital mortuary.

Then, a few hours later, the SAS, their faces blackened and covered with balaclavas, burst into the embassy and within minutes put an end to the siege. The speed with which they did this was amazing. We received another call and once again set off for Kensington, this time in two ambulances. When we neared Prince's Gate we were stopped at a police checkpoint. The ambulance was inspected, our ID carefully checked by the police and we were then waved through. Driving slowly on, there was an eerie silence along what is usually one of London's busiest roads. Police cars and fire engines were lined up on the park side. Scaffolding and floodlights had been erected in front of the embassy. Smoke still hung in the air.

Explaining that the fire had now been put out and it was safe to enter the building, a senior policeman directed us to the entrance. We took three stretchers and a shell out of the back of the ambulances and walked through the front door. The dreadful stench of death hit me immediately. The wonderful winding staircase, the chandeliers, Persian carpets, the marvellous paintings, they had all been burnt, while on the walls slogans had been scrawled in Farsi, Arabic and English.

In the telex room, we found two bodies lying in pools of

blood. I saw another body at the foot of the staircase and a fourth a little way up. The bodies were still hot because of the fire. Looking around, I realised how close I had been to being caught up in the siege; how close I had been to death. We put the three bodies on stretchers and one in a shell, carried them out and then loaded them into the ambulances. We were given a police escort to Westminster Coroner's Court, where the autopsies were to take place. Arriving there, we were met by a pack of TV crews and journalists, all anxious for a glimpse of the men responsible for the siege.

Afterwards, I went to the Westminster Hospital to visit Mr Ali and Mr Dani, who had both been shot during the siege.

'You saved my life, Mr Barry,' Mr Ali said with emotion when I walked into his room.

'How?' I asked, puzzled. Perhaps he was suffering from some kind of delusion, I thought to myself. I wasn't even at the embassy during the siege.

'Do you remember that fifty pence piece you gave me on the morning of the siege?'

'Yes,' I replied, wondering what the connection was.

'Well, if it had not been for that I would not be sitting up talking to you now. When the man fired the gun at me the bullet hit the fifty pence piece in my top pocket.' He paused and with emotion in his voice said, 'That coin you gave me saved my life.'

I was amazed and stood there in silence, not knowing what to say. I thought back to when I handed him the coin. Ever since, Mr Ali has always sent me a card and some pistachio nuts at Christmas.

Recalling the terrifying moment the SAS stormed the

embassy, Mr Dani told me one of the terrorists then opened fire, hitting Abbas and another man. Everyone then fell to the floor and the SAS burst in through the wall and through the window and shot one of the terrorists straight away. An SAS officer then shouted out, 'Who is the terrorist?' One of the terrorists had thrown away his gun and had lain down on the floor with the hostages. Then someone pointed to him. The SAS man asked him if he was a terrorist. When he admitted he was, he picked him up by the scruff of the neck. 'You've caused this country nothing but trouble, you bastard,' he said. The SAS were livid when they realised that the police had taken the sixth terrorist away.

I have often asked myself how the terrorists had got past the police officer standing between the inner and outer doors. It emerged later that throughout the siege he was carrying a gun, unknown to the terrorists. They assumed British police officers didn't carry guns and didn't know that the diplomatic police did.

The Iranian Embassy asked me to conduct the funeral of Abbas, the press officer. My friend Taslim Ali was given the job of conducting the funerals of the four terrorists. The following Saturday I found myself at the head of 10,000 chanting Iranians who were marching from Hyde Park Corner to the mosque at Penzance Place, about two miles away. I had planned the route with Scotland Yard, who were concerned about the possibility of violence breaking out, given the volatile political situation resulting from the siege. Apart from a few scuffles and someone spitting at the hearse, the funeral passed off without serious incident. Afterwards, I drove the hearse to Heathrow, and was directed on to the tarmac to a waiting Iran Air plane.

Little did I know that four years later I would myself be in a hostage situation. I was having a business meeting upstairs at the Iranian Consulate in Kensington Court one morning when, all of a sudden, I heard the cry of 'Allah Akbar' followed by a great commotion. The diplomat I was talking to told me not to panic and ordered me to stay where I was, and then raced out of the room. Curious, I followed him. Coming up the stairs was a man, screaming and wielding a chair leg. A struggle ensued and he was overpowered by myself and the diplomat, who barked that I should go back upstairs to the office.

I sat around anxiously in the office, listening to the shouting downstairs, wondering what on earth was going on. Was this going to be a repeat of what had happened at the Iranian Embassy? Suddenly, a vicious-looking man appeared in the doorway and began making threatening gestures. As he tried to come in, I rushed across the room, put my body against the door, and pushed him out, slamming the door.

I was on the telephone, speaking to one of my staff at the funeral home and explaining what had happened, when through the window I saw a policeman on the roof pointing a gun at me. I can tell you that having a gun pointed at you is a marvellous way of focusing the mind. With my pulse racing, I made signs to him that I wasn't a terrorist. I didn't know whether to put my hands up or get under the desk. Then the phone rang. It was the Iranian Embassy. They wanted to know what was happening. Before I could explain, the call was intercepted by a police officer who wanted to know who I was and what the situation was inside. I told them the consulate had, it appeared, been stormed.

I had to wait in the room for about four hours while the situation was brought under control. It was a nerve-wracking time, even though the consulate staff had assured me that none of those who had stormed the embassy were carrying guns. Eventually I was asked by one of the consulate staff to go downstairs. When he asked me to be blindfolded, I refused. Instead, he tried to prevent me seeing by holding a coat in front of me as he led me downstairs. I did agree, however, to place my hands behind my back. But I could see people tied to chairs with tape and being interrogated by consulate staff. I saw blood on the carpet and overturned furniture. I was then told to leave the consulate through the basement. As soon as the door to the street was opened I was grabbed by the police, bundled into a squad car and whisked away to Kensington police station.

I was taken into an interview room and questioned about events at the consulate. I learned that eleven unarmed anti-Khomeini students had gained access to the consulate by pretending to want immigration documents. The students had been overwhelmed by the diplomats. Sitting there, explaining to two surly detectives about what I had seen at the consulate, I began to feel as if I was guilty. They adopted an offhand and aggressive manner with me, and asked me to draw a map of the layout of the embassy building and indicate who was in each room. Then my voice bleeper suddenly went off and the voice of Mahmoud, one of the officials at the embassy, could be heard.

'Mr Albin, I forgot to tell you. Don't tell the police anything,' he said urgently.

Oh, no! I wanted the floor to open up.

The older detective screwed up his face and said, 'Yeah, do that. Don't tell us anything. And then we'll have more policewomen like Yvonne Fletcher shot in the street and foreigners will be running the country.'

Of course, I did tell them all I knew. After about eight exhausting hours I was released, tired and angered by the attitude of the two detectives. On my way back to Bermondsey, I reflected that I had been treated far better by the Iranians than by the police.

Apart from conducting the funerals of Iranians and arranging for their repatriation, I have also helped many Iranians to find medical treatment in private hospitals and accommodation during their stay. For instance, I helped a number of mustard gas victims of the Iran/Iraq war. I remember speaking to one thin sixteen-year-old whose brother had already been killed in the war. He was burnt all over: his face, arms, legs, even genitals. His breathing was very bad.

I asked him, 'When you go back to Iran, what will be the first thing you will do?'

I expected him to say that he would go to his parents to convalesce. He replied, 'I will get a rifle and go straight back to the front, because I want to die for Islam.' I then realised that what mattered most for these young men, more than even their family, was sacrificing their life for their beliefs.

The boy never made it back to Iran, and a few weeks later I conducted his funeral. I led the cortege, consisting of several thousand distraught mourners, from Hyde Park Corner to the mosque in Penzance Place. We marched all the way. After the service in the mosque we took his remains to Heathrow, where he was loaded into an Iran Air plane and sent home as a martyr. During the following six weeks, I conducted another six funerals of young Iranian war victims.

On a lighter note, I remember the time when an Iranian man phoned the owner of the garage in his village in a remote corner of Iran to let his family know that one of their relatives had died in hospital. The village had clubbed together to send the man to London for medical treatment (Iranian families are very kind to one another). When the owner took the call, he shrieked and dropped it on the floor. He knew the other man was in London and he couldn't understand what was happening. It was as if he had spoken to him spiritually, and he refused to come back to the phone.

# 4

# CEMS, CREMS OR OUTER SPACE?

'Well, Barry, all quiet on the western front,' whispered Freddy Collins, one of my drivers, as we walked, shivering in the snow, into the chapel at Honor Oak Crematorium.

'Don't be so sure, Freddy. It might be the calm before the storm,' I replied.

I knew, from my meeting the week before with the family, that they were embroiled in a bitter feud after one member had attacked another. I was very worried that feelings might come to the boil during the funeral. But, so far, things had run smoothly, although I had noticed dagger looks among some of the mourners when we were leaving the deceased's flat in Walworth.

After the service, the family trooped out and I could sense that there was tension in the air. Several of them were exchanging threatening looks. Just as I was about to usher people back into the limousines, one man suddenly aimed a kick at another and floored him.

What happened next was like something out of a film. I

stood there stunned as thirty people tried to trade punches in the snow. I was trying desperately to hang on to the brother who had started the fight but I couldn't keep my balance and keeled over backwards with him in my arms. The shouting and screaming was incredible. As they lunged at each other, rarely connecting, they fell over as if in slow motion. Some fell into rose bushes, others on to the hearse. All you needed in the background was Perry Como singing 'Have Yourself a Merry Little Christmas'. It was like *Come Dancing* on ice. From a distance it must have looked very funny, but, of course, it was very upsetting for many of the family, and I had to intervene to bring the fight to a halt. This wasn't easy, especially in the snowy conditions. Nevertheless, eventually my team and I succeeded in calming everyone down and we managed to usher them into different cars for the journey home. As I was getting into the hearse, I went to remove my glasses, but I couldn't. They were frozen to my face. I had to call one of the men to unhinge them for me.

Another very tense funeral was that of an elderly lady who had been cared for in her last years by her son-in-law, a Czech brain surgeon who lived on a boat in Rotherhithe. He said to me that there were people at the funeral he didn't want: his mother-in-law's three daughters. He added that if they turned up they would be ignored. Outside the church one of the daughters gave me a wreath and he snatched it from me and threw it in the dustbin.

When we arrived at the crematorium he told me he wanted to say a few words. 'Do you think it's wise?' I asked, knowing his strong feelings about the daughters.

'Absolutely', he replied boldly and strode resolutely over to the coffin. 'You're going now,' he began. 'You are very lucky. Your daughters are here. But I don't know why they have bothered to come because they never bothered to come and see you when you were alive.'

The daughters were outraged and one of them threatened to leave. But the others argued that they should stay.

'They're having an argument now,' he went on, ignoring the polite request from the priest to sit down. 'You knew this would happen, didn't you, my darling. I suppose they've come because they think there's some money for them. Won't they be surprised when they realise that you have left everything to me and I'm leaving everything to the hospital. You bitches at the back here, you will be getting nothing. And that's what you deserve. And mother will be so pleased to see this day. You care nothing for her; only for yourselves.'

Afterwards, he requested that he should be cremated and the ashes of the two of them were to be sprinkled in the Thames. And when he died ten years later I did this.

Yet, I have to admit, I know from my own experience how easy it can be to lose your cool during a funeral. Once, at Streatham Park Cemetery, I was walking the cortege down the road to the chapel when, to my astonishment, a hearse and a car from another well-known funeral firm overtook me and drove straight up to the doors of the chapel. I was incensed. They should have been there half an hour before. Cemetery and crematorium chapels are busy places and they usually run a very tight schedule, booking in funerals at thirty- or forty-five-minute intervals. The cemetery attendant had called me in on time because they hadn't turned up. Not wanting to cause a scene that might upset the mourners, I decided to wait until after the service before challenging the men from the other company.

When the men from the other funeral directors came out I went up to the hearse driver and the conductor and politely, but firmly, asked them if they would come around the side of the chapel for a word. They looked a bit surprised but, nevertheless, followed me obediently around the corner.

'How dare you be so rude and so ignorant,' I said angrily, trying to keep my voice down but never taking my eyes off them. 'I won't accept this. It's unprofessional. You were late. If you can't get there on time, that's your problem, not mine. You took a right liberty.'

'Sorry, we didn't mean to upset you, Barry,' apologised the taller one, clearly taken aback at my outburst.

'We didn't think, did we,' added the other, timidly.

'Well, next time make sure you do think,' I replied, stepping back, knowing that I had made my point. 'I won't tolerate such behaviour in front of my mourners. Do you understand?' They both nodded. 'We all have to work together, so don't take the piss. Just show some respect.'

Afterwards, I felt somewhat ashamed of my actions. I had lost my cool but, thankfully, it wasn't in front of the mourners. Anybody can be late, but it's how you behave that matters. As I've said, when it comes to arranging and conducting a funeral I will let nothing and nobody interfere with it, and if this means I have to get into a confrontation, then I will, as I did once in the middle of Lewisham High Street when a workman suddenly began drilling and scared the living daylights out of the horses pulling the hearse. I'm not saying this is the proper way to go about things, but it is, rightly or wrongly, my way. Fred Albin took the same approach when he ran the business, and I suspect there are other funeral directors up and down the country who would react in a similar way. Unfortunately, there are some people in life who because of ignorance won't listen to reason and only understand one sort of language.

Another confrontation, this time at Honor Oak Crematorium, caught me completely by surprise. After the Baptist minister concluded his service in the chapel I took him aside and told him that he had run into my time by fifteen minutes and this was unacceptable. He gave me a supercilious look, turned his back and walked away. I turned to the Church of England vicar who was with my funeral and shook my head, 'If there's one thing that gets my back up apart from late clergy it's ignorant clergy.' The next thing, the vicar went bounding off like Lynford Christie and grabbed the Baptist minister around the neck and slammed him up against the wall.

'You fornicating old bastard,' he said angrily.

'What do you think you are doing?' exclaimed the Baptist minister, looking terrified. 'Let me go.'

Then, to my astonishment, the vicar began lifting the other minister up and pushing him against the wall.

'Steady on, there's no need for that,' I said with alarm, as I grabbed him around the chest and began to pull him off. But he just kept lashing out. The Baptist minister was now cowering with his head in his hands, pleading for his fellow clergyman to stop. As I dragged the vicar away and tried to calm him down, the Baptist minister fled, shaken but not seriously hurt. But if this clerical punch-up had continued much longer, I mused afterwards, we might have had another cremation on our hands.

Cemeteries are sacred places, and these sorts of incidents are rare, I am glad to say. In a cemetery people remember their loved ones in silence and reflect on their own mortality. Tending the grave, bringing fresh flowers, these actions are expressions of love for the deceased and can be a part of the grieving process.

I can never forget the funeral of the wife of a local Jack-the-lad character. We were all standing around the grave when one of the old aunties said, 'I didn't see our flowers and cards. I hope they arrived.' The Jack-the-lad character replied, 'Well, there's two cards on the coffin.' And with that he jumped into the grave. 'Are these them?' he shouted up to the old lady. I had a job to keep a straight face.

When I conduct a funeral at somewhere like Kensal Green or Highgate Cemetery, I always reflect that, with their flamboyant sculptures, tombs and mausoleums, these cities of the dead illustrate the flair the Victorians had for commemorating death. Interestingly, though, they took their ideas from countries such as France and Italy, where cemeteries were designed with tomb-lined avenues.

We take public cemeteries for granted nowadays but they only originated in the Victorian period after concerns that some churchyards posed a health risk. Despite being only sixty metres square, it was estimated that as many as sixty or seventy thousand people were buried in the churchyard at St Martin-in-the-Fields. The Burial Act of 1852 closed churchyards and required the General Board of Health to open cemeteries in the London suburbs. The Romans, in fact, forbade the burial of bodies inside a city's walls. Their catacombs in Rome are a superb example of how an ancient culture looked after its dead.

London, in fact, has a number of specialist cemeteries. For example, there is the Army cemetery at the Royal Hospital in Chelsea and a Royal Navy cemetery in Greenwich. There are

Catholic cemeteries at places such as Kensal Green and Leytonstone and numerous Jewish cemeteries, reflecting Orthodox, Liberal, and Reform traditions in areas such as West Ham, Edgware and Willesden, and Muslim cemeteries in Tottenham and Walthamstow. There is even a pet cemetery in Sevenoaks, Kent.

One of my greatest fears has always been not being able to find a cemetery, even though I have a very good knowledge of London. It's very easy to get lost in London. I will never forget the time I looked in my wing mirror and saw behind me the funeral cortege from another firm turn not into Putney Vale Cemetery but into the adjacent Asda car park. I often wake up in the middle of the night to a nightmare of being lost on my way to a funeral. In fact, I have an alternative map of London in my head, made up of funeral homes, cemeteries and crematoriums. But the majority of the funerals I conduct are in south and east London.

So, when I was asked by an Iranian Muslim family living in Finchley to conduct a funeral that would end up at the Great Northern Cemetery in New Southgate, I knew I needed to work out my route well, as I hadn't been there for a long time. When Lee, my hearse driver, and I left the funeral home in the hearse that morning (the family had decided to provide their own cars), I felt somewhat apprehensive but, I thought, between us we would have no problem in finding the cemetery.

The deceased had died the day before and the family wanted him buried immediately. This tradition of immediate burial originates, so I gather, from Islam taking root in hot countries, where a body would soon begin to smell and decay after death. Islam is about good practice and the Koran about living a good life.

After walking up and down a street of shops for several minutes, I eventually found the flat, which was above a launderette. A middle-aged Iranian woman with an American accent came to the door and said there was no one to drive her car to the cemetery. So would I drive it? I agreed and she gave me the keys and told me where the garage was. But I was concerned about Lee finding the cemetery without me sitting beside him.

When I opened the garage doors I was taken aback to find that it was a large, blue, American, left-hand drive car. Now, while I've always loved cars and admired American ones in particular, this, I felt, was not the time to be familiarising myself with controls that were in different places to British cars. But what could I do?

Before we set off, I gave Lee detailed directions on how to get to the cemetery. It involved travelling through a winding route across north London and then along the North Circular Road. I told him that I would flash twice for a left turn, three times for a right, and four times to remain in the lane. But I could see from the look on his face that he wasn't very sure about the route.

With the A–Z perched on my lap, the Iranian lady with the American accent sitting next to me and three other women in the back, I followed Lee into the traffic. Suddenly, the four women in the car began wailing and screaming. I had to concentrate hard to make sure I didn't lose the hearse in the, by now, heavy traffic. Then one of the women lit up a cigarette. Not being a smoker, I fumbled with the dashboard to find the button to open the windows. While I was doing this the woman sitting next to me slotted in a tape of prayers.

As arranged, I flashed Lee each time we had to make a

turning. I nearly lost him when a bus cut in between us at a busy junction and then again at the roundabout near New Southgate station. Finally, I saw the sign for the Great Northern Cemetery and I breathed a huge sigh of relief.

Cemeteries nowadays offer a range of graves available to families. For instance, the large and very attractively landscaped City of London Cemetery and Crematorium, in Manor Park, east London, offers a choice of seven types of graves. Lawn graves are level with the ground and usually have a simple headstone, while a classic lawn grave has a different memorial design. There are also classic lawn graves for cremated remains only. Traditional graves come in three varieties: fully constructed, non-constructed and semi-constructed. All three types may be covered by a substantial memorial on a concrete landing, which covers the area of the grave. You can also have a coffin placed in the crescent shaped catacomb. When this is done, the cell is sealed with a tablet, which can be inscribed as a memorial. The cemetery also offers the option of being buried without a memorial in one of its wooded areas.

And, of course, there are also common graves, sometimes referred to as 'paupers' graves'. These are graves that might take up to six people, marked by tiny memorial stones.

But if I am taking a funeral to the City of London Cemetery and Crematorium, for example, I will never drive the hearse through the Rotherhithe or Blackwall Tunnel. And the reason is that you never take anyone underground before their time. It might sound strange, but I have always followed this tradition. If Tower Bridge is closed I'll go to Southwark Bridge and if that's closed I'll go to Blackfriars Bridge. I've never had a family complain about this. If they ask why we are going a long way round to get to the cemetery I tell them it's because Arthur Albin told me, 'Never go underground before your time.' And they love it. If anyone ever told me to go under the tunnel I wouldn't.

The weather plays a key part in a funeral. I've seen cases where water has flooded graves and they have caved in and once the vicar and I slipped and disappeared into a grave after the head of the grave gave way at the edge. I remember once doing a funeral at Nunhead in thick fog. You could only see about a foot in front of you. We must have looked like monsters from the swamp. The gravedigger walked ahead with a lamp, while I drove behind in the hearse with the headlights on. It took us about an hour to find the grave and two hours to find our way out.

One thing that can often cause embarrassment at a cemetery is when someone wants to respond to the call of nature. The very old cemeteries don't, generally, have public toilets. When I was a kid accompanying my dad on a funeral at Nunhead Cemetery I can remember the hilarious sight of all the men hurrying off to the bushes on one side and all the women going to the other side. They had all made the fatal mistake of having a few drinks before they left the house. I remember a particular horse-drawn funeral we did one winter some years later. As we were putting the flowers on the hearse, a horse decided to relieve himself. Its urine ran down between the cars and within a few minutes had frozen over. Unaware of this, I then walked through the middle of the cars, hit the floor but came straight back up again, as if I was on a trampoline, and just carried on walking. And my top hat never even fell off. Unbeknown to the mourners, my son Jonathan had to fight hard to prevent himself bursting into laughter; and when he gets the giggles he is infectious. In fact, due to having 'elasticated' ankles, I fall over regularly.

I have arrived at cemeteries to reopen graves, and after sending the cemetery superintendent the deeds, the correct number of the grave and correct name I have discovered that the wrong headstone has been removed and the wrong grave opened. This once happened when I arrived with a bereaved family at one south London cemetery. We spent ten minutes making our way through the graves and plots until we reached the far end where the family's grave was.

'Mum's not buried there,' shrieked the daughter.

'Are you sure?'

'Yes! She's not buried here,' she repeated in a distraught voice.

I marched into the superintendent's office. Looking up from his desk, he could tell from the expression on my face that something wasn't right.

'This is unacceptable,' I said angrily. 'Your men have opened the wrong grave. My family are extremely upset. Now, I am going with everyone to the Greyhound pub and I am going to make sure they have sandwiches and something warm to drink. And this will be at your expense. My hearse driver will stay here with the deceased and when you have found the right grave and reopened it you will phone me and I will then bring everyone back.' The way I saw it was that I was just changing the order of the funeral and starting the wake a bit earlier.

When we returned to the cemetery a couple of hours later, it was dark. So we had to position the cars around the grave and switch the headlights on full beam so that the mourners – who now felt relaxed after a few drinks and some food – could find their way to the grave. The scene resembled a floodlit football pitch.

Over the years, I have successfully exhumed a number of bodies, and it always seems to be at 4 a.m. when you have the mist floating across the cemetery. Exhumations are usually carried out because a family is dissatisfied with the cemetery or they want their loved one nearer home. In some cases, a family might have bought a larger plot and want to have all their family together. The reason why exhumations are done at such an early hour is so that it doesn't take place in view of the public.

Permission from the Home Office must be obtained before an exhumation can take place. You fill out a form stating who owns the grave, whether there are any objections to the exhumation, whether the grave contains anyone else, why you want to do the exhumation and where the body is to be moved to. If someone is buried on top of another in a public grave then there is no problem in opening the grave. However, if they are buried beneath other bodies, then permission from the other families must be sought before an exhumation can take place. Once the Home Office clears the application they issue the funeral director with a licence to exhume and they write to the cemetery. If you exhume a body from a Church of England cemetery, for example, you need to obtain a faculty from the local bishop.

There's always a mystique to exhuming a body, no matter how many times you have done it. You wonder what it will look and smell like and how you are going to get it out. And the smell when you open a coffin is so bad it makes you sick. This is because of the gases from the body. The coffin is disinfected and lime sprinkled around the grave to prevent the spread of disease.

Not everyone is buried the traditional six feet under. In some cases, the last interment in a grave might only be a foot or so from the surface. In these situations, the law requires that the top end of the grave be sealed off with concrete.

Shortly after the film *Pocahontas* was released in Britain in 1998 I received a request from the American Office for Indian Affairs asking me if I would be prepared to undertake the exhumation and repatriation of Pocahontas to her home land. Soon after, I received a similar request, this time from the settlers in the area where she came from. Although she's buried in a churchyard in Gravesend in Kent, the site of her burial plot has been lost. It's certainly within a quarter of a mile of the church. The vicar of the church is adamant that he doesn't know where she is and that she shouldn't be moved. I expect he makes a fortune out of the tourists who go to the church in search of the grave. I explained to both parties that for us to carry out research into the resting place of Pocahontas would cost about £10,000. It would require someone to be employed scouring maps and documents at the British Museum. So far, they haven't been back in touch with me.

The fear of premature burial is a deep one. Since the time of Duke Ferdinand of Brunswick in the late 1700s, there have been numerous cases where the deceased has been buried in what is known as a security coffin, which would often have an air hole and a rope attached to the hand of the deceased and linked to a bell above. And as recently as the mid-1990s it was reported that an Italian watchmaker had marketed a coffin equipped with a bleeping device, a telephone, a flashlight, an oxygen tube, and a heart stimulator.

Once, at an exhumation at Nunhead Cemetery, I discovered scratch marks on the inside of the coffin and pieces of fingernail in the bottom of it. I was told this was the result of someone being buried alive a couple of hundred years before. I don't know if it's true or not, but the explanation certainly had the air of authenticity about it. I once conducted the funeral for a man who was buried with an alarm bell in his hand, a fully charged mobile phone and some food, in case he woke up. As we carried the coffin I couldn't help but think what if we bumped it and the alarm went off – or the phone rang!

But I am certain that I have never buried anyone alive. I say this because before an embalming begins we always take the pulse of the deceased person, look at their eyes to see if there is any movement and on occasions make a small pin prick to see if the circulation system is working, or hold a mirror in front of the mouth to see if the deceased is still breathing.

I believe, however, that there have been times when people have been buried alive, for example, on the battle-fields during the Second World War.

In December 2000 I carried out one of the most unusual funerals I have ever done: that of the bones of between thirty and forty people who died in south-east London in the eighteenth century and were discovered by staff from the British Museum during an archaeological dig. The vicar of St Paul's, Deptford, approached me one day and explained that he wanted the remains given a proper funeral.

We collected the bones from the church and placed them each in an individual small coffin. Two coffins were placed in each hearse and we drove to the church, which was then in the middle of renovation, for a service. I and my team formed a circle around the open coffins and the vicar stood in the middle and individually blessed each set of human remains.

Later, when the renovation work has been completed, the remains will be buried in the churchyard at St Paul's. Some people might think all of this unnecessary and that we should have simply put the bones in a black bin liner. But the vicar and I both believed in the sacredness of the body.

Human remains have, for various reasons, always attracted the interest of some unsavoury people. At one time, grave robbers such as the notorious Burke and Hare made a lucrative living by selling human remains to medical schools. Most famously perhaps, in March 1978 grave robbers took the body of Charlie Chaplin from the Swiss cemetery where he had been buried three months before. Police said that the marks on the ground at the graveside indicated that the heavy casket had been dragged several feet before being heaved on to a truck. There have also been many stories, some apocryphal perhaps, of Satanists robbing graves. (I once exhumed a body at Nunhead because the family were convinced Satanists were gathering in the cemetery.)

Late one night, a worried vicar rang to say that a vault at a Camberwell church had been broken into by some men looking for jewellery and would we go there immediately. When Fred Albin and I arrived, the vicar told us that the vault contained the body of a famous car inventor. Leading me through the dark, dirty, dusty vault, which was crawling with insects, he took me to the far wall, where a coffin on a shelf had been broken open. I was amazed to see that the inventor was in perfect condition and was wearing a suit and bow tie and had thick ginger sideburns and a ginger moustache. He remained like this for ten hours before he became dehydrated and very leathery. We resealed the coffin with lead, reburied the remains in another more secure part of the vault and bricked it in. Moving these lead shell coffins, even though we had rollers, was not easy, I can tell you.

Similarly, I was once asked to move the bodies in the crypt of St James' church, Bermondsey, as the vicar wanted to open up the crypt for the parishioners to use as a meeting place. He had been quoted thousands of pounds when he asked building companies what it would cost to move the remains from one side to the other. I agreed to do it as a charitable venture as that was the church I had known as a child and where I had been married. Over the next three months, I, my sons and some of my staff came along in the evenings and moved the oak and lead coffins to the other side of the crypt to be sealed up. Many of these interments, it turned out, had been carried out by Albin's. We found a number of coffins that had been unsealed or broken. It's amazing when you see a body that has been sealed in an air-tight container for a couple of hundred years. For the first few hours, before they start to shrink in the atmosphere, their hair and skin all look perfect. Apart from decorating rooms for the elderly in Bob a Job week, this was the first charitable thing I did as a young man. We have a plate on the wall in the funeral home and, as a memento, we were given the old hand barrow that was used to wheel coffins through the churchyard.

Soon after, we did the same thing at St Mary's church in Rotherhithe. Christopher Jones, the master of the Mayflower, the ship that took the Pilgrim Fathers to

America in 1620, is buried here. The churchyard also contains the tomb of Prince Lee Boo from the Pacific Islands. The inscription reads: 'Stop reader, stop! Let Nature claim a tear / A Prince of mine, Lee Boo, lies buried here.'

I love reading gravestone inscriptions, some of which are very amusing. Take these, for example:

Remember me as you pass me by,
As you are now once was I.
As I am now soon you will be,
So be prepared to follow me.

Not Dead. Only sleeping.

I have only this small stone because I knew there were no pockets in the shroud. I enjoyed every moment.

How happy we will be in a hundred years from now
The centipedes crawl up your nose
They lay their eggs between the toes
How happy we shall be in a hundred years from now
So don't be buried; be cremated
Or you'll end up aerated
How happy we will be in a hundred years from now.

Pass this way quietly, if you please. I'm dead not deaf.

The last trumpet sounded
They banged the big drum
The gates of Heaven opened
And in walked mum.

One of my biggest business failures was when I turned down the opportunity to buy a share in a cemetery, Brookwood, near Woking in Surrey. Originally opened as a private cemetery by the London Necropolis and National Mausoleum Company in 1854, Brookwood is the only cemetery to have its own railway station. Trains from Waterloo still stop there. During World War Two many of the people who died during the bombing and couldn't be identified were buried there. My dad used to take bodies to Waterloo Station, which had a special coffin-loading platform, and every Friday morning what was known as 'the death train' would depart for Brookwood. Once it reached Brookwood all the bodies were then buried in a mass grave.

One afternoon, I was cleaning up in the mortuary when a call was put through from reception. It was Ramadan Gunay, a Turkish businessman whom I vaguely knew. After a bit of chit chat, he said, 'I have a proposition for you.'

'I'm listening,' I replied, wondering what this was all about.

'Would you be interesting in buying Brookwood Cemetery with me?'

'Brookwood? Why would I want to buy half of Brookwood?' I replied, laughing.

Brookwood was a huge cemetery and as such had high maintenance costs. If it wasn't maintained properly, you would be dealing with the complaints of the families. It could only be a loss maker, like those cemeteries sold off for fifteen pence by Dame Shirley Porter when she was leader of Westminster city council in the 1990s.

'They only want £200,000. I need someone to put up the other half. Believe me, it's a good deal,' he insisted.

'Ramadan, I wouldn't buy it for £2,' I replied emphatically. 'Come on, it's a dead duck. It will make you old and stressed.' I wasn't going to start looking around for this kind of money for such a risky venture.

'You'll regret it, Barry,' he predicted.

Some time later those words came back to haunt me. Chatting to a business colleague over lunch one day I discovered that Ramadan had indeed bought Brookwood, for £250,000, and was also the owner of the fire station, the police station, the school and hunting lands. It turned out that Ramadan had found some ancient deeds, which identified the owner of Brookwood as owning other tracts of land in the vicinity. I was gutted. That cemetery was recently on the market for £28 million. I think Ramadan's good fortune was, though, more luck than judgement. So for a £125,000 investment I could have had land valued at £14 million, as he still reminds me even to this day. He now also owns a funeral business, an airline and hotels. Ramadan was also the man who put up £1 million bail for former Polly Peck director Asil Nadir, after the collapse of his business empire in 1993. But Nadir fled Britain, to Turkish northern Cyprus, rather than face fraud charges relating to the theft of £34 million, and I guess Ramadan lost his money.

This brings me to what many believe to be a chronic shortage of burial space, especially in the capital. Today, some inner London boroughs have an average of only seven years' supply of burial spaces left, while Hackney and Tower Hamlets have no space left at all. In leafy Bexley on the edge of London there is no shortage of space, while the neighbouring borough of Greenwich has very little. It is estimated that by the year 2010 London will have no burial space left at all. In Southwark, where around 40 per cent of people choose burial, far higher than the national average, this is a particularly acute problem. There is a lull now in the death rate because there are fewer people in their seventies and eighties as a result of a whole generation being lost during the war. In the next ten to twenty years we will have the highest ever reported death rate because of the post-war baby boomers. This is why an urgent solution to the shortage of burial space needs to be found.

Crucially, the Greater London Authority (GLA) has no London-wide strategy for the disposal of the dead. Instead, each borough makes its own arrangements. Many people are unaware that, because of this pressure of space, most burial plots in cities are sold on a leasehold system. Remains can therefore legally be moved to another part of the cemetery once the lease has expired, usually after fifty-five to ninety-nine years. But I have never known this to be done. In 2000, though, there was public outrage when the remains of 15,000 victims of the Blitz were relocated from Wood Grange Cemetery in Manor Park to make way for luxury flats.

In my opinion, we operate a ludicrous system of digging graves in England, which is partly because local authorities have seen cemeteries as an obligation rather than an opportunity to do something creatively. They dig one grave one day, another the next and so on. Why? It would be more sensible and cost effective to bring in machinery to dig a trench of, say, 200 yards long, which would hold about 150 graves and then cover them with metal sheeting and grass matting or Astroturf, making sure they looked decorative. You would then simply open one grave at a time, inter the remains and fill it in. In fact, they used to do something similar at a London cemetery, where they had what are called public, or 'paupers', graves. These were very deep because each could hold up to eight people. They used to dig a grave that was only six feet deep. After the body had been interred, two men would pop up at the bottom of the grave and they would lower the coffin down on to a little trolley in a tunnel underneath and then wheel it to a space 100 yards away, where the bodies would be stacked in a public grave, which was like a long trench, and then filled and marked.

And there is no need, as some suggest, to exhume remains and disrupt the dead, in order to create new spaces. What would be much simpler would be to flatten some of the very old cemeteries, mound them up in steps with sand and bury people at a higher level. Some of the old chapels could also be converted into mausoleums above ground. The funeral historian Julian Litten, whom I respect very much, argues that it isn't human remains that are responsible for the shortage of burial space in cemeteries but headstones. This is a view I share. Memorials that were, say, 200 years old could be removed, used for rubble and one single memorial erected to all those buried there. Something similar to this has been done at St Patrick's Cemetery in Leytonstone.

Another problem is that municipal cemeteries are run by individual local authorities, who have rules about who can and cannot be buried there. The situation in south-east London illustrates this point. Before the borough of Southwark was created by the Greater London Council in 1965, the area consisted of three boroughs, Southwark, Camberwell and Bermondsey, each with its own town hall and services. What this meant in terms of funerals was that if someone in Bermondsey wanted to be buried in Camberwell Cemetery, then a triple fee had to be paid because it was in another borough. To get around this many people chose to be buried in private cemeteries, such as St Patrick's, Manor Park, across the river in east London.

Interestingly, Lambeth Council set up a web site to help people trace old graves dating back to the nineteenth century at West Norwood Cemetery. Amongst others, the cookery writer Mrs Beeton is buried there. The council had been criticised by the Church of England diocese of Southwark for illegally re-using graves, known as 'lawn conversion'. Many of the dead listed on the web site are thought to be buried under other bodies. Stacking corpses happened in order to save burial space.

Today, we can use any of Southwark's three cemeteries, Nunhead, Camberwell or Camberwell New. The average cost of a grave in London is around £1,000, more than in many other parts of the country. If, for example, a person lives across the road from Camberwell New Cemetery, but they are in the borough of Lewisham, then it will cost them three times more to get buried there than at, say, Grove Park Cemetery, at the other end of the borough. Despite opposition from local residents, Southwark will, eventually, have no alternative but to use some of its recreation ground adjacent to Camberwell New Cemetery or make other arrangements. The solution, I believe, is to fund cemeteries nationally, or in London's case through the GLA, rather than locally, along the lines of the Post Office. A person could then be buried anywhere rather than restricted by the regulations of a particular borough. I have written papers on this and lectured on this. But, unfortunately, nothing changes. It seems that when the government research the issue of burial space they don't ask people like myself who have knowledge, insight and ideas.

Today, two thirds of funerals in the UK are bound not for the cemetery but for the crematorium. Arthur Albin could not accept cremation because he held to the traditional Christian view that it was incompatible with the resurrection of the body. He believed that Sir Henry Thompson, the surgeon to Queen Victoria and the founder of the Cremation Society, had a lot to answer for. Cremation is not new, however. Many cultures have used it. The Vikings, for instance, used to burn bodies on a boat out at sea. And they believed that if you died with a sword in your hand Thor would welcome you into Heaven. Although cremations account for the biggest part of our work, I, like Arthur Albin, believe the body is sacred and would not want to be cremated.

The legalisation of cremation was also due, in part, to the eccentric Dr William Price, a chartist who had escaped to France dressed as a woman. At the age of eighty-three he fathered a child, whom he named 'Jesus Grist'. When the child died, aged five months, Price attempted to cremate the body at the top of a hill. At his trial in Cardiff in 1884 the judge ordered the jury to find Price not guilty, as no British law forbade cremation unless it was carried out in a manner that would cause a public nuisance or prevent a coroner from holding an inquest. Soon after, at Woking, 20,000 people turned up to watch William Price become the first person in Britain to be publicly cremated.

When I meet people at social gatherings and I tell them I'm a funeral director very often the conversation turns to cremation. They want to know if we actually cremate the coffin and if we take the handles off beforehand. These questions are tied up with a general suspicion that funeral directors remove valuable personal effects, such as jewellery, before a cremation or burial. When I tell them that, yes, the coffin is cremated and, no, we don't take off jewellery, unless requested to do so by the family, and, yes, they are the genuine ashes of the deceased person concerned, they often give me one of those disbelieving looks. But it is perfectly true.

Many people are unaware that it's not the cremator that produces the ashes of a deceased person. After a cremation a number of bones are still left. The ashes are created by placing the bones in a container with some ball bearings and then putting it into a machine, which rotates very quickly. The ball bearings contact with the bones, gradually grinding them into ashes. Afterwards, a magnet is used to extract the ball bearings, leaving only the ashes of the person cremated.

Many crematoriums are computerised and more environmentally friendly. For example, the heat from the cremator can be turned into steam, which can provide heating to the local area. Some environmentalists argue against using certain polishes on coffins or even a deceased person being buried in clothes or a child with a teddy bear. This kind of thinking makes me angry. It has no justification. What is the amount of pollution caused by a teddy bear compared to the effects of such a ban on a parent's mental health? The emissions from all UK crematoriums over a whole year is probably less than that produced by a large car factory in a week.

With growing environmental concern, woodland burials have become more popular. However, there are people who opt for a woodland burial for environmental reasons, but still want to bury the deceased in his or her own clothes, something which is perfectly understandable. At the end of the day, many people are just paying lip service to green issues, because to be truly green is too painful. Who wants to bury a loved one naked and smelling badly because they have not been embalmed?

I have scattered ashes at football grounds, from a mountain top and from an aeroplane. Sometimes seamen, dockers or Hindus request that their ashes be scattered at sea or in a river. Once, I drove down to Portsmouth with the remains of an old sailor. At the docks we transferred the body of the deceased on to an ex-Navy trawler. The coffin was weighted with concrete so that it would fall to the sea bed. Holes had been drilled into it. When we had sailed a few miles out to sea the coffin was slid down a plank at the back of the trawler.

One of my major successes was in 2000, when I opened the UK's first private cremation cemetery, the Albin Memorial Garden, on land next to my funeral home. It is open to anyone and has space for the ashes of nearly one million deceased persons. My dream only came true after a seven-year battle with Southwark Council and with London Underground, who were then building the Jubilee Line Extension, which runs under my funeral home. At the opening in November 1999 the local MP Simon Hughes, who had supported my fight, said, 'The Jubilee Line has taken ten years to build. Barry has built this garden in three months after being given permission and beaten the Jubilee by a short length. This is a triumph of private enterprise over corporate bureaucracy.'

I had become aware that for many people, particularly the elderly, travelling to Honor Oak or Lewisham

Crematoriums to visit the place where the ashes of their loved one had been scattered was quite a journey. Frequently people would phone up and ask for information about bus routes and times. Furthermore, many people wanted the ashes of a loved one to be laid to rest in their own community.

In the late 1980s I had urged the local churches to open an area where ashes could be scattered. The then vicar of St James' gave permission for ashes to be scattered in an area of the churchyard. Two other Anglican churches, St Mary's and Holy Trinity, both in Rotherhithe, soon followed suit. I really felt we had achieved something. However, neither church would permit families to place a large memorial to their loved ones. So I bought a head-stone and had inscribed on it, 'In memory of all those whose ashes have been scattered in this churchyard,' and received permission for it to be erected at St James'. Yet, what was really needed in Bermondsey was a garden, with seats and flowers and a water feature, where people could deposit the ashes of a loved one and erect a memorial plaque or place a vase; somewhere that families felt belonged to them.

In the cremation cemetery, remains of between four to six people can be deposited in niches, which are sealed with a granite stone. The underground ashebarium is the first of its kind in the country. One third of it is above ground and two thirds below ground. Inside it is a memorial book in which for £20 you can record the name of a loved one. Around the walls are shelves for depositing ashes. In the rose garden we move a slab and scatter the ashes into shingle and sulphur. Eventually the ashes go to feed the roses – part of life's great plan, I like to think. The memorial wall is a much smaller version of the one in Washington D.C. that records the names of those killed in Vietnam. The Albin-Dyer Bermondsey and Rotherhithe Foundation, a charity I set up, provides vases for families who want to lay flowers along the floral wall.

Families don't need me to have been their funeral director in order to make use of the garden, and their ashes don't have to be recent. In some cases they may not even have ashes. For example, someone may have lost their brother in the war and want to have him remembered in Bermondsey. What's more, through the Internet you can take a guided tour of the garden and visit your loved one.

I had got the idea of the sanctuary, named after my nan, Elizabeth Dare, who took such great care of me when I was a boy, from my travels in Italy and the film *Once Upon a Time in America*. There was a marvellous moment when one of the characters sat inside a gated sanctuary, which contained the remains of his friends, thinking back over their childhood together and, at the same time, wondering which of the urns the money was in.

At the time of writing, it looks possible that the cremation cemetery might contain the ashes of pioneering local GP Dr Alfred Salter, who did so much to alleviate poverty, slums and poor health in Bermondsey in the early part of the century. Elected MP for West Bermondsey in 1922, one of his many achievements was to oversee the planting of 9,000 trees in the streets of Bermondsey. When Dr Salter died in 1945 Albin's conducted the funeral and his ashes were interred in a tomb in a small park in Druid Street. Because of building work, his ashes may have to be removed and placed elsewhere. My cremation cemetery has been spoken of as a suitable resting place. Should this happen, then I would feel very proud and privileged, as Dr Salter was such a great man.

On a lighter note, shortly after the ashebarium opened, Georgie, a local totter, a sort of Del Boy character, drove into the yard in his van.

'Bal, I've got a bit of gear for you. It'll be lovely for the new garden at Christmas.'

'What is it?' I enquired, knowing that Georgie, who used to clear out places such as offices and banks, often found some very useful stuff.

'Just you wait and see,' he said excitedly, opening the back of the van. 'Here you are. Ten quid each, that's all I'm asking, Bal.'

He was holding up a two-foot Santa Claus figure that lit up. But it had no hands. 'George, you must be joking if you think I'm going to put those in my garden.'

'What's up with 'em?' he asked, puzzled.

'What's up with them? They've got no hands, Georgie. That's what's up with them. And they're tacky.' No sooner had I said this than Freddy Collins came out of the garage and immediately bought two! There's no accounting for taste, is there?

On another occasion, I bought six boxes of carpet tiles off George. I thought I had a good deal until I discovered that the tiles in each box were a different pattern. When I told Georgie, he just replied, 'It's alright, Bal. Just mix 'n' match.'

Because they have witnessed a badly conducted funeral in the past, some people have begun opting for private burials. Princess Diana was, of course, buried in the grounds of the Spencer family estate in Althorp. There is nothing in the law to prevent a person being buried privately. So long as authorisation is obtained from the registrar of births and deaths, or a coroner, registration carried out at the land burial registry, and planning permission obtained, anyone can do it. Guidelines from the Environmental Agency recommend that no body be buried within ten metres of standing or running water, or within fifty metres of a well.

However, planning permission is not required if you want to have your ashes scattered in outer space. Celestis, an American company, will do this for you. So, if you never achieved your ambition to go into space during your lifetime, you can do this in death using a 'memorial satellite', that will take two grams of a deceased person's ashes in a container the size of a lipstick case. The satellites stay in orbit between 50 and 240 years, after which they burn up in the atmosphere. As the company say, this is a matter of ashes to ashes, star dust to star dust; an 'uplifting experience'.

A question many bereaved families have when they meet the funeral director is whether to have the deceased embalmed. I will never carry out an embalming without the permission of the bereaved family. As with every aspect of a funeral, it is their wishes that come first. Where an embalming is not being carried out we will still wash and dress the deceased. However, we will have to keep the deceased in the refrigerator in our state of the art mortuary (one of the most modern in the UK) and we will transfer him or her into the chapel when a family want to come to the funeral home for a viewing.

When Albin's began over 200 years ago embalming was unheard of, at least for ordinary people. In the nineteenth century it was common amongst the poor for bodies to be left in the house for weeks. It was not unheard of for a wife to kiss her deceased husband, contract a fever and then die. As late as the 1960s embalming was still not that common amongst funeral directors in Britain. On the occasions when it was carried out, the embalmer would virtually bleach all the skin and the body would become hard. This went some way to preserving the body but did nothing in terms of presentation.

Today, the British Institute of Embalming offers a three-year embalming course, consisting of theory and practice, in conjunction with firms of funeral directors and various academic institutions.

Although Jews and Muslims choose not to be embalmed (unless there are legal reasons to do so), there has been a tradition of embalming in many different cultures. We only have to think of the ancient Egyptians, for example. Several accounts of forms of embalming appear in the Bible. Isaiah called the physicians to embalm his son, while on Easter morning several women took oils to anoint the body of Jesus. Before the advent of modern scientific embalming, oils, vats of wine, spices, honey, glycerine and salt were all used.

Scientific embalming is more about protecting the living than the dead. Put another way, embalming is about the three p's: preservation, presentation and protection. Embalming is carried out to preserve the body from the decaying process. I believe that embalming has changed the world forever. I see it as the first form of inoculation. In other words, the correct treatment of the dead is the first form of preventing diseases spreading.

Embalming, which should only be carried out after a death certificate has been issued, is a process similar to a blood transfusion or dialysis. Apart from slowing the process of decomposition, embalming removes the harsh physical effects brought about by an accident or illness and restores a person's natural appearance. Soon after death the body begins to decompose and it might turn green in some parts and blisters form in another part. The break-down of body tissues releases various gases, which cause blisters under the skin and swelling of the stomach and torso. If the body isn't embalmed or refrigerated, the swelling can cause it to burst open. It was common years ago to have a body explode on you because of the gas that had built up. Sometimes the side of the coffin would blow off. On other occasions the stomach would inflate, or you'd be carrying the coffin downstairs only to find that it was leaking.

The first time this happened was when I was about ten years of age. With five minutes to go before the funeral my dad and Uncle Fred couldn't get the lid on the coffin. Panicking, my dad told me to sit on the coffin. When I did I could feel myself going up in the air. 'Dad, I'm moving!' I cried out. 'Just sit here, boy. You're doing a good job,' he replied coolly, as he struggled to fasten down the lid. If you were unable to get the lid on, there was only one thing for it: you had to pierce the body in order to release the gas and deflate it. Can you imagine what that was like?

Embalming is best carried out as soon after death as possible when the body is still warm. This is because after death the body begins to change. The muscles relax causing defecation and urination. Later, they become tense and rigid, producing rigor mortis, usually lasting between twelve and twenty-four hours. During this period, the body cools to the temperature of the surroundings and the blood collects in the lowest parts, often causing the skin to turn to a light blue colour. The bladder, the bowels, the kidneys, and the heart all have to be drained and the muscles have to be exercised to break down the rigor mortis. When I have embalmed I have always talked to the deceased person in front of me. This is a way of showing respect.

Embalmers can face health risks in their work. When you go to collect a deceased person you don't always know what disease a person might have. I know several embalmers who have caught TB. Other diseases such as hepatitis, smallpox and cholera can pose a threat. If a body comes from a hospital and it is highly infectious it should have a red or yellow label attached to it. But these procedures have not always been followed.

When Aids and HIV first came to public prominence in the UK in the mid 1980s the government did not issue any directives regarding precautions that should be taken in mortuaries. Aids and HIV were not notifiable diseases. In other words, if you had a deceased person who had contracted smallpox you would have to notify your local health authority. A death might be recorded as pneumonia but Aids might well have been a contributory factor. Some embalmers wouldn't touch a person if they know they were HIV positive. This has never been my approach. I think people who contract this disease are stigmatised enough in society without me adding to it.

We have a belief that it takes somebody a couple of days to settle down after they have died. When you put somebody in the chapel of rest their face changes dramatically in the first forty-eight hours. The pain seems to go and their features soften and relax. I believe visiting people after their death is very important, as is how you present them.

There's nothing worse than for someone to walk into the chapel of rest and to say, 'That's not my mum. It doesn't look anything like her.'

There was one memorable time when I was showing two sisters, Joan and Daisy, their brother in the chapel of rest. He had died while on holiday at a holiday camp at Hayling Island. When they saw him they withdrew in horror. I froze. What was the matter? Oh, no, had I shown them the wrong body? Then one of the sisters said, 'Oh, Daisy! Don't he look well.' The other replied, 'Gawd 'elp us, Joan, that 'oliday's done him good. Look at his colour. Beautiful.'

Another time, I can remember my dad was showing a family into the chapel. 'I think he looks very peaceful,' he said. 'Peaceful,' exclaimed the wife. 'Peaceful! The old bastard should have been dead years ago.'

Jackie and Elaine will use a photo of the deceased to style their hair. We only apply a minimal amount of make-up to keep the skin clean and prevent it from being too dry. Whenever possible, I employ a female embalmer for the ladies, particularly Muslims, and a male embalmer for the males. The reason I do this goes back to when I heard a woman say that she wouldn't let Albin's do her funeral because she didn't want us 'looking at her ha'penny'. Although she said this in fun, I thought about it afterwards and concluded she was absolutely right. She felt she would be embarrassed in death.

Many years ago I took a course in embalming at King's College Hospital, taught by the marvellous Ronald Judge, known as 'the professor', and later I learnt new techniques at Campbell's Funeral Home College in New York. But my first introduction to the subject came from a mortician at Guy's Hospital, who carried out all of Albin's embalming.

Although he never allowed me to observe him carrying out an embalming, he would often spend a few minutes explaining various aspects of his craft. I didn't know it at the time, but I think the reason he refused to let me watch him was that, knowing how keen I was to gain knowledge, he was worried I might learn too much and take the Albin contract away from him and he would lose important income.

He showed me all his tools: a Spencer Wells; spatula; scissors (an embalmer never uses a scalpel); athesium hooks, which were used to separate the arteries from the vein; forceps; arterial clamps, which keep the artery tubes in position once they had been stitched; vein drains; and trochar, a long thin metal object with holes on the end, which looked like an arrow and was used to extract deoxygenated blood from the body. He used two fluids, a red one for the arteries and a green one for cavities. Both were formalin based, but the green fluid was by far the strongest and it would make your eyes water within seconds.

When the rich, deep voice of Professor Keith Simpson, the Home Office pathologist, was heard in the corridor outside, the mortician would suddenly stop in mid-sentence and push me in the fridge and shut the door, in case Professor Simpson caught me hanging around the mortuary. As I listened to their muffled conversation, I would be shivering and praying for Professor Simpson to hurry up and go, which he always did after about five minutes. I think I was more frightened of being seen by Professor Simpson than I was of freezing to death, because if Professor Simpson discovered that I was hanging around the mortuary he would probably have told my dad and Fred Albin, who were both good friends of his, and I would have been in serious trouble for bringing the firm's name into disrepute. Albin's had enjoyed a long and distinguished relationship with Guy's. Looking back, it was like something from a *Doctor at Large* film.

On occasions, both the mortician and his wife, who also worked at the hospital, used to sleep in the mortuary. They were good people, but how they were able to do this with such an overpowering smell of formalin, I will never know. It used to make me gasp every time I went in there. He was so dedicated to the hospital that when he went in to have one tooth out and they took them all out, by mistake, he refused to take any action against the hospital because he loved it so much. He didn't smoke, however, unlike an Irish pathologist I once knew who never wore gloves and used to conduct postmortems with a cigarette hanging out of the corner of her mouth.

In 2001 there was widespread shock and outrage at the disclosure that Alder Hey and a number of other hospitals in Britain regularly removed body organs for medical research, without the permission of families. This has been going on for many years in hospitals, as many funeral directors, if pressed, would have told you. A mortician at St Olave's Hospital, for example, used to sell pituitary glands, which come from brain stems, to a laboratory. They were used in the production of growth hormones. He would store them in little jars and when he had a certain amount the laboratory would send someone over to collect them. He did this for one reason: in order to pay for his holidays. This was accepted practice in those days. As a child, when I asked him what was in the jars, he replied, 'Pickled onions.' All I can say is that I'm glad I never sampled one.

Despite this, it is a foundation stone of embalming that

during the process no organs are to be removed. Neither embalmers nor funeral directors are allowed to do this, under any circumstances, nor do they ever do it. True an embalmer opens up a body and removes various parts but it is understood that, after they have all been treated with cavity fluid, usually in a large plastic container, he will replace each one.

A funeral director is certainly surrounded by death all day but not by dead bodies. He has many other tasks: managing staff, running a fleet of cars, meeting with families, collecting flowers, assisting in the church service, handling legal documentation and so on. Having contact with dead bodies is only one element of his work. His main work is with the living.

By way of contrast, morticians do little else. I have to say, some of the most eccentric people I have ever met have been morticians. I think this must have something to do with working in an enclosed space and being surrounded by dead bodies all day.

For example, I knew a mortician who would strip off every day at 3 p.m. and sit in the mortuary sink and wash himself with carbolic soap. He would then rinse himself off on the table where he had done all his postmortems. Worse still, he kept all his butter, milk and meat in the fridge with the bodies – between their legs – and he never wore gloves for postmortems. A resourceful man, every Monday and Friday he would take some of the flowers from the mortuary chapel and take them home to his wife, wrapped up in paper. He would keep them fresh by dropping an aspirin into the vase. She thought he had bought them.

Another mortician, a hippy type in his twenties, who played in a pop group and used to take his guitar to work, built a train set around the shelves of the mortuary. He had built bridges where there was a gap between shelves. I used to stand there in disbelief and amusement as he would break off from a postmortem to announce, 'The 9.30 to Victoria is about to depart.' He would then flick his control box and, with a satisfied smile, watch entranced as a tiny train would whizz around the track. 'Isn't it great, Barry,' he would enthuse. 'Yes, it is,' I would murmur, thinking: what on earth is he doing in this job? But he wasn't at the mortuary for very long. I like to think that perhaps he got a job on the railways. It would have suited him better.

One final mortuary story. I had gone to Guy's one day to collect a body with Eddie, who had worked for Albin's for a few years. Now, Eddie had no teeth. The mortician used to keep the dentures of deceased persons in a box on one of the shelves. They should have been destroyed. So he asked Eddie if he would like a set. Eddie's eyes lit up. What happened next was revolting. Eddie stood there in the mortuary trying on all these different dentures until he found a set that fitted. True, the dentures had all been washed, but the thought of them having been in the mouth of a deceased person – can you imagine?

With my mother on the beach at Ramsgate, 1953

Mum and Dad on their first
holiday together.

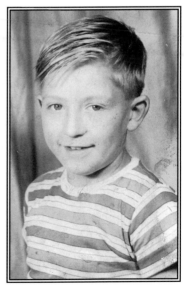

By the age of nine I was used to
the sight of coffins.

Albins are a familiar sight on the streets of London. Here are two scenes
from days gone by: in Marigold Street (late 1920s) and the Mayor of
Bermondsey's procession on Tower Bridge Road (1930s).

Two more recent processions: mourners come to pay their respects to
Canon David Diamond (top) and to 'Del Boy, Captain of the Ship'.

Accompanying Donald Pleasance's widow, Linda, from the church, following the great actor's funeral.

Outside our funeral home in Culling Road in 1990. Police mounted a high-security operation when Category 'A' prisoners Dennis and Mehmet Arif came to pay their last respects to their father in the chapel of rest.

A death that shocked the nation: murdered Peckham schoolboy Damilola Taylor.

Images of one of Britain's oldest family funeral firms.
On duty are: Arthur Albin, at the time of the First World War (top left);
Dad, in the 1960s (top right); and myself, in 2001 (centre).
The painting shows Fred (holding the pen), Dad and me with the next
generation: my sons Simon (top left) and Jonathan.

Pride of the fleet: the Queen Mother's limousine,
now owned by F.A. Albin & Sons.

James Bond, eat your heart out! The modern-day hearse
contains more than you might expect, from video camera
and tripod to portable keyboard.

Work, rest and play: wearing traditional uniform (top left),
Polytechnic's colours – before Fisher Athletic's days (top right)
– and very little else (in Majorca with the boys)!

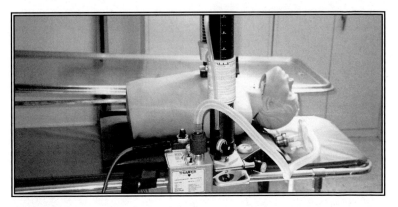

Gone but not forgotten? Scenes from the Cryonics Institute in Detroit: portraits of some of those already frozen (top); a mannequin under the heart support machine (middle), which keeps a body's blood circulating until perfusion; and one of the cryostats (bottom), in which a body is then entombed.

# 5

# MURDERS AND GANGLAND

The first murder scene I ever attended was at the age of fifteen when I went with my dad to remove the body of a bookie who had been shot dead in his shop on Jamaica Road. Getting out of the private ambulance, I remember feeling a mixture of excitement and fear. What would the bookie look like? Why had he been murdered?

The policeman standing outside the door greeted my dad in a jovial manner. He gave me a brief glance and then asked, 'Is the lad going to be alright?'

'He's a keen lad and he's got to see his first murder at some point if he's going to make it in the business,' replied my dad.

In those days funeral directors would be called to a murder scene immediately, as the police relied upon them to provide the body bags. Unlike today, we knew all the police, police doctors, coroner's officers and pathologists by their first name.

We went into the small shop, where an inspector

informed us that some youths had broken in and demanded money. When the bookie said he didn't have any, one of the youths shot him through the chest. I was shocked at this.

The inspector then lifted up the flap of the counter and motioned us through. Lying there in a pool of blood, was the bookie. He looked about the same age as my dad. Around him were screwed up betting slips, which reminded me of confetti. A police photographer was carefully record-ing the scene, while a fingerprint expert was busy dusting the handle to the door that led to the flat at the back. Today, a murder scene would be sealed off until all this work had been completed.

After we had placed the bookie in the ambulance, we got in the front, but my dad didn't start the engine.

'What's up, Dad?'

'We've got to wait, son,' he replied looking at his watch.

'What for?' I asked, puzzled.

'For the police escort,' replied my dad without even a hint of excitement.

A police escort? My heart pounded. This was brilliant. Shortly, a police officer came out of the shop, signalled to my dad, and got into a police car. With the blue light flashing and the siren on, he moved off and we followed. As we threaded our way through the streets of Bermondsey to the mortuary at Guy's Hospital, I felt so important and concluded that being a funeral director had to be the best job in the world.

The next day, two police officers turned up at our funeral shop and asked me to accompany them to Tower Bridge police station in order to eliminate me from their enquiry. My fingerprints had, it transpired, been found in the bookie's. Dad didn't seem too alarmed and reassured me that it was just routine.

Sitting in a small, bare room at Tower Bridge police station, dipping my fingers in ink was a frightening experience, even though I knew I had nothing to do with the murder. At the same time though, to be part of a murder enquiry was fascinating.

The following week at school, the boy who usually sat next to me in my class was absent. I assumed he was ill. Then during the afternoon break one day I overheard two other boys discussing him in hushed tones.

'What's happened to him?' I asked.

Their eyes widened as they looked at me. 'Don't you know?'

'Know what?' I replied, wondering if he'd had an accident.

'He's been arrested.'

'Arrested! Why? What's he done?'

'They reckon he shot dead that bookie on Jamaica Road last week,' replied the taller one. 'Can you believe it, Barry?'

I couldn't believe it. The boy didn't have a reputation as a real tough character. True, he had been in a few fights, but that was common in Bermondsey. I later learnt that the boy had carried out the murder in a moment of madness and stupidity. I still see the wife of the bookie today and when I do I reflect how that moment of madness had changed her life forever.

Since then, I have conducted numerous funerals of murder victims. This part of south-east London, it has to be said, has more than its fair share of murders. In most cases, the victim knew his or her killer. All murders are shocking but, for me, there is something particularly evil about a child being murdered and laying to rest a murdered child is one of the hardest things I ever have to do.

One of the most traumatic funerals I have ever conducted was for four-year-old Stacey Kavanagh from Rotherhithe. The bodies of Stacey and her friend, seven-year-old Tina Beechook from the East End, were discovered under a pile of leaves in Southwark Park, which backs on to my funeral home. I, like everyone in the community, was deeply shocked. The children had both been strangled. Watching the two mothers make a tearful and emotional appeal on TV for the killer to be caught really cut me up. As my two sons were around the same age, I felt I could, to some extent, share in their grief.

Stacey's funeral, at St Mary's church, near the flats where she lived, was one of the biggest seen in the area for many years. In a display of sympathy, people lined the whole route of the funeral. Murders in Bermondsey and Rotherhithe have usually been the result of gangland feuds or domestic situations. The murder of an innocent child was unheard of. People were angry and were asking why this had happened. When I heard about the Moors murders in the mid-1960s I remember thinking the same thing. How could someone do this?

There were so many floral tributes, some in the shape of teddy bears, dolls and slippers, that we were unable to place them all on the sixteen limousines and hearse and had to provide an open-back lorry for the remainder. In a poignant moment, the cortege paused outside the corner newsagents on Brunel Road, where Stacey was last seen alive.

It goes without saying that there were many tears as Stacey's father, trembling, helped to carry the tiny white coffin down the aisle of the packed church. Standing there, listening to the vicar talk about Stacey's brief life, about how she helped her mum wash up but was really a daddy's girl, I struggled to hold back the tears.

The person to be charged with both murders was the mother of Tina. A final sinister twist was that a few months before, the workshop at my funeral home had been broken into and some babies' coffins stolen. When the police searched the mother's flat, they found one of the stolen coffins under a bed. I found this news spine-chilling.

I have always kept in touch with Stacey's parents. I have found the way they coped with her terrible death inspiring. Every five years I clean Stacey's headstone at Camberwell New Cemetery.

The murder of eleven-year-old Nigerian schoolboy Damilola Taylor in a stairwell on the North Peckham Estate on 30 November 2000 was an event that shocked the whole nation. What made this murder particularly horrific was that Damilola was apparently killed by other children. Witnesses had reported seeing a group of teenage boys running away from the scene. Parallels were immediately drawn between Damilola's murder and that of toddler Jamie Bulger a few years before.

When I heard about the murder I immediately contacted the police family welfare officer and offered to conduct Damilola's funeral. This was not out of any desire for cheap publicity but simply a gesture of kindness and support to Damilola's family in their hour of darkness. Damilola's family had decided that they didn't want any publicity and no one would know where the funeral would take place. I knew that Albin's would provide for them the best funeral they could possibly hope for and we would do everything to make it a day that would live on in the memory for many years to come. Damilola's family were grateful for the offer to conduct the funeral.

It took two days to embalm Damilola as he had been dead for some time. After this, we dressed him in his own clothes and placed him in a white coffin.

Damilola's parents then decided that they had changed their mind over publicity about the funeral. They did this, I think, to draw attention to the terrible death their son had undergone. I met with the police to discuss the funeral route and security. There were fears not only that some groups might cause problems at the funeral but also about the number of TV crews and journalists expected. A chief inspector said to me, 'When we knew it was you doing the funeral we were delighted, because your reputation precedes you.' I took this as a great compliment.

The cortege set off from Culling Road and was met near Woolwich barracks by two police outriders, who escorted us to All Saints church, Plumstead. MPs, including Paul Boateng, Simon Hughes and Ann Widdecombe, the Nigerian High Commissioner and leading figures from the Nigerian community were among those who packed the church, as Damilola's white coffin, adorned with a cross made of white chrysanthemums, was carried up the aisle by six bearers. Also present were a number of black police officers and Doreen Lawrence, mother of Stephen Lawrence who was stabbed to death a few years before in Eltham.

High above, a police helicopter hovered while outside, other mourners, including a number of children, stood silently in the street, listening to the service via loudspeakers.

The police took their cue from me throughout the funeral. It was clear that I was in charge. Afterwards we took Damilola to Plumstead Cemetery for a private burial, away from the glare of TV cameras and the prying eyes of journalists. At the graveside I was handed a box and asked to release a dove. This was the first time I had ever done anything like this, and I felt quite privileged.

But I think what really sticks in my mind from the funeral was when I was walking the funeral towards the church. There was total silence in the street and then suddenly you heard click-click-click-click. Photographers were everywhere: on roofs, leaning out of windows, on balconies. The sound was almost deafening. At that moment I realised for the first time the magnitude of the effect of this funeral on the nation.

Another murder that made an impact on me was that of a young woman who I used to occasionally speak to when she took her two children to school each morning. She was bright and cheerful, just an ordinary mum doing the school run. One day she told me that she had split from her husband. For whatever reason, their marriage had hit problems and they felt they couldn't continue living together. As is not uncommon in situations like this, the children stayed with their mother during the week and their father at the weekend. But the husband wasn't happy with this arrangement. One evening he went berserk, forced his way into the flat, locked the children in a bedroom, and stabbed his wife to death. After this, he went to his own flat and hung himself with a rope. The children were then taken into care. What became of them I don't know.

I was asked to conduct both funerals, the wife's in Sussex and the husband's in Bermondsey. But I didn't allow myself to sit in judgement. I had to show just as much respect to the family of the husband as I did to the family of the wife. A funeral director is a bit like a doctor in the sense that you don't judge a person you simply carry out your professional duty and treat each person the same. In death we are all equal.

What made this funeral very hard to do was that apart from being given the job of conducting the funeral and being an acquaintance of the mother I was also chair of governors at St James' primary school, which her daughter and one of my sons attended. I had to deal with the press, organise floral tributes from the school, provide bereavement counselling from two of the teachers and organise a memorial service, which was attended by all the pupils. I had to handle the situation with great sensitivity and tact.

When I think about the many murder victims for whom I have conducted funerals what comes to mind is the look on their face. They all have a look of what I can only call disbelief; an expression of utter and complete amazement, as if to say, 'No! You can't really mean to kill me.'

My job is to undertake to care for and bury the dead, whoever they might be and whatever they may have done or not done. I have often reflected that there can be few professions where you work with such a cross-section of society, and in such an intimate way.

One afternoon in 1987, a man turned up at the funeral home and asked me to conduct the funeral of his mother. His name was Dogan Arif and he had a reputation as one of the leading gangland bosses in London. Little did I realise that, as unlikely as it sounds for someone who was to go on to be a magistrate, this encounter was to be the beginning of a warm friendship and it was to cause some raised eyebrows amongst those who knew me.

The Arifs were a well-known gangland family in south London. They were one of the leading London firms. When they arrived from Cyprus they were the only Turkish Cypriot family living in their part of Bermondsey and not everyone welcomed them. As a result, the family learned the importance of sticking together and standing up for themselves. They got involved in crime and went on to build up an empire of clubs, pubs and restaurants. The five brothers, Ozer, Mehmet, Dennis, Bekir and Dogan, had, in the 1970s and 1980s, accrued a list of unsuccessful prosecutions and convictions that included, in the case of the latter four, armed robbery, which became their speciality. Unlike their more famous gangland predecessors, the Krays, the Arifs have kept the slate clean of murder.

'I've heard you are very good at what you do. I respect that in a man. I want the best for my mum,' said Dogan, sitting down in my office.

'Well, Dogan, I always give of my best, that you can be sure of.' I could see that he was studying me very closely. 'At F. A. Albin we will take care of every aspect of a funeral. Whatever it is you want, a horse-drawn hearse, special floral tributes, memorial cards, headstones, photographs of the day, we can provide it.'

Dogan was a lean man of medium height and with an olive complexion. He was dressed in a smart suit and he was a couple of years older than me and had, I knew, gone not to Bacon's School, where I went, but to Tower Bridge School – a really tough place, very near to being approved – in Riley Road. In my teens, kids used to boast that Dogan Arif was the best fighter in Bermondsey. Word soon gets round in a close-knit area like Bermondsey. Yet when Dogan was very young he looked nothing like a kid who could handle himself, what with his big glasses and skinny frame. But by the time he was in the third year at Tower Bridge School he was feared, not because he was such a good fighter, more because he had no fear, a characteristic that has stayed with him to this day.

Some years later, I remember hearing that three heavies turned up at a flower shop he had bought for his daughters after the previous owners went bankrupt. They told him they had to collect some fittings. Dogan just stood there, staring menacingly at them. His look frightened them and they walked away without him laying so much as a finger on them. He gives off such a feeling of self-confidence and danger that people immediately back off.

As we talked through the funeral arrangements, he explained that his mother had been taken over to a mosque, but seeing the shabby conditions there, and the unprofessional attitude of the staff, he wanted someone else to take over the care of her and of the funeral arrangements. I was a little flattered that he had come to me.

'So, will you do it, or do I have to find someone else?' he asked, coming straight to the point. This was, I knew, a simple question and contained no hint of a threat.

'I'll do it. Of course I will. That's my job.'

He smiled. 'Good.'

When Dogan told me that there would be several hundred people there from the Turkish Cypriot community, most travelling in their own cars, I explained that we preferred private cars in the cortege to keep together, that the owners shouldn't slam the doors and that all mourners should remain in their cars until I instructed them to get out. He booked a hearse and ten (a hearse and ten limousines). It was arranged that I would collect the body of his mother from the mosque the next day, bring her back to the funeral home and place her in our Islamic chapel of rest overnight. The funeral would be held the following day, leaving from her house in a street off Southwark Park Road.

While I had conducted gangland funerals when Fred owned Albin's, this was the first time since buying the business that I had taken on such a funeral. I realised that the buck stopped with me if things went wrong. So I had to make sure things didn't.

The morning of the funeral came and the cortege set off for Dogan's mum's house. When we turned into her street, I could see that crowds had begun to gather and, as is traditional in this part of London, a number of neighbours were standing at their doors. The pavement outside the house had been carpeted in flowers, wreaths and floral tributes. There were so many that I had to phone the office and ask for a second hearse to collect them all up.

'Everything going smoothly, Barry?' It was Dogan, looking extremely sharp in his suit.

'Fine, Dogan. I've sent for a second hearse so that we can take all the flowers. It'll be here in a few minutes.' A few minutes later, the second hearse appeared at the end of the street. I motioned some of the team to gather up the flowers. My team know how important it is to handle floral tributes with care and discreetly dispose of any broken flowers and petals.

Drawing on his cigarette, Dogan then said somewhat sheepishly that the mullah, a Muslim teacher, had told him that they had to leave for the service at the mosque straight away, so there wouldn't be time to gather all the flowers.

'Well, Dogan, there's no way I'm leaving all these flowers,

wreaths and tributes here on the street, that's for sure.'

He looked surprised. 'Look, Barry, will you go and have a word with him, then?' I was slightly taken aback that a man with a fearsome reputation was reluctant to speak to the mullah.

'Of course I will. We're taking them all with us,' I said emphatically. As Fred and my dad told me on many occasions, and as I tell my sons, you always have to be strong and authoritative when you conduct a funeral. And this was one such situation. The mullah soon backed down when I confronted him, as I knew he would. Ministers of religion rarely argue with a funeral director about how a funeral should be conducted. They know their professional boundaries and we know ours.

My staff took out the ladders from the hearse and began to carefully secure the flowers, wreaths and floral tributes on the roofs of the hearse and limousines. We then set off for the mosque, where prayers were said, and then on to Beckenham Cemetery. Apart from the hearse and ten limousines, there must have been fifty other cars in the cortege.

After the burial, the cortege drove to one of Dogan's clubs, where food and drink had been laid on for the mourners. As I often do when invited, I stayed for a short while and had a soft drink and a few nibbles. The place was packed and the atmosphere was relaxed and, as you tend to find with Turkish Cypriot funerals, almost celebratory.

Dogan wandered up to me and expressed his appreciation. 'Thanks, Barry. You did a great job. My information was correct.'

I permitted myself a moment's glow of pride. 'Nice of you to say so, Dogan. But how are you feeling?'

He shrugged and pulled a face. 'She was a great lady, Barry. A great lady.'

oOo

'Sorry, sir, you can't come in here,' said a policeman in a flak jacket, his machine gun looped over his shoulder.

I shook my head in bewilderment. 'I beg your pardon. What do you mean I can't come in?'

'You can't come in, sir. The building's a high security zone.'

'But I own the place!'

He gave me a blank look and adjusted his gun.

'Check with the staff. I'm Barry Dyer, but everyone knows me as Barry Albin,' I explained.

I was standing outside the gates of my funeral home in Culling Road in 1990. Inside, armed police were circled around the yard, while on the roof and in Southwark Park next door police marksmen stood motionless, their guns pointing at the funeral home. A police helicopter whirled incessantly overhead. It was a virtual siege. Once the policeman had verified my identity with my staff, he opened the gates to let me in.

The reason for such security was that Dennis and Mehmet Arif were being brought from HMP Brixton to pay their last respects to their father, who was in our chapel of rest. The brothers were awaiting trial for their part in an alleged armed robbery on a Securicor van delivering £750,000 to branches of Barclays Bank in Surrey. The police had ambushed the gang, shooting dead Kenny Baker and wounding Mehmet.

Dennis and Mehmet were double category A prisoners

returning to their roots in south-east London, where they had countless friends and associates. The police, no doubt fearing an attempt could be made to free them, had mounted a high security operation. Dogan had decided not to attend the funeral because he knew the fuss it would create, and he didn't want this.

Once the police allowed me into my own funeral home I was ushered into my office and told to wait there until the brothers had paid their last respects and left. Sitting there, looking through the window at all the armed police outside in the yard, I reflected on how unnecessarily costly it was bringing high security prisoners to a funeral home. It would be far cheaper for the funeral director to take the deceased to the prison chapel.

Then there was a flurry of activity as a police Range Rover, motorbikes and an armoured police van pulled into the yard. Dennis and Mehmet emerged from the back of the van and were frog marched by armed police towards the entrance of the funeral home. After a few minutes, I heard Dennis shout, 'Thank you very much, Bal,' from the other side of the door. I watched as the brothers were shepherded back into the prison van and the convoy left the yard.

Many of those who move in the underworld are, like Dogan and his brothers, extremely tough. But when they and other underworld figures deal with a funeral director they are very humble, grateful and respectful. I am sure that English's, the Bethnal Green funeral directors who have conducted the funerals for the Krays, would say exactly the same.

There is a tradition of the heads of gangland families, or firms, being on first name terms with the local funeral director. For example, we buried the father of the

Richardson family who, with the Krays, controlled much of the organised crime in London. He was a great character who used to feed all the Bermondsey stray cats and dogs and on the day of his death had visited the local pet shop.

The Arifs, like the Richardsons and other gangland families, understand that the funeral director is the protector of their dead. At a gangland funeral I become the all-powerful person, listened to and respected and, of course, with power comes responsibility. That was why Dogan asked me to speak to the mullah. There have been times during a church service when I have had to tell some of the villains not to talk or to switch off their mobile phones. In another situation, such as in a pub, they might become aggressive or violent, but not at a funeral. They are very apologetic.

When I got to know Dogan better, I discovered that his attitude to the mullah came out of respect and trust, not fear. Once when we were discussing the relationship between gangland and funerals he revealed that when he is in an unfamiliar situation, and doesn't know how to control it, he stands back, watches, listens and learns, and lets the professionals get on with it. 'Bal, only a fool will tell a pro how to do his job,' he observed. 'A tough guy will be tough in his own environment, say if he is in a room with armed robbers or fighters. He'll be comfortable in that room and he will be tough in that room. But take him out of it and put him somewhere he is unsure of and he will be a very ordinary person and will shrivel up.'

Some people find it strange that I have a friendship with Dogan. What has really formed the basis of our friendship is football and in particular Fisher Athletic, the local non-league club, which Dogan managed in the 1980s and then returned to in the 1990s. When the club hit rock bottom, and was on the verge of bankruptcy, Dogan asked me to become president and use my business expertise to help turn it around. I worked alongside him for five years, renegotiating the lease with the council, drumming up sponsorship, redeveloping the ground, finalising transfer deals, and so on, eventually handing the club over to another businessman. He was unable to take the club forward and I have since returned.

At the age of forty-nine I was given a game in the first team for Fisher, in a game with no consequence. The crowd loved the idea of an undertaker turning out for the team. Every time I touched the ball cries of 'Put it in the box!' and 'Bury it' could be heard from around the supporters. I had a bit of luck and scored in the first few minutes. That silenced the crowd.

In fact, although my two sons have followed me into the funeral business, they could have been successful footballers. Their mother was brilliant in taking them to football practices when they were young. Jonathan played for Millwall at schoolboy level and Simon played for the Wimbledon youth team for three years. Although he was the leading goal scorer, Wimbledon decided to let him go. Instead, they kept on Jason Ewell, who has gone on to become a first team regular. And they both turned out for the Fisher first team.

On one occasion, as Dogan was driving out of the yard after popping in for a cup of tea, someone with whom he had fallen out was coming in to discuss the funeral of his father.

'Look, tell me straight. Does Dogan own this business?' he asked with a stony face.

144

'No,' I replied. 'Whatever gives you that idea.'

'Because if he does, I can't have you conduct my dad's funeral.'

'No, it's my business. But I have to tell you that Dogan is my friend. We have a shared passion for football and we work together at Fisher Athletic.'

He shrugged his shoulders. 'I don't have a problem with that, so long as Dogan isn't running the business.'

Dogan has now turned his back on a life of crime, or 'blagging' as he calls it, and instead runs a leisure and hotel complex in northern Cyprus. 'In prison you have a dead life. It doesn't matter who you are or what you were, it's dead. I don't want to finish up that way,' he once told me. He added that he had reached the point where he didn't want to continue living on the edge any more. Having risen to the top in the underworld, he shrewdly realised that there was only one way to go: down.

Although I have never ever been involved in any criminal activity, with Dogan or anyone else, I was once accused of planning the escape of a prisoner. A local villain had been let out for a family funeral at Nunhead Cemetery. As he was a small time crook, the prison officers hadn't bothered to handcuff him. They had agreed that after the funeral he could go back to the house where his family were giving a reception. I opened the door of the limousine for the man to get into and, lo and behold, he legged it out the other side and made off, zig-zagging between the gravestones. The prison officers gave chase, but the man was too quick. That night his mother phoned me up and blamed me for his escape. When I tried to explain that I was an undertaker not a prison officer, she wouldn't listen, insisting the door on the far side of the car should have been locked, while ignoring the point that he should have had more respect than to escape during a funeral.

On one occasion, the hearse had just pulled away from the old Midland Bank on Jamaica Road, and as it did four armed robbers came running out of the bank. One of them put his foot on the front of the limousine, waved his gun at Mick, the driver, and ordered, 'Stay there!' At the same instant, the other three bundled themselves into a getaway car and sped off down Jamaica Road towards the Rotherhithe Tunnel. Mick had immediately put his hands up in the air and as he did so the limousine I was in behind him accidentally hit him and the gunman. Before they had time to recover from the shock, two police cars suddenly appeared, screeching to a halt, doors flying open, and the man was swiftly arrested. It was just like a scene from the Keystone Kops.

In many ways the funeral of Dogan's mother was a major turning point for the Turkish Cypriot community in London. The hundreds of mourners who turned up from all over London were not only amazed that the funeral combined what you might call the English way with Turkish Cypriot customs, but also at how well organised and dignified it was, all the way through from the house to the mosque to Beckenham Cemetery to the reception at Dogan's club. Afterwards, a number of people phoned Dogan to ask who had conducted the funeral. As a result of this, I have since conducted many other Turkish Cypriot funerals and also supplied Turkish Cypriot funeral directors with materials and ideas. At one such funeral in 1998 I erected a marquee in the yard of the funeral home and laid on food and drink, because the family had nowhere to hold a reception.

A few months after the funeral of Dogan's mum I was asked to conduct the funeral of Tony Ash, a well-known so-called Bermondsey villain who, unlike the Asifs, appears to have been the sole member of his family involved in any criminal activity. When his brother came to the funeral home to give me the certificate for burial, he told me that it was not only going to be a big send-off but it was also going to act as a showcase. All the top underworld 'chaps' would be there as a mark of protest against what they saw as a police shoot-to-kill policy. Tony had been shot dead by a police marksman in 1987 when he walked into an ambush, while attempting to rob a store in Woolwich. Tony wasn't a major underworld figure. His one spell in prison had not been for armed robbery but for giving short measures when he worked as a coalman.

The police had got wind of what was planned and were, understandably, nervous that with so many underworld figures in one place the situation could explode. A few days before the funeral, I met with a chief inspector at Southwark police station to discuss the route. He wasn't very happy when I told him that the family had requested that the cortege drive around Bermondsey first before going to Camberwell New Cemetery. But, in the end, he agreed to let it go ahead.

There would be, he said, a significant police presence on the day, but they would try to keep it low-key, as they didn't want to incite trouble.

With the funeral of Dogan's mother, my only worry had been that we might do something wrong. The funeral of Tony Ash, however, contained within it the possibility that the funeral could disintegrate into violence, either between villains who were locked in feuds, or between villains and

147

the police. At the south London gangland funeral of another robber, shot dead by police the previous year, mourners had turned on the journalists present.

There have been times when the funeral home has been guarded because there has been the risk of the body of the deceased being desecrated. One of these occasions was when a man had murdered someone and then had been murdered himself. His family and associates feared that certain individuals would try and enter the funeral home to spit at the deceased or do worse. I gave them permission to have two very tough-looking characters stand guard over the deceased until the day of the funeral. I wasn't pressured into this. I felt that, given the circumstances, it was appropriate. Had I thought otherwise, then I would have told the family that this was not appropriate, whatever the consequences. A similar thing happened when an Iranian gangster-cum-nightclub-owner died. What I particularly remember about that funeral was the six carloads of minders who acted like a police escort all the way from Bayswater Road to Brookwood Cemetery. Cars screeched ahead, blocking off side roads and then waving me on. They were fearful of an attack from Iranian revolutionaries.

For the funeral to erupt into violence would be awful for the family of Tony Ash. I outlined these concerns to my team over our staff breakfast on the morning of the funeral and urged them to be extra vigilant. At times like this, I always say the same: just do your best. I reminded them to be very aware of everyone around them at the funeral.

As the funeral was to be so big, I had hired extra limousines and staff from Martin Green, who runs a funeral support company in Forest Hill. Martin has a fleet of around forty limousines and hearses.

On the morning of the funeral, family, friends and associates began turning up to pay their last respects to Tony, who was in the chapel of rest. A steady flow of tough-looking men wearing sharp black suits, long black coats, chunky jewellery and sunglasses, and blondes in bright red lipstick and decked with jewellery came and went. Amongst those paying their respects was Big Dave Courtney, another man who made a name for himself in the south London underworld as a tough character, although he has now turned his back on crime and put his hard man image to use in a new career as a writer and celebrity. I have met Dave at funerals several times over the years and he has always seemed very well mannered and respectful, although I don't know him well. I have to admit, I found it strange that for a time he often drove around London in a Daimler hearse! For the life of me I could never work that one out. Also there was Nosher Powell, a famous bare knuckle fighter, whom I had met at the funeral of Jim Wicks, Henry Cooper's manager at the time. 'Done well ain't I, young Albin?' he said cheerily, referring to his many TV appearances. Today, I gather he is in charge of security at Manchester United.

At 11 a.m., I drove the Rolls hearse slowly out of the yard. On top were three large floral tributes: 'Daddy', 'Brother' and 'Tony'. The Daimler limousines, which were parked on Culling Road and on Rotherhithe New Road, started their engines and began to form the cortege. One of the mourners had attached a photo of another man who had, allegedly, led Tony into a police ambush, to one of the limousines.

By the time I turned off Jamaica Road into Southwark Park Road there must have been thirty or forty BMWs,

Jaguars and Mercedes behind the limousines. Shoppers gawped as the cortege snaked its way through, turning into St James' Road and on to the Thomas à Becket, a famous boxing pub on the Old Kent Road, and a local of Tony's. After a brief halt there, we drove further up to the Green Man. When we reached the Frog and Nightgown, where Tony had worked as a bouncer, a man came out of the crowd which had gathered outside and stood in front of the hearse and poured half a light ale in front of it before walking around to the back and placing the empty bottle next to Tony's coffin. We then drove up to the Bricklayers Arms roundabout and back down the Old Kent Road. Across the road a vanload of police officers watched this little ritual with anxious faces. After a final pub stop, this time at the Henry Cooper, we continued down the Old Kent Road towards New Cross and then up through Nunhead and on to Camberwell New Cemetery.

The cemetery chapel was packed for the service, while hundreds more stood outside. The mourners stood reverently as recordings of some of Tony's favourite songs, including Frank Sinatra singing 'My Way' and Tony Bennett singing 'I Left My Heart in San Francisco' were played. It was all too much for Tony's girlfriend, Jackie, and his two daughters. They broke down in tears.

After Tony had been buried in a grave under a tree on the top of a mound the mourners stood around chatting and my team arranged the floral tributes around the grave, making sure, as always, that the cards faced outwards. A card attached to one of the wreaths read: 'With sorrow and regret may your executioners live long and suffer every day.' Handshakes took place, cigarettes and cigars were lit and groups of men began to huddle in deep conversation.

If anything was going to happen, it was probably going to happen now. The plain clothes police were easy to spot. Police always seem to look like police - especially when they are trying to be anonymous amidst hundreds of London's most notorious villains. I knew there would be countless police officers sitting expectantly in cars and vans parked in the streets nearby. Everyone, it seemed to me, was aware of the tense situation. I ushered Tony's family back to the limousines, praying that trouble would not flare up.

But then the mourners began to drift slowly away, stubbing out their cigarettes and cigars, and getting into their cars. They had done what they had intended to do: register a silent protest against what they saw as the police's shoot-to-kill policy. Having done that, they were leaving. Driving the hearse back to the funeral home, I have to admit that I felt a sense of relief. It had been a nerve-wracking funeral, to say the least. Had trouble broken out, there was no telling what might have happened.

Throughout all my years as a funeral director neither Dogan nor any of the local villains, some of whom I grew up and went to school with, have ever attempted to compromise me by getting me to break the law. And I mean this. Never once has anyone asked me to cover for them. The villains respect me too much to put me in a compromising position. We both move in different under-worlds. Mine is the underworld of the dead; theirs is the underworld of organised crime. At the end of the day, the villains like to think that one of their own - someone who comes from the same background as them - has done well legitimately.

I have often thought that the film *The Godfather* captured perfectly the relationship between a funeral director and a gangland family. For example, at one point in the film, the funeral director goes to see the godfather and tells him that he wants revenge on the men who raped his daughter. The godfather says that he will make sure the rapists pay for what they did and then adds that he may need a favour one day from the funeral director. A few years later one of the sons of the godfather dies in a hail of machine gun bullets. The godfather goes to see the funeral director and tells him that the time has now come to return the favour. He asks that his wife doesn't see the son in his present state but that the funeral director makes him look presentable.

In the underworld a funeral home is seen as a sacred place. Because this is the place that cares for the dead of their families, professional criminals would never attempt a break-in. Yet, we were broken into once and had a number of computers stolen by drug addicts. A week later, however, the computers were returned in an unusable state. When the thief had bragged about his haul to some tough villains in a local pub, he was told in no uncertain terms to return them and given a slap for his disrespect. Sadly, the thief was stabbed to death some years later in the early hours of the morning near an illegal drinking den. I conducted his funeral.

If you've grown up in a place like Bermondsey, a tough working class area, you know that there is an unwritten code that operates. You don't squeal to the police and you settle disputes among yourselves. Personally, I find it hard to subscribe to this view. I remember when a young man was stabbed to death in a local nightclub. Despite there being about a hundred people in the club that night, a wall of silence was put up, and not for the first time. Local MP Simon Hughes appealed for witnesses to come forward.

Later, the man who was thought to have committed the murder was himself stabbed to death, illustrating once again that if you live by the sword you often die by the sword.

# 6

# FROM HERE TO WHERE?

If you go and buy one thousand marbles, put them in a jar and then each day take one out and throw it away, you suddenly start to realise how quickly three years passes. Tellingly, after the death of Princess Diana in 1997 I was inundated with people wanting to take out pre-paid funerals. Our business increased five fold during a three-month period. This I put down to the impact the death of Diana had on people's perception of their own mortality.

I have always seen my role as a funeral director as being to carry out a corporate act of mercy. I think there is something very special, or sacred, about laying a soul to rest, and I am sure that the soul, or spirit, of the person who has died remains present through those days before the burial or cremation.

When Fr Power, a former priest at the church of The Most Holy Trinity, Dockhead, was dying of cancer of the liver in King's College Hospital, I went to visit him. Sitting there at his bedside, I was taken aback when he admitted to me that he was frightened of death. Fr Power was a tough character who had been in the Marines before entering the priesthood.

'But Father, you believe in God. Where's your faith?' I asked.

He looked up at me and said, 'Barry, there's nothing more frightening than going into the unknown.'

At the time, I was shocked by his fear of death. I assumed that a priest's faith would overcome this. But I now know that this is not the case. No matter who a person is, or how strong his faith is, there will always be a fear of death because death is the ultimate mystery and we are human beings. It doesn't matter how wealthy you are, how intelligent, or what you have done or not done in your life, whether you are a saint or a sinner, when you are confronted by death fear will grip you.

Fr Power was, in fact, influential in my decision to become a Catholic. Catholicism seemed to me to be the religion that best made sense of the world. The memory of the care provided by Fr McManus and the Sisters of Mercy at Dockhead when my mother died has always stayed with me. I remember Fr McManus putting his arm on my shoulder and saying, 'Dying is just as much a part of life as living. And you've got to live.' I've never forgotten those words.

Over the years, I'd talked to various priests about Catholic beliefs and teachings. Some had drawn me nearer to the Church; others further away. Gradually the desire to share in Communion grew in me. I didn't see Communion as just a re-enactment of the Last Supper. I really saw it as the Body of Christ; a chance to be one with Him.

However, I found the Church's teaching on issues such

as birth control a stumbling block and, furthermore, I
didn't want to indoctrinate my children. When I told a
priest about my difficulties, he replied, 'Do you think that I
agree with everything the Church teaches? I don't and
can't. But I realise that Catholicism is available for everyone
but you have to find your place in it. You have to accept
what you can. God still accepts you because he can understand what you can't accept.' This gave me the encouragement I needed.

I attended weekly instruction but, nevertheless, still
found it hard to make the final leap of faith. What's more,
I was the chairman of governors of a Church of England
school. However, I eventually made the decision after a
priest said to me, 'Come on board and see where it takes
you.' I was received into the Church at the Church of the
Most Holy Trinity, Dockhead.

It took me a long time to become a Catholic. I never deny
I'm a Catholic and I always make it clear what I believe in. I
have some main teachings that I use in my daily life. The
easiest thing in the world should be to put God first every
time. In fact, it's the hardest thing. In everything I do, I
always try to think what's right for that other person I'm
dealing with, not just what's right for me.

I've never been attracted to Evangelical or Pentecostal
Christianity with its emphasis on emotions and idea of
God as a benign chief executive. I remember once going to
deliver some flowers to the house of an Evangelical minister.
When he opened the door, he ushered me quickly into the
living room, where his wife and two children were holding
hands. He rejoined them and then said, 'Dear, Lord, I'm
sorry for this interruption but we're going out in a few
minutes to buy a new coat for Judith. Please give us a good

buy.' I was incredulous. There are people with problems and here's this minister asking God for a good buy at the market! I just can't believe that the Lord wants to hear me moaning about buying a coat. I'm sure He's quite happy for me to make those sorts of decisions.

Amusingly, at a Salvation Army funeral that I conducted at their hostel in Spa Road, all the lights suddenly went out. Major Trump then stood up and announced, 'Now, we're going to sing "Abide with Me". But because the electric's gone you'll all have to be patient because I'm playing the organ and the pumps have gone. Because of this, Sister Anna is going to have to pump up my organ by hand.' Priceless.

I have become very good friends with Fr Alan McLean, parish priest at the Church of The Most Holy Trinity. He's a man with a sharp mind, a good sense of humour and a real awareness of the needs of bereaved families in Bermondsey. Mind you, we got off to a bad start when he first arrived. We had a disagreement over the position of the trestles at one particular funeral. But unlike the mullah at the funeral of Dogan Arif's mother, Fr Alan didn't immediately back down. He was the first priest who had challenged my professionalism. A brave man.

However, since then, we have worked together fantastically well on making the funerals at Dockhead dignified and a reflection of the wishes of the families concerned. When we work together in conducting a funeral we both want to leave the bereaved family and their friends with a lasting memory. The secret is we respect each other as professionals and both want to do the best for a family.

Like me, Fr Alan enjoys an occasional good meal and a bottle of wine. Picking up on the relationship between priests and funeral directors, we were invited to take part in the TV programme, *Dinner Dates*, in 1999. It was highly enjoyable. We both got togged out in our best bib and tucker and were taken by a black cab to a mystery destination. It turned out to be, appropriately, a restaurant in the crypt of a Brixton church. The wine bill was three quarters of the cost of the food!

In 2001 Peter Hindley, head of Service Corporation International's (SCI) UK operations, phoned me to ask if he could borrow my grave-lowering machine for the funeral in Glasgow of Cardinal Thomas Winning. No problem, I told him and then quipped, 'Fr Alan said I would always bring the Church down.'

Most, but not all, Catholic funerals are Requiem Masses, that is a service where the Eucharist is central to the worship. Where a family's link with the Church is not strong, a simple service may be held, either in the church or in the cemetery or crematorium chapel. Nowadays, many Catholic priests have abandoned black vestments in favour of white or purple and, in these more enlightened times, a person who has committed suicide is no longer denied a full Catholic funeral. Generally, eulogies are not common at Catholic funerals. Instead, the priest will preach a homily with the intention of making it personal to the deceased and his or her family. As is traditional, the priest will always bless the grave with holy water before the prayers of farewell are said.

The Church of England say that if someone dies and the family want a C of E funeral, then I must contact the vicar or priest of the parish where the deceased person lived. But what if the vicar or priest is incompetent, as has been known? If I book an incompetent priest, then I am opening up myself to a lawsuit. I have told the rural dean for

Bermondsey that if I know that a priest or vicar is incompetent when it comes to funerals, then I won't use him. When a bereaved family come to me and ask for a religious minister they trust that I will find them one who conducts a service in a dignified and thoughtful way. Nowadays in Bermondsey we are blessed with first class clergy.

An example of an insensitive vicar was a former incumbent at a certain Bermondsey church. I had first met him at school, where he ran the choir. He seemed very normal then, cheerfully greeting all the pupils and asking us all how our studies were going. However, he became very odd during his later years, perhaps because he had lived alone for so long, with just his dog for company.

Fred Albin and I turned up at the vicarage one morning to take him to Honor Oak Crematorium to conduct the service for an elderly man. When the vicar emerged from the vicarage, he went up to the limousine in which the wife of the deceased was sitting, opened the door, stuck his head in and said, 'Ah, Flo, I didn't think it would have been Eddie who went first; I thought it would have been you.' Fred and I stood there speechless. The poor woman was distraught when she heard him say this and she burst into tears.

During the service in the chapel, we were even more astonished when he refused to begin until the lady stood up. She was in her nineties and very frail. Fred told him that the lady was unable to stand. Very reluctantly he proceeded with the service, which little thought had gone into. Afterwards, Fred, who by now was fuming, took him aside and told him how rude and obnoxious his behaviour had been. 'I will never have you take a service for one of my funerals again,' he said angrily. Fred felt so strongly about the vicar's behaviour and attitude that he wrote to the bishop demanding the he reprimand the vicar. The bishop gave Fred permission not to use the vicar again.

This vicar was an example of someone who was full of his own self-importance and with no genuine interest in the needs of a bereaved family, unlike Fr Alan, Fr Power and countless other clergy I could name. In these type of situations, caring for the bereaved family and conducting their funeral can be difficult, to say the least. And I don't mind admitting that my tolerance level plummets to zero if I encounter such an individual.

But Canon David Diamond was as far removed from that vicar as you could get. When I received a phone call asking me to conduct the funeral of Canon Diamond, who had died of a heart attack while on holiday in Scotland, I was deeply saddened, as I had known him ever since he was appointed parish priest of St Paul's, Deptford.

I had never met a more saintly man than Canon Diamond, and it was a view shared by many in this corner of south-east London. He was a born priest, in the same way that I am a born funeral director, and, no matter how busy he was, he always had time for people. I think what made him so popular was that it didn't matter who people were, rich (Princess Margaret was a good friend), poor, living on the streets or in the lap of luxury, loved or unloved, he always treated them the same. It didn't seem fair that his life should be cut short at just fifty-six years of age.

The morning of the funeral came, and, looking at the sun shining, I felt God was looking down on one of his faithful servants. Followed by a lone bagpiper, a pipe and drum band, the hearse and cortege, two bishops and over 100 priests, I walked the funeral along the length of

Deptford High Street. Crowds lined the length of it and several TV crews were in attendance. It was one of the biggest funerals in the area for a number of years. At times like this, I am so proud to be a funeral director. The dignitaries and ordinary south Londoners who packed the church for the High Mass knew, as I did, that they were saying farewell to a very holy and special man.

As a mark of the affection in which he was held, special permission was given for his body to be laid to rest in St Paul's churchyard. This was the first burial there since 1854. That was when the Burial Act closed urban churchyards, such as St Paul's, because of health risks from decaying corpses.

At home that evening, I watched the Thames TV News report of the funeral. Asked by a reporter why Canon David was so special, an elderly woman shook her head and replied, 'There'll never be another like him.' Others interviewed spoke affectionately of the annual trips to the seaside he organised for pensioners, the rose garden he established for the scattering of the ashes, the care he showed to families, and his acceptance of people, whoever they were, whatever they had done. Even to this day, people still talk fondly of Canon David, but Fr Peter Fellows, his successor, is an equally devoted priest and has also become a legend in Deptford. There is, I have often thought, something very special about that church.

Music plays an important part in a funeral service and can express much about a person's life. In recent years many Christian denominations have allowed bereaved families a much wider choice of music than traditional hymns such as 'The Lord's My Shepherd' and 'Abide With Me'. I wonder if Frank Sinatra realised that he was recording one of the all-time, top ten hits for funerals! I have lost count of the times that I have heard My Way played at a funeral. Mind you, the songs some people choose to be played at funeral services are, let's say, somewhat unexpected. 'The Chain Gang', for a man who died in prison; 'YMCA,' at a gay funeral; 'Hello Mother, Hello Father', for a mum and dad; 'Magical Mystery Tour'; 'Please Don't Talk About Me When I'm Gone'; 'Always Look on the Bright Side of Life'; and 'Shep the Dog'. Believe it or not, in crematorium chapels I have heard, 'Heart's On Fire', 'Smoke Gets in Your Eyes' and Elton John's 'Love Lies Burning'.

Once, at the Requiem Mass at Dockhead for a young man who died of a brain tumour, we carried the coffin out to the beat of 'It Must be Love' by Madness. Although he is wary of turning a Mass into a pop concert, Fr Alan thought this move was appropriate, given that the church was packed with young people and that the particular song chosen, he felt, did have a spiritual dimension.

Another time, at the funeral of an old Bermondsey lady at Lewisham Crematorium, a tape of her singing 'Wish Me Luck as You Wave Me Good Bye' was played as the coffin was committed. It was fantastic. All her family and friends were tapping their feet and singing along. Afterwards, the minister led everyone in a round of applause for the lady.

It's not uncommon for ministers to forget to turn up at a cemetery or crematorium. This is every funeral director's nightmare. The Funeral Ombudsman has ruled that if this happens the funeral director should be held responsible, something I agree with, unlike some of my fellow professionals in the industry. When a certain Catholic priest failed to turn up on a number of occasions I never spoke to him again. He may well have had a drink problem, as a colleague of his told me, but, in that case, he shouldn't have been exercising his ministry – at least not with bereaved families. Fortunately, he is no longer around. He now has, I believe, a peaceful retirement. There but for the grace of God go others.

On occasions when clergy haven't turned up, or at the request of the family, I have conducted services. This is something I enjoy and put a lot of effort into. To prepare for this and make it meaningful and personal, I will always visit the family to get some details about the life of the deceased and prepare a eulogy. For instance, I might look at the significant years of a person's life and refer to who he or she shared their birthday with, what music was popular and what the major world events were and so on.

For example, I delivered a eulogy at the funeral of Derek Turner, known to all, because of his ducking and diving, as Del Boy, the landlord of The Ship pub in Rotherhithe. I talked about the time Derek once sold me a camel-hair coat. When I told him all the buttons had come off after a week, he said there was no refund. Holding up the coat, I said, 'Derek, here is the coat and as far as your funeral is concerned: no refund.' I must have struck the right note as everyone gave Derek and I a round of applause at the end. In the cemetery, I threw the coat into the grave.

Sometimes I will lead the mourners in the Lord's Prayer because even people with little or no religious affiliation usually know the words and can agree with the sentiments expressed. 'Footsteps' and John 14, where Jesus says that in His Father's house there are many mansions, are two other texts I will often use, again for their universal appeal. And since seeing the film *Four Weddings and a Funeral*, I have sometimes recited W. H. Auden's poem 'Stop All the Clocks'.

But there was one occasion, while giving a eulogy, when, for a few seconds, I froze in front of the mourners. Halfway through somebody's mobile phone went off. That was bad enough. But what made matters worse was that it played the theme music from the film *The Sting*. I was completely thrown by this unexpected interruption and lost my place. All I could see on the paper in front of me was a load of jumbled up words. Those few seconds when I struggled to find my place seemed like an eternity.

While I consider myself, generally, to be quite a good public speaker, I am not in the same league as actress Diana Rigg. At a funeral at Golders Green Crematorium – which might well be called the crematorium to the stars – she read out some of her deceased actor friend's letters. She did it with such feeling and passion, as you would expect from an actress of her calibre. I sat there at the back of the chapel absolutely enthralled by the way she brought the man to life. It was as if he was talking himself.

The first time I really became aware of how different cultures view death differently was when I was a teenager and a Filipino family came to the chapel of rest one day to pay their respects to a deceased relative. I was fascinated as I watched them place pearls in his mouth. This was, my dad informed me afterwards, to symbolise his wealth for the journey ahead.

Over the years, I have conducted numerous funerals for people of other faiths. As I've already said, Albin's have a very special relationship with Britain's Iranian community, the majority of whom are Muslims.

In Islam, simplicity is the hallmark of a funeral, which

should normally take place as soon as possible after death. As I've explained, generally bodies are not embalmed, unless they are travelling abroad, but they are washed and then sprinkled with perfume. It is not uncommon for somewhere such as the East London Mosque to have prayers said for several diseased persons at once. A deceased person will be wrapped in white sheets called a kafan, three for a man and five for a woman. Generally, there are no flowers or floral tributes, as this is seen as waste. It is prayer, not flowers, that the deceased person needs, in Islamic thinking. In Islam, to be involved in a burial is one of the greatest kindnesses you can do. This is because a person cannot repay you.

I was once asked to go to Cambridge and bring to London the body of a Muslim boy who had been killed in a boating accident. The arrangement was that his body would be taken to Heathrow at 10 a.m. the following day and then flown back to Iran. When the family asked me if they could come to the shop early that morning for prayers, before the cortege left for the airport, I said, yes, that was fine. At that time my family and I lived in a flat above the funeral home.

I woke early the next morning to the sounds of banging and shouting. Rubbing the sleep from my eyes, I looked at the alarm clock. It was just before 5 a.m. Our dog was barking his head off. What was going on? I ran out on to the patio to discover a heaving crowd of 200 Iranians at the gates. Some of them were trying to clamber over, while others were screaming, or chanting the name of Allah. Considering this was Bermondsey, it must have looked a bizarre sight to those people going to work on the early morning buses.

I dressed quickly, hurried downstairs, dashed into my

office, grabbed the keys to the gates and went out into the yard. When I appeared the shouting grew louder. Looking at all the wide-eyed, emotional faces pressed to the gates, I felt like some film star going to meet his fans. It was abundantly clear that they wanted to come in – all of them. What on earth was I going to do?

When I unlocked the gates the crowd surged past me and headed straight for the chapel. I doubt even Clint Eastwood would have stood a chance of stopping them. I ran after them and had to push my way through the crowd in order to get to the front. The screaming grew louder in the chapel and some people had begun to bang their heads against the walls.

Did I have a camera asked one of the family. 'We want photos,' he explained. Everyone wanted to be photographed standing beside the deceased. In such a small chapel this was not easy, as you can imagine. As I stood there with my camera, fending off elbows and feet, people pushed each other out of the way, as they tried to get in the frame. How I kept a straight face when I looked through the viewfinder and saw all these smiling faces leaning sideways, I don't know.

Then one of the family asked me for tea and coffee for everyone. I know Jesus fed the five thousand with a few loaves and fishes, but miracles were something I hadn't quite mastered. In the middle of all this, the unsuspecting milkman arrived in the yard. Seeing a crowd of Iranians running towards him, he panicked and tried to reverse out. But the crowd surrounded his float, eagerly grabbing bottles of milk. Eventually he managed to get away. A few minutes later a police car appeared. I explained to the puzzled looking officers that the crowd were not terrorists but mourners and that everything was under control. As they got back into their car, they warned me not to let the situation get out of hand.

The family then lifted the coffin high above them and began to carry it out of the chapel. It was wobbling all over the place and I was seriously worried that they would drop it. To my relief, they managed to slide the coffin into the back of the hearse without any mishaps, apart from two broken lights on the chapel ceiling.

I walked in front of the hearse and out into Lower Road. The crowd followed, chanting and shouting. It was now the morning rush hour and the procession soon caused a tailback. A man on a push bike coming the other way was so stunned by the sight of all these frenzied Iranians that he accidentally rode his bike into the crowd and hit one of the party. The mourners walked all the way down Jamaica Road as far as the junction with St James' Road. I then stopped the hearse and they all ran back up Jamaica Road to where they had parked their cars.

The rest of the funeral passed off uneventfully. At Heathrow, the deceased was put on board an Iran Air plane while all the mourners then waited in the viewing gallery for it to take off. When I arrived back at the funeral home I had an interesting conversation with my staff about events earlier that morning. Under all the empty milk bottles I discovered money covering the cost of all the milk.

Through my work with the Iranian community I have also conducted a number of funerals for Britain's 6,000-strong Baha'i community. The Baha'i faith originated in Iran (then Persia) in the 1840s as an offshoot of Islam. According to Baha'i beliefs, the deceased person should be buried as close as possible to where he or she died, no more than an hour's travelling distance from that place. So, if a person dies overseas they will not be brought back home.

Many Baha'is ask to be buried at the Great Northern Cemetery in New Southgate, where Shoghi Effendi, the guardian of the Baha'i faith and great-grandson of its founder, was buried after he died while visiting London in 1957. Baha'is from all over the world come on pilgrimage to the guardian's grave, which is looked after by two custodians in a small hut nearby.

As with Islam, cremation is not allowed and, unless the law requires it, embalming is not recommended. The deceased is usually wrapped in either silk or cotton and, for Baha'is over fifteen years of age, a ring may be placed on the finger. At a Baha'i funeral there is often poetry, readings, a eulogy and songs. When what is called the obligatory prayer for the dead is read all present must stand. As there are no clergy in the Baha'i faith, an elected local spiritual assembly will often help the family with funeral arrangements.

I have only ever conducted a few Jewish funerals. On the whole, the various synagogues in Judaism handle their own funerals and Jewish burial societies provide white shrouds and simple coffins. Because the origins of Jews in Britain go back to the twelfth century they have very strong social and religious structures in place. Many of the more recent ethnic communities in Britain don't.

I was deeply touched when I once moved a deceased Jewish man from London Bridge Hospital to our funeral home. The family were concerned that the deceased would be left on his own and that his soul wouldn't be protected. Then the son noticed that we had a dog to protect the premises. He walked over to it, sat with it, prayed and then said gently, 'You have a soul. Please protect my father's soul. I leave my father in your protection this night.'

Unless a postmortem is to be carried out or the coroner becomes involved, Jews will usually be buried within twenty-four hours, either in a Jewish cemetery, of which there a number in London and other cities with a long Jewish presence, or in Jewish sections of municipal cemeteries. Services – levayi – are usually held not in the synagogue but in the cemetery hall (Jews don't like the word 'chapel' because of its Christian connotations).

Like Islam and Baha'i, Orthodox Judaism doesn't allow cremation and tends not to go in for embalming the body. In cases where a deceased person may have to be shipped to America or Israel, they may opt for embalming, for purely hygienic reasons. They believe in a physical resurrection of soul and body. One of the interesting rituals Orthodox Jews have is the tearing of a garment at the graveside. This is because bereavement is seen as something that can induce anger, so, Jewish thinking runs, it is better to take the anger out on a garment than another human being or God.

Hindus do allow cremation and it is quite common for a member of the family to assist in placing the deceased in the cremator and even to press the button to start the fire. Several times I have sailed up the Thames estuary in a tug belonging to a friend and scattered the ashes of a Hindu. On other occasions the family will ask for the bones and transport them back to India, where they might be thrown into the river Ganges.

Because of the presence of so many ethnic communities, with different customs, traditions and rituals, death is less of a taboo in British society today. Vietnamese funerals are very colourful affairs and usually have a barbecue and joss-sticks. The family, who usually mourn for a week, give out sweets and lucky money to the mourners. Everyone chants and wears white and ties rags around their head. There was one occasion in Rotherhithe when a Vietnamese Buddhist family sat outside their flat for a week, in mourning. People came and went throughout each day. They must have taken a lot of stick from the neighbours. And I remember the time a group of gypsies from Yugoslavia spent the night in the funeral home, playing music and singing. Most West African families, on the other hand, send the deceased back home for the funeral. It is quite common for us to keep the body of a deceased in the freezer for two or three months while arrangements are made for the funeral.

I will never forget a funeral for a Greek family where, as is the custom, they smashed plates on the casket as it was lowered into the grave. One of the plates bounced back up and, quick as a flash, one of the mourners dived like a goalkeeper in an attempt to catch it, thinking he was at Wembley, no doubt.

Surprisingly, some of the old south London customs and superstitions surrounding death remain. Some people still put white sheets up in the windows after a death, the reason being that it is thought unlucky to have any reflections in a room where someone has died. Others will not have red and white flowers together because red and white are equated with blood and bandages. And even today I have seen some children touch their collar when a cortege passes through Bermondsey. In the old days, the kids would sing, 'Hold your collar. Walla, walla, walla.

Never catch a fever.' Today, while the kids still hold their collar they don't know the rhyme.

My dad always used to say to me, 'Barry, when you get to the cemetery, up you get with the brush. We don't want any petals falling off the hearse.' This was because of the belief that a falling petal means there is another death to follow. But the old tradition of placing pennies over the eyes of a deceased person was not, as was thought, a payment for going from this world to the next. It was simply because pennies were heavy enough to keep the eyes closed.

From Victorian times, black has been the traditional colour for funerals. This is because in the spirit world it's a colour you can't see through. In other words, you can't see through death, which is a veil behind which lies the ultimate mystery of existence. The mausoleums and elaborate memorials in cemeteries such as Highgate and Kensal Green tell you much about the pride the Victorians took in representing death. If you travel to Italy, Cyprus, Turkey, or many other parts of the world, you will see that everyone there also wears black at a funeral.

In the popular imagination funeral homes are associated with the supernatural and seen as spooky places (think of all those horror films or the undertakers in the films *Oliver!* or *Billy Liar*). In reality they are very ordinary places. As in any profession, what most people would consider abnormal becomes normal to you. However, I must admit I have witnessed several strange incidents over the years.

One time, a young man was brought to the funeral home after being killed in an accident. His body was in a terrible state and his mouth was still open. I had just come back from New York, where I had been learning new methods of embalming at Campbell's Funeral Home, and I was keen to try them out.

His mother, a university teacher, came to see him the next day. As you might expect, she was heartbroken. For the next week she came early every morning and would sit beside him until the evening. When I would walk past the chapel of rest I would hear her inside, talking to him softly.

On the day before the funeral she came out of the chapel and said to me, 'He's very pleased you know. He's very happy where he is. And he said that you helped him on his way.'

'Really,' I replied, unsure exactly what she meant.

She nodded and told me she was a Spiritualist. 'He had asked me to stay with him but now he's told me I can go home because he feels safe with you.' Smiling, she then told me he had laughed when I'd put his shoes on the wrong feet. She was right. I had got his shoes mixed up. But how did she know?

'You've had to do something to his mouth,' she continued. 'But he was pleased you did it because he knew I wouldn't have been happy to have seen him like he was when he came in.'

Then she told me in detail exactly what I had done to his mouth. No one in this country knew what this technique was and there was no way she could have seen what I had done as it was concealed. I was astounded. How did she know this?

When she died ten years later I received instructions from her family that she was to be buried with her son. They gave me a letter she had written to me. In it, she thanked me for the care I gave her son and ended by saying that after her death she would be my guardian angel.

Knowing she is watching over me is reassuring and gives me faith in what I do.

Then there was the day a man, slightly the worse for drink, turned up at the funeral home. 'Hello, Mr Albin,' he said, slurring his words and doing his best to stand up straight. 'I've come to see the missus.'

'Now, I can see that you've had a bit of a drink, so why not go home and come back later, or in the morning,' I said.

'Mr Albin,' he pleaded, 'I've had a good drink, I know, but I won't be any trouble. Honest.'

He didn't look like someone who was intent on causing trouble, I thought to myself, so I agreed he could spend some time with his wife, and I took him into the chapel. 'But you must behave yourself,' I reminded him as I opened the door. 'Remember this is a funeral home and you placed your wife in my care.'

'Honest, I'll be as good as gold. Thanks, Mr Albin.'

I paused outside the door. The man was talking to someone. But who? Then it dawned on me. He was talking to his wife as if she was asking him questions. 'So I've had a drink. What do you think I've had? What I always have. Light and bitter. No, I didn't have a scotch. No. Don't keep on. You've kept on at me all my life. All I've had is a drink. Yeah, I've done the washing up.' It was extraordinary. It sounded as if he was having a conversation with the deceased. It would be easy to dismiss this as the behaviour of a drunk, but I wasn't entirely convinced. There was something about that conversation that was eerie.

Another time, I was dressing a Nigerian chief in his gown. Two of the other men were assisting me, while Jonathan, who was very young at the time, looked on, clearly fascinated by the fact that this big man was a chief.

I said to him, 'You hold his head, son, and we'll lift.'

As we pulled the chief up, he smiled at me. His whole face in an instant lit up with a huge grin and then went back to its previous expression. I went cold. 'Did you see what I just saw?' Like me, the men were stunned.

'Dad, the chief just smiled at you,' said Jonathan excitedly. 'He's very happy.'

Fred Albin told me of how, in the old workshop at the Jamaica Road shop, the atmosphere would go cold, the windows rattle, the fire in the stove would blow itself up again when the embers were about to die. It was, he said, a dreadful feeling. Nevertheless, one evening he decided to stay to try and find out what was behind all of this. He waited patiently for several hours. There suddenly was a loud bang and doors began to open and close. He spoke to whatever was there and told it that it couldn't remain there. This was a place were other people came to pass on. From that moment he never saw anything again. I believe that these incidents were a result of someone who had passed through our care and was angry about dying and could not pass on.

And in the old garage at Snowsfield the sheets covering the doors would swing frantically, with no assistance from the wind, until they turned over. When this happened there would be an eerie silence. I believe this was due to a man who had committed suicide there.

All the staff believe that my office at the funeral home in Culling Road is haunted. There's a coldness in it, even when the heating is on, a musky smell and a strange atmosphere. The door slams on its own and sometimes the lock won't undo. Joanna, my receptionist, has seen an arm come through the door and slam it. Some days when I've come in I've noticed that the pieces on the chessboard have been in different positions, or pages in my diary have been turned over. In the nineteenth century a workhouse stood on the land. Whether these occurrences have something to do with this, I don't know. But I never get frightened. I feel protected by the spirits who have passed through my funeral home (which I liken to a transit station). I see it as a place marked by goodness rather than evil. Apart from my office, the funeral home is, I have to say, very peaceful and serene.

The case of the mysterious priest easily has to be the strangest thing I have ever experienced. I arrived with a funeral on a grey, cold afternoon at Nunhead Cemetery, expecting the service to be taken by old Mr Black, one of the rota ministers there who always gave the same five minute service for everyone. He was a rather strange looking man with a grey face and a big pointed nose that always seemed to have a dew drop at the end of it. On this particular day, however, he was nowhere to be seen.

All of a sudden a priest appeared at the door of the chapel, wearing one of those Canterbury caps, which were once popular with clergy in days gone by and a long, heavy black cloak with a gold clasp. When I asked him who he was, he just nodded silently. He did the same when I introduced the family. He then walked slowly into the chapel. Sitting in the hearse while I waited for the service to finish, I remarked to my driver on the odd behaviour of the priest.

The family eventually came out of the chapel and got into the cars to go to the grave. I was expecting the priest to do the same, as was the usual protocol, but without saying anything, and much to my surprise, he set off along an old footpath. He stood solemnly at the graveside, then made the sign of the cross and muttered, 'Et cum spiritu tuo' as the coffin was lowered. After this, he bowed his head, turned, walked away and vanished into the bushes.

As we were driving out of the cemetery, I stopped at the superintendent's office. 'Who was that priest who just took the service in the chapel?' I called through the window of the hearse.

'What priest?' asked the superintendent coming to the door of his office.

'The elderly man in the cap. The one who looked like Bela Lugosi in *Dracula*. He used Latin in the service. The family didn't understand a word of it,' I said.

The superintendent shook his head and looked at me quizzically. 'I don't know any priest who fits that description, Barry.'

'But we ordered a rota minister.'

'No, Barry, we didn't receive any instructions for a rota minister.'

I was baffled. And to this day I still do not know who that priest was. Was he a man or was he a ghost?

These incidents – and the time an Armenian businessman-cum-clairvoyant left me speechless in a restaurant by telling me that I couldn't stand foam (for some inexplicable reason, I can't even say the word without shivering) – all point to another dimension to life: the spiritual. The belief in a soul is common in many cultures and religions. For me, the body is a piece of apparatus. If the heart stops, for example, does it mean that is the end of the person? I don't believe it does. I believe that life goes on, somewhere. It would be ridiculous to think that just because a tube breaks in a television the programme ends.

It doesn't, of course. I believe in a soul and that it leaves the body. In the near-death experiences people report they often talk about a white light and a feeling of peace. And I see the funeral as conveying someone to that light. Sometimes the soul, or spirit, doesn't know how to move on and maybe they don't even know they are dead. Who really knows? I feel these strange experiences, perhaps, come from this.

Death is the eternal mystery; the door through which kings, presidents, paupers, saints and sinners, all have to pass. And it is frightening, even for someone who has faith. But I don't see it as the end but rather as a continuation or a new beginning. In some ways, a funeral home is a bit like a departure lounge in an airport. People come to us when they are about to begin the next stage of their journey.

This reminds me of the time a local Jack-the-Lad character was lying in the chapel of rest, dressed in a flash suit with a dickie bow. Looking down at him, one of his friends shook his head and remarked, 'He never believed in heaven and he never believed in hell. And there he is, all dressed up and nowhere to go.'

I wonder if you have ever asked yourself what words you would like to hear when you die? I know the words I want to hear: 'Hold on, you're still alive.'

# 7

# THE THIRTEEN-MONTH ILLNESS

It was a dark, cold, windy afternoon at Nunhead Cemetery. The occasion was the funeral of an elderly Bermondsey gentleman. He had, I think, been ill for some time, so his death had been expected. The only mourner in the stark chapel was his wife, a small, frail lady whose lined face spoke of hard work and sacrifice. After the rota minister had finished the short service, probably his third or fourth that day, she remained motionless in her seat in the front pews. Aware that another funeral party would be arriving within a few minutes, I walked over and gently placed my hand on her arm to lead her back to the limousine outside. 'Come on, love. Shall we go?'

She looked up at me, with tears in her eyes, then said, 'Me and Billy we've been together for' – and then she began to sing softly – 'fifty years. And it don't seem a day too long.' As she sang the song the whole way through I struggled hard to keep my composure, feeling I was going to cry in a minute. Looking at the tears running down her face, I felt so sad. Billy and she had been such a devoted couple and now she was facing life alone. I knew what was going through her mind. How can I cope? Will I cope? He was my life. What kind of future faces me?

As often happens in situations like this, she didn't live much longer. A few months later I was helping to bear her coffin into the same chapel, knowing that she had what she wanted: to be reunited with her husband. And as I sat there at the back of the chapel, all I could hear was her sweet, cockney voice singing, 'Me and Billy, we've been together for fifty years, and it don't seem a day too long.' Although it wasn't recorded on her death certificate, what she really died of was a broken heart.

I remember also a young man who was absolutely devastated when his mother died. As he sat by the coffin in the chapel of rest at my funeral home I tried to console him as best I could. But he just kept saying that he couldn't live without her. I told him to take every day as it came, and reassured him that he would manage to live again, eventually. The next day he returned and, again, just sat there beside the coffin, crying. On the third day he did the same, and seemed to be even more distraught. He looked pale and gaunt and was unshaven. We had a cup of tea and I tried to offer words of comfort as he left that evening, but he just shook his head silently. The next day I was shocked to learn that shortly after leaving the funeral home he had jumped off a nearby tower block and was killed instantly. I wondered could I have done more. But the truth was there was nothing anyone could have done. He had decided to be with mum.

That elderly lady and that young man had come face to face with one of the hardest challenges you encounter in life, how do you live without someone after they have died, leaving behind a huge emptiness in your life? It is said that much mental illness is connected with a bereavement. When you have lost a loved one, it doesn't seem to matter what anyone says. In a well-meaning way, people sometimes say, 'I know how you feel.' But, of course, they don't. If, for example, a parent loses a child the first thing I say is, 'I can't imagine how you feel.' How could I, never having lost a child?

It is well known that after the death of a loved one the person left behind will often act as though the death hadn't happened, for example, continuing to set a place at the table and talk to the person. I remember a woman who still cooked her husband's tea each night even though he had died ten years previously. This is a way of denying the death.

When many people step through the doors of a funeral home they do so apprehensively, not knowing what to expect. What goes on behind the doors of a funeral home is shrouded in mystery. And often people are in shock or are numb after the death of a loved one. I have tried to make our reception area at Culling Road, our offices in Deptford and Mottingham and Hitchcock's funeral home in east London, which I own, as welcoming and warm as possible. The emerald green carpet at Culling Road was inspired by a visit I made some years ago to Rosewood's funeral home in Houston, USA. The colour helps to create the right kind of comfortable atmosphere for the funeral home, as does the lighting, type of furniture and soft background music we often play. On the walls are photos of past funerals, a portrait of Fred Albin, my father, my sons Simon and Jonathan and myself, and a painting of our old shop at 62 Jamaica Road. These, and the other memorabilia around our funeral home, emphasise our over 200-years-long tradition of conducting funerals. It is to say to bereaved families, don't worry, you can trust us. We are very experienced. And life goes on.

There are times when I arrive at a house on the day of a funeral only to find that the wife or the mother refuses to come to the funeral because she is too distraught. This is where I use the counselling skills I gained on a course at Morley College and from Fr Frank Carter. I will sit down opposite the lady, sometimes holding her hand, and get her to look at me. Then I will gently encourage her by saying something like, 'You've got to do this. You've got to do this for George. You've got to show people you can do it. We're going to do it together.' I will then ask her to lean on me and, when she's ready, slowly walk her to the car, encouraging her all the way.

One such occasion was when I arrived at a house to collect the deceased for the burial at Streatham Park Cemetery. I went into the flat and said to the family that it was time to leave. Several members started screaming and clutching the sides of the coffin. Now, on occasions like this you can't rush someone's goodbye. Tact and sensitivity are required. On the other hand, you have to do your best to arrive on time at a cemetery. But with the traffic conditions in London it is sometimes impossible to get there on time.

'Listen to me,' I said softly to the daughter. 'I understand that at the moment you can't let mum go. Well, that's fine. I'm going to wait for you outside and then in about twenty minutes we will leave.'

She nodded. This, I knew, gave the family some time. Fr

Frank Carter told me this approach was called 'time therapy'. The idea is that you give a person a specific amount of valuable time. This way, a person calms down. I had phoned the cemetery superintendent to explain what was happening and after fifteen minutes reminded the lady that she had five minutes before we left.

When we eventually arrived at the cemetery, an attendant, standing outside the office, told me that we had to wait for Mr Smith's funeral to arrive before we could go into the chapel. We were fifteen minutes late. Mr Smith's funeral was due in the chapel at 2.30 p.m. There was no way I was going to have my family waiting around for an hour, I decided.

Most cemeteries and crematoria only allow you a ridiculous thirty minutes for a service, but Streatham Park allow you forty-five minutes, even though services usually take no longer than thirty minutes. This extra quarter of an hour makes such a difference because services in cemetery and crematoria chapels nowadays often include a eulogy and more music than, say, twenty years ago. Today, people are more involved in a funeral.

'Now, we're going to use some common sense here,' I insisted. 'I'm going to go straight into the chapel, to keep things moving, then clear my cars out of Mr Smith's way, do my flowers as quickly as possible, and when Mr Smith arrives I will apologise to him for making him ten minutes late. But that won't be a problem. I know Mr Smith.'

But the attendant was adamant that I wasn't going into the chapel. I was frustrated by his lack of imagination and lack of sensitivity to my mourners.

'Look, I won't delay Mr Smith's funeral by more than ten minutes,' I said. But I'm not going to have my family waiting around for an hour and a half. And I've told your man this. If we have to wait you are going to have to deal with thirty cars of very upset people.'

The attendant begrudgingly waved me on, not wanting a confrontation. When Mr Smith did arrive he was fifteen minutes late, which meant that no one was delayed.

On the whole though I have very good relationships with cemetery staff. They recognise, I hope, that I am thoughtful, helpful and professional. What's more they know I am very respectful. I recognise the importance of the funerals before and after mine. And I know that digging a grave, for example, is hard work, and I always express my admiration for this. If ever I want a special favour at a cemetery I will nearly always get it.

Although I have cried at funerals, I have a barrier inside me that prevents my feelings becoming too involved in the death of someone and the grief of their family. It's not that it shuts you off, but it enables you to empathise. If you become too personally involved you are unable to do your job. When that happens you are no good to anyone.

Yet, despite this barrier, you have to be able to understand what a bereaved person is feeling. When people say 'I'm sorry' when they hear of a death they are being polite. They don't feel the sorrow. If you don't know what to say, then it is better to say nothing or, 'There is nothing I can say except get up tomorrow and put one foot in front of the other and see what the day brings. But you may not be able to do this for a year or more.'

If you can feel something of what a bereaved person is going through you can relate to them. In my opinion, to be a complete funeral director you have to have experienced bereavement and understand how devastating it can be.

When I was a young man learning about funerals, we never talked about death and its effects; either its effects on us or on the families. It was a bit of the stiff-upper-lip syndrome the British are supposedly famous for. Death happened. Grieving happened. That was reality. True, the families who came to our shop on Jamaica Road or our chapels of rest in Tranton Road would be treated with sympathy and understanding by Fred and Ernie Albin and my dad, but, back then, little was really understood about loss and the term 'bereavement counselling' hadn't been coined. Today, it seems as if the bereavement counsellors are the first people to arrive at the scene of a train or air crash.

I first came face to face with the pain and darkness that the death of a loved one brings when my mother died. I was just seventeen at the time, and even though I grew up in a funeral home the finality of death hadn't really hit me. I had seen deceased persons, acted as a bearer at funerals, polished coffins, removed bodies to and from mortuaries, and yet death seemed to be something that happened to someone else.

I had come home from school one day to find that, unusually, my mum was in bed. Dad told me she wasn't feeling well and that the doctor was going to call to see her after the surgery closed. Mum had been burping a lot, he explained, and her tummy had swollen. Dr The, the family doctor, examined her and then suggested she went to see Mr Wass, a surgeon at Guy's who was also a friend of my dad. Mr Wass recommended that Dad took her on holiday for a change of scenery. They flew off to Italy for a fortnight and I went to stay with my nan who lived in a flat near the Bricklayers Arms. But they cut short the holiday as mum had got worse. She was immediately admitted to Guy's for some tests.

The next morning at about six o'clock I was in the bathroom when I suddenly heard my nan shout, 'No! No!'. Grabbing a towel, I leapt out of the bath and ran into the living room to see what was the matter. My dad was standing there, looking ashen-faced and my nan was bent over the side of the armchair, sobbing.

'What's happened?'

He looked hard at me for a few seconds and then burst into tears. 'Barry . . . mummy's died. She's dead, Barry. She died this morning.'

I stood there, trying to take in the words, but I couldn't. 'No, Dad. She can't be. You've got it wrong.' Then I began to shake. 'No! She can't be. She can't. How can she be?'

My dad shook his head and said weakly, 'She is, son.'

To be told at seventeen years of age that your mother has died is something you can't comprehend. You think your parents, like you, are going to live forever. My mum was just forty-three and had been full of life. I tried to let the words sink into me but my mind was all over the place. All I could think was, 'How could she have died? It was impossible. She couldn't have. This must be a dream or a mistake.'

Dad and I then drove up to Guy's, both of us in tears. On the way, Dad told me that mum had got up out of bed in the middle of the night to go to the toilet and had collapsed as a result of a blood clot. She had had a massive stomach cancer. Walking through the hospital corridors, on the way to the ward, we passed several people who knew us. 'I'm so sorry,' said one woman, crying. Reaching the ward, the first thing that struck me was that the curtain had been pulled round mum's bed. I slipped through it and saw her lying motionless on the bed, her eyes open. I cuddled her. No, she couldn't be dead. She was just sleeping. My dad stood behind me, trying to control the tears.

'Well, what do we do?' asked my dad, staring at the floor.

I looked at him, but didn't know what to say.

'What do we do, son?' he repeated.

'I don't know, Dad. I don't know.'

So, here were two people experienced in death and organising funerals, and we didn't know what to do. Mum's death had paralysed us both, and we couldn't think straight. This is, I have discovered over the years, one of the things the death of someone you love can do to you.

Then I remember mum lying in our chapel of rest in Tranton Road in a Garratt oak casket with people popping in and out to pay their respects, flowers arriving, and my dad phoning people to tell them that mum had died of a pulmonary embolism (blood clot). It had been decided that Fred Albin would conduct the funeral. To this day, I don't know how he did this because he loved and respected mum very much.

Mum was brought from the chapel to the shop the night before the funeral. It was a big funeral with about twenty limousines making their way from the shop in Jamaica Road and then down Abbey Street to St Mary Magdalen church at the end of Bermondsey Street. Neither Mum nor Dad were particularly religious, but they had both been brought up in the Church of England.

There wasn't a spare seat to be had. Sitting there were all my extended family, friends from school, Professor Keith Simpson, the Southwark coroner, the registrars, police officers, florists, Mr Wass, the surgeon from Guy's, old Mr Smith, a funeral director who had a shop in Borough and two staff from Tadman's, a funeral firm with a shop off the Mile End Road. Some were crying, while others were coming up to Dad and I to offer condolences. As I sat there through the service, staring at mum's casket and the flowers and floral tributes that surrounded it, two things suddenly hit me for the first time: I never said goodbye to her and she died alone. Tears flooded down my face when I realised this.

As we walked out of the church to the limousine, Ernie Albin squeezed my arm and whispered, 'Barry, be strong. Be strong.' Sadly, this was the last time I was to see him alive. He died a year later.

After the cortege had driven past Weston Street, where we had lived, it made its way down the Old Kent Road to Camberwell New Cemetery, where a plot had been reserved in what was called the rosary section, a beautiful floral area. Standing there as the vicar said the funeral prayers, I looked around me at the headstones and saw so many names from Bermondsey. As mum's casket was lowered into the grave by Fred and the men, all I could think about was that I hadn't said goodbye and that she had died alone. There was so much I would have told her. Most important of all, I would have said how much I loved her, even though I had told her that many times during her life. And it suddenly dawned on me that, up until then, all the deaths I had been involved in hadn't touched me as real. But mum's death was real. And I became aware of my own mortality. It chilled me to think that I wasn't going to live forever. Now, much older, this is a comfort – and if we all lived forever, I would be out of business, of course.

When I trained as a bereavement counsellor I realised that I had denied my mother's death inside of me; I had shut it off, out of fear of what those feelings might do to me. Years later, when my family gave me a Christmas present of a videotape containing a collection of cine film featuring my mother during my childhood I cried like a baby.

The thousands of families I have conducted funerals for have taught me that the sooner you face bereavement, the quicker you can move your life on. When people say, 'I'll never get over it,' they are absolutely right. You never get over the death of someone you love dearly. Even though I am now fifty, I have never got over the death of my mother.

But, of course, no two people grieve in the same way, something I learnt early on when I conducted the funeral of that child in Brixton, and something that has been brought home to me again and again over the years. For example, after the death of Prince Albert in 1861, Queen Victoria became the 'Widow of Windsor' and remained so until the end of her life. She demanded that Royal servants wore black armbands for at least eight years after Albert's death, and she reprimanded her daughter, the wife of Kaiser Fredrich III, for not putting her five-month-old baby into mourning when its great-grandmother died. When Queen Victoria died in 1901, aged eighty-two, it was said at the time that over £80,000 was spent on flowers. The wreath from the 7th Hussars comprised their regimental shield composed of 60,000 dark Russian violets.

The outbreak of public mourning over the death of Princess Diana in August 1997 caught the nation by surprise. Seeing a beautiful young woman, who was both wealthy and popular, die tragically in a car accident was a poignant reminder to millions of people not just in the UK but around the world that we are all vulnerable; that, one day, no matter who we are, or how wealthy and powerful we are, we will die.

Murray E. Parks, the author of *Stages of Grief*, outlined four stages of grief: numbness, denial, deprivation and depression. He was the first to refer to bereavement as an illness, and described grieving as a thirteen-month illness. The reason for this is that a person had to pass through all the first anniversaries associated with a loved one – Christmas, birthdays, holidays, and so on – before they could begin the process of recovery. My experience with bereaved families supports everything he said.

But bereavement doesn't begin at death. It can begin when a person knows that they have a terminal illness. In such circumstances, when death is imminent, it is not uncommon for the person and their family to plan in advance for the funeral. This can be of enormous help to the family.

Bereavement, however, isn't just about the death of a loved one. People can experience bereavement over the loss of a limb, a career or something else precious to their life. Grieving properly and learning to move on after a death is crucial, and also difficult.

This is where the role of an experienced and caring funeral director comes in. As I have said, the main focus of 50 per cent of our work is the living not the dead. My job in arranging and conducting a funeral is to provide a vehicle where the bereaved can safely express their grief, and in whatever way they want. We aim to provide as many options as possible. Being involved in the planning of a funeral can have a therapeutic value for those who are able to do it.

I allow the bereaved to visit the chapel of rest whenever

they want. I am lucky in having Carrie and Bill, my caretakers, living in the flat above the funeral home. They are a dear retired couple who display kindness, patience and sympathy to the bereaved families who visit our funeral home at all hours.

When a family are not allowed to lay their loved one to rest and say their final goodbyes this can intensify their grief. In the case of a murder in England the body can be kept until the time of the trial, which could be a year, before it is released for burial or cremation. This is because the accused has the right to request a second postmortem. In Northern Ireland, on the other hand, the body will be released for burial or cremation in forty-eight hours. This, in my opinion, is far more sensible. It seems to me that we need an independent panel set up. They could authorise a second postmortem by an independent team of pathologists, and the report could be confidentially withheld until the time of the trial in case such a postmortem is requested, thus allowing the burial or cremation to go ahead straight away.

The murder of a father of six in Bermondsey was an example of a family not being able to grieve properly. After the man's bloodstained clothing was found in a burnt out car under a railway arch a murder enquiry was launched. Even though the police didn't find his body, they arrested and charged three men in connection with what they concluded was a murder.

It was nearly a year before the man's remains were discovered in a sandpit in Rainham, Essex. During this time, his wife and family regularly left flowers on some railings opposite the St James' Tavern. This became a sort of shrine to the man. While it appeared that he had almost certainly been murdered, there was still that 1 per cent chance that he might still be alive, somewhere.

The three men were eventually tried at the Old Bailey and convicted. Two received life sentences and the third eight years for conspiracy to murder. The man had suffered a terrible death, it emerged. After an evening drinking in several local pubs, he had gone back with the three men to the house where one of them lived. An argument ensued and the man was shot. His body was cut up into pieces before it was driven to Essex and dumped in a sandpit. At one point, the men were contemplating putting him through a mincing machine.

His funeral was a big affair. His wife had requested the horse-drawn hearse and five limousines. I had placed a violet flashing light (which I had bought in Canada) on the lead security car, which drives in front of the horse-drawn hearse to stop the traffic and run the funeral through traffic lights.

Given the nature of his death and the bad feeling that was still there in the community, the police shadowed the cortege throughout the funeral. After collecting his wife, six children and other family members, from their house on St James' Road, we proceeded the short distance to the church.

His wife gripped my arm tightly. 'You know, Barry I've had a drink.'

'Listen, love, you do whatever you want; whatever helps you through the day,' I replied. It was a terrible day for her and her family. If a drink helped her through it all, then that's fine by me.

As we were entering the gates to the churchyard, I turned around only to see two men lounging against the wall near the Royal Mail sorting office. I knew instantly from the posture that they had turned up to antagonise the family. This was the last thing they needed. Before I could do anything, several of the mourners walked towards them, gesturing in no uncertain terms that they should leave. And, wisely, they did.

Holding the wife by her arm I entered the church ahead of the bearers. As soon as we walked in a piece of music began. 'You'll never guess what,' I whispered to her. 'The theme from *Once Upon a Time in America* is my favourite music of all time.' She smiled through her tears. There were in fact ten pieces of music that day, double the number you would normally have at a funeral. Afterwards the cortege made a tour through the streets of Bermondsey before making its way to a local cemetery.

I kept a special eye on her at the graveside. Experience has taught me to always do this in case someone is so distraught that they might throw themselves in. That's why today we carry smelling salts in the hearse. As a rule, it's not the person who threatens to do this you have to watch but those who don't. Certain people want to make a show, but they will only do this if they know there is someone there to catch them. I will often stand behind someone like this and gently place a hand on each shoulder. Often they will be screaming and then, once they have made sure there is someone there to catch them, faint. I haven't lost one yet, I'm happy to say. But Roy's wife did not make a show and, as the earth was scattered over the coffin, she felt a release. She had been allowed to say goodbye and she behaved with great dignity.

Cemeteries and memorial gardens play an important part in the grieving process. The gravestones and memorials exist for the benefit of those left behind. Compared to the imaginative way in which the Victorians remembered the dead, modern memorialisation is, on the whole, pretty bland, I feel. Simple tablets of stone are the order of the day.

It goes without saying that the way a person grieves is also shaped by their beliefs about what happens beyond death. Religion, of whatever variety, can provide enormous consolation. I have lost count of the times that someone has come up to me after a service or in a cemetery and said, 'You know, I don't think I could have coped with this if it hadn't been for my faith in God.' For the non-believer, the death of a loved one is, perhaps, more difficult to face, because they have no faith in there being another life other than this.

No death can be harder to come to terms with than the death of a baby or a child, so young and so innocent; their whole life ahead of them. When I was a young man training to be a funeral director the first jobs I was given were with children. Life expectancy was much lower then and there were a great number of infant deaths. And if you look at our early records you will see that it was nothing for a family to have seven or eight children who had died. This was often through deprivation, poverty or malnutrition. Every week you would get a child of five or six dying. And even in the 1960s it was common in a family to have one or two children who had died. At one time, some foetuses and stillbirths would not be buried individually but placed in the same coffin as a pauper. This practice had stopped by the time I came into the funeral business but I was still very aware of it. Today I would never consider sending someone to learn about funerals by doing children's funerals. Times have definitely changed, and for the better.

Once, when I was doing a removal from Guy's Hospital, a midwife asked if she could visit the funeral home because she had never been to one before. So, the following week I gave her a guided tour. When I asked her what happened to the dead foetuses, she had to admit that she didn't know. When I made some enquiries through Fr Cooley, one of the Catholic chaplains at the hospital, I was shocked to discover that foetuses were disposed of with the clinical waste.

Not long after, I was at a dinner party with some friends. We were talking and joking about local gossip, politics, football, all the usual things, when the conversation at one point turned to babies.

'Everyone should know where someone they love is, if they have died. It's that important,' I suggested.

The wife of one of my friends went quiet and stared at me for a moment. I wondered if I had said something wrong and looked at her husband. He nodded at me awkwardly and then looked away.

She said, 'You're right, Barry. I lost a baby once. It was many years ago when I was in St Olave's Hospital. And do you know, I don't know what happened to it. Years later I felt I wanted to know what had happened. But when I contacted the hospital no one was able to tell me.'

I listened silently as she talked emotionally about the pain she felt at not knowing the whereabouts of her baby. I said that it had probably been buried in a parish grave, at a local cemetery such as Nunhead. She said she wanted to know where the baby was so that a couple of times a year she could visit the grave with a few flowers.

This brought home to me not only how important it was

to know where a loved one was buried, but also the importance of having a funeral for foetuses. When I proposed this
to the management at Guy's and St Thomas's Hospitals
they all agreed it should be provided.

When a hospital has a number of foetuses they will
phone me up and ask me to come and collect them from
the mortuary. Not all foetuses have a name. Some have a
number, if they are as a result of an abortion, for example.
I put each foetus in a tiny white box, about the size of a
hand, a midwife signs a paper confirming the death and I
take them away in a small carrycot. Years ago funeral
directors would have gone with an old case. I do this because
I believe each life is sacred, whether it's a one-day-old foetus
or someone who is a hundred.

The foetuses are brought to the funeral home and put in
a refrigerator until the burial or cremation is arranged.
They are all buried individually in one grave or cremated.
One of my staff will attend and say a short prayer, such as
'suffer the little children to come unto me'. The mother is
always invited to attend. If she wants to come, we meet her
at the cemetery or crematorium. At Honor Oak Crematorium a baby's ashes are scattered on a stretch of lawn,
known as 'the babies lawn' and we also have a baby section
in our cremation cemetery. Every burial or cremation is
recorded in a book and every foetus has a memorial card
printed for it. Over the last four or five years I must have
had approximately fifty people who have contacted us
through the hospital wanting to know what had happened
to their baby. Sometimes this might be a year later. And I
can tell them by finding the details in the book. They take
great consolation from this.

Since setting up the foetus burial service, other

hospitals have followed suit, and I have given lectures to midwives and trainees about infant deaths, along with bereavement and my life as a funeral director. The midwife who came to visit the shop is now based in a Birmingham teaching hospital and each year she invites me to give a lecture to her students.

In order to improve the funerals of babies, I bought a rocking horse, repainted it by hand, took it off the rocker and secured it to a glass shelf. This gives the impression that the coffin is on a rocking horse and helps parents to realise we are human and caring. These little touches are very important.

My sons once had to remove a baby who had been born deformed. The parents had put the baby in the care of a foster mother, a hospital nurse, who kept him alive for eighteen months. When my boys arrived at the house they placed it in a carrycot, just as a mother would do if she was taking it out for a walk. The foster mother contacted me to say how grateful and touched she was at the way my sons handled the baby. I was proud of them, as any father would have been.

That children should have the opportunity to participate in a funeral is, I believe, very important. During my childhood, children never went to funerals. My earliest memory of a funeral was when my Uncle Bill died. I wasn't allowed to attend and could only watch events with my cousin Janet through the window from the house across the road, where we had been put up. Jonathan and Simon, on the other hand, read John 14 from the Bible at their great grandmother's funeral when they were very young.

But I also believe that a child should only participate in a funeral if that's what they want. And their parents need to explain properly what's happening. Jonathan and Simon once did some drawings about a funeral home and what happened when someone died. I printed these out and gave them to the clients to show their children to help them understand what was happening. Later in America I saw that someone had done a similar thing with children's drawings.

Apart from the death of children, suicide must be one of the hardest things for a family to come to terms with. Interestingly, I was once told by an Iranian minister I met that according to Islamic belief there is no such thing as suicide. Such a death is seen as killing something inside yourself that you hate. In other words, you are not in your right mind. I tend to agree with this. On the other hand, the Catholic Church used to teach that someone who commits suicide could not go to Heaven and could not be buried in consecrated ground. My dad used to say to me that people who commit suicide are the brave people. But I'm sure it's the reverse. You have to be brave to continue living through and beyond an event such as the death of a loved one. I know that I did.

# 8

# MAKING A LIVING OUT OF DYING

'Barry, I'm going to make you an offer. How does £1.5 million sound?' asked the voice at the other end of the phone.

I gave a sharp intake of breath. 'Did you say £1.5 million?'

'That's right . . . £1.5 million.' He said the figure slowly for maximum effect.

In the late 1980s Howard Hodgson was gobbling up funeral homes around the country at a phenomenal rate and he wanted to add mine to his list. He had made an earlier attempt when he had sent former England and Warwickshire cricketer Dennis Amiss down to Bermondsey to sweet talk me. I enjoyed our meeting and listening to his stories about his long career in professional cricket, but even Dennis Amiss couldn't sway me.

But could Albin's be worth this much? 'It sounds about right, Howard,' I responded, unable to think of anything else to say. I really wanted to walk out of the room and scream, 'I've got the winning lottery ticket.' But I quickly realised that because Albin's meant so much to me I could never cash it.

'What do you say then?' he said expectantly.

I was still gobsmacked.

'But that's not all. I'll also give you £40,000 a year, your own office, a Jaguar, medical insurance, and an expenses account, and you can work for me in America.'

'America?' I was flattered. Howard had done his research: he knew I liked America – but he didn't know that I loved Bermondsey more.

'Yes, I'm setting up a chain of funeral homes there. And you would be the man to run them.' From the tone of his voice, he clearly expected me to accept his offer.

'I'm sorry, Howard. I can't sell Albin's. It's everything to me, you know that. And I couldn't leave the business here to work for you in the States. And I wouldn't want to have to move my family over there.' At the time, my two sons were still at school.

'Well, think about it. It's a good offer,' he added seductively.

He was right. It was a good offer, more than generous, in fact. But, for me, while money has been important, it has never been the primary driving force in my life as a funeral director.

In many ways, Howard was very much a man of the Thatcher era. *The Sunday Times* in 1987 named him as one of 'Maggie's Dozen of the Decade'. Some people mistakenly saw Howard as a wide boy. In fact he was a very clever and shrewd businessman. His entry into the history books of funeral directing in the UK occurred when he obtained money from the City and by 1990, after a frantic acquisition spree, owned 546 funeral directors, making his company the largest funeral director in the UK, along with the Co-op. Before he came along funerals were very much part of a cottage industry: small family businesses in the local high street, a bit like corner shops.

He was, it has to be said, a difficult man to work with because he talked so much – especially about himself – and he had a radically different view of the funeral business to me. He saw it primarily about making money; I see it as providing a service to bereaved families and more a way of life.

But I liked Howard and we both agreed that funerals were underpriced and that there had to be changes in the industry. He was all about doing as many funerals as possible. He used to get fifty brilliant ideas a day but could never make one of them work (his introduction of blue cars was one idea that never caught on). While he was buying up funeral businesses all over the country, to keep the Stock Exchange happy, he often ended up with related companies he didn't want. For example, he ended up with a kitchen manufacturer, warehouses and shops, which were of no use to him at all.

In 1991 he sold his business, for over £120 million, to Pompes Funebres Generales and walked away with a fortune. After becoming chief executive of a brewery, he bought Ronson plc, the famous lighter company. If I sold this business I would be in shock for years. That's the difference in our approaches to funerals. After other business ventures, Howard went on to become a writer, publishing his autobiography, *How to Become Dead Rich*, and a novel *Six Feet Under*. He also presented two BBC TV documentary series about the single European market and became a regular member of BBC Radio 4's *Business Quiz*

*Show,* and *The Board Game.* Howard left his mark on the funeral industry and on me.

But, despite our radically different views on running a funeral business, I learnt a lot from Howard: the importance of eye contact, the importance of listening to people (because he never did) and the importance of taking just one good idea and concentrating on that. In the bigger picture, Howard made people realise that they were getting funerals on the cheap. He pointed out what they paid for a settee or a car and what they got in a funeral. When he sent me his first book he wrote on the flyleaf, 'Barry, you were right not to sell. You were one of the good ones.'

I could never have sold Albin's to Howard. And when, a few years later, SCI, the world's largest funeral directors, offered first, £4.7 million then £6.5 million for the business plus a huge salary over ten years connected to very high performances, I still said no. SCI wanted to take the Albin formula and franchise it in about twenty big towns, making it a sort of Marks and Spencer of the funeral business. But to have sold up would have been to have sold my soul. I realised though that I could, for the first time in my life, be a millionaire. But there are more things in life than money. F. A. Albin & Sons was a historical mantle I had picked up on 1 November 1986 when I bought the business from Fred Albin. It was also a dream come true. In fact, I really picked up the historical mantle when I was born.

My personal motto is 'carpe diem', which means seize the moment. When I took the plunge and purchased the business (thanks to the encouragement of Johnny Raven, a close friend and fellow funeral director) I was determined to seize the moment and turn Albin's into the most modern and best firm of funeral directors in the country without losing any of its traditions. It would be hard work, I knew, and it would involve taking risks and maybe dealing with a few disasters along the way. But anything worthwhile is worth working hard for. And, after all, I had my sons to follow me into the business. It was my task to sow the seeds, which they could cultivate.

While F. A. Albin & Sons had a very good reputation, and a 200-year-old tradition of undertaking to care for the dead and the living, the company, in my opinion, needed to take a big leap forward. And with large companies such as SCI and the Co-op providing serious competition to small, independent funeral directors, it was more important than ever to examine where the company could improve its service from good to outstanding; so from the outset I developed a long-term strategy for change. I knew exactly what I wanted.

One of the first areas I turned my attention to after I became the owner of Albin's was the staff. There were kind but difficult employees who had been with the firm so long they were in a rut. They refused to change with the times. Any company is only as good as its staff. It doesn't matter if you are talking about funerals, supermarkets, car manufacturers or banks, it's just the same. But obviously working for a funeral director requires different skills and attributes to working on a car production line or in a bank, for example. What sets funeral directors apart from many other businesses is that you are dealing with people who are often at the most vulnerable moment of their life. Selling a car to someone and selling a coffin to someone call for very different approaches. Tact, sensitivity, patience and empathy are just some of the interpersonal skills required to work in a funeral home.

Looking around, I could see that there were many gaps in my staff's understanding and knowledge about death, bereavement, funerals and all the various professions linked in some way to caring for the dead and their families and friends. This might not be a problem for some funeral directors, but it wouldn't do for me.

While in America it is common for men and women to undertake studies at funeral colleges, in Britain it had not been the case. Most of those working in the funeral business had little, if any, formal training. They had learnt everything on the job. So I decided to form an in-house college. I have always believed that some people are naturals in life; others need to be taught. But all of us can benefit from education at certain points. And I have always seen education as a lifelong process, not something that ceases once you leave school, college or receive a qualification.

At the time of writing, I am still finalising details for the college. But the plan is that once a month at 7 a.m. a lecture will be given. Staff will have to attend at least eight of the twelve lectures, which are given by various professionals on subjects such as health and safety, basic first aid, basic car mechanics, chemicals used in embalming, bereavement and religious rites. At the end of the year, staff will receive certificates and medals and then at the end of five years' service they will receive a silver award and at the end of ten years a gold award. I have already revived the apprenticeship scheme, taking on local youngsters and training them in various aspects of the funeral business.

Often, priests are surprised that when my bearers carry a coffin into a Catholic church they will genuflect to the Blessed Sacrament when it is reserved in one of the side chapels rather than on the sanctuary, which is the usual case. Even though not all my men are Catholic, I have taught them to understand what they are doing, not to simply go through the motions but to actually acknowledge the Body of Christ, which is signified by a sanctuary lamp. To me, this seems right and proper. In the same way, we always take our shoes off before entering a mosque (even if they might get stolen!).

Apart from having the necessary skills or training, someone must also be able to fit in with the team and the philosophy of the company. Because of my reputation in the funeral industry I am always receiving enquiries from people wanting to work for me. For example, Paul, one of my current staff, first came to me for a job when he was employed by SCI. I told him I didn't have a vacancy at that time but to keep in touch. He wanted to work for Albin's so badly that for the next three years he came to the funeral home every month to see if there was a vacancy. By the time a vacancy did arise Paul knew a number of my staff. So when I asked them whether they thought he would fit in they all said yes. My key staff are always involved in the selection process. It is vital they feel that the person applying for a job has the right knowledge, aptitude and personality.

Before the advent of the drinking and driving laws funeral directors had a reputation as hard drinkers. Even I used to take the odd glass of brandy while I was on duty (until I learned to deposit it in the flower pot). Today, I don't allow my staff to drink alcohol while on duty. If invited by the family, we will sometimes attend a reception afterwards. But we will only drink tea, coffee, soft drinks or mild shandy. I was gutted when I once had to sack a member of staff after he turned up for work at 7 a.m. blind drunk. The reason I felt this way was because he had been with me for eight years and I had given him the best training available. And he knew well my strong views on alcohol at work.

This is a long way from when funeral directors would often supply two mutes to welcome mourners to the home of the deceased person. I remember Fred Albin once telling me about when Arthur, his father, conducted a big funeral for a publican. The mutes were sent around at 12 p.m., two hours before the funeral party was due to depart. By the time Arthur and the bearers arrived the mutes could hardly stand as a result of all the rum and whisky they had been given by the mourners, who kept enticing them into the house. Is this where the expression 'pissed as a newt' came from? Should it really be pissed as a mute?

The only place where success comes before work is in the dictionary. I remember the time Mick Collins, the foreman at the old garage in Southwark Park Road, once asked me to make the tea while the men washed the cars. I thought to myself, 'I don't mind doing this. It's easier than washing the cars.' But when I told my dad he was furious. 'Don't you ever think that work is easy! Don't ever take the easy job. Do the hard things. Never be lazy.' I stood there dumbfounded. I didn't think I had said anything wrong. But, like the time my dad stressed that on no account do you ever drop the coffin, I never forgot that incident.

But in case I come across as a sergeant-major type, driving his men on until they drop, just let me say that I have always had a mischievous sense of humour and have enjoyed playing practical jokes with the men. I once sent an apprentice to the post office on Jamaica Road to buy a Penny Black stamp. The man behind the counter told him, 'If I had one of them, mate, I wouldn't be working here.' Another time, I gave a young lad working for me an order for a Chinese take-away and wrote down a restaurant address in Beijing. It took him five minutes of flicking through the south-east London area telephone directory before he realised what I had done. Having a sense of humour and being able to share it with your employees is, I have always believed, an important element in running a successful business. And I have been on the receiving end of practical jokes, such as the time I walked into the kitchen one morning, expecting to find all the staff there. It was deserted. I walked around the funeral home and there wasn't a soul to be seen. I went out into the yard and as I did I heard a giggle from somewhere. It turned out that all the staff were hiding in the limousines, crying with laughter.

All my staff meet for breakfast in the kitchen of the funeral home every morning. The reason is two-fold: to build up the sense of being a team, or a family, as I like to think, and to provide a place where we can discuss the day ahead and any pressing issues. And doing this over tea and toast – or a fry-up on Friday mornings – creates a much more informal atmosphere than having a meeting in the office. I got this idea after visiting a Pearce Brothers funeral firm in Kentucky where each morning the staff at the four branches had a ten-minute meeting using the phone.

Furthermore, I've always believed that if you treat your staff well and provide a good financial package they will never leave you. The key to keeping staff, making them care about their work and creating loyalty, is running a company that is good to the staff and where everyone appreciates each other. At one time, Marks and Spencer held to this philosophy. A Marks and Spencer girl was superior to a Woolworth girl or a C & A girl. Today, Marks and Spencer have abandoned this approach.

Hairdressers, chiropodists and all the other staff services have disappeared. And look what has happened to the company's profits and image.

In fact, I have often felt that picking my team for a funeral and making all those decisions about who should talk through the funeral arrangements with a family, drive the hearse and the lead car, act as a bearer and deal with the floral tributes and so on was not too dissimilar to being a football manager. The key to good management is knowing the strengths and weaknesses of your team, not putting a square peg in a round hole, and establishing good communication. For example, Reg, one of my hearse drivers, always travels at one steady speed, whether he is driving through south London or up the motorway. On the other hand, Lee, another of my staff, would start off at a slow pace and then increase speed. So I don't like to use Lee as a hearse driver. I prefer to play to his strengths and use him as a limousine driver.

I have eight fully trained, part-time men and women to call on to cover for holidays, absenteeism or when we are extremely busy. I refer to them as second stringers. I know that when I put a second stringer with three of my first team men he soon becomes as good as them. In some ways it's a bit like the Liverpool squad. Each of those twenty or so players in the squad is able to step into the first team and perform well. But if I put four second stringers together on a funeral the performance would be below par.

I will admit that finding the right kind of staff has not been easy, and my search has placed a tremendous strain on me at times, but I believe I now have the best team in any funeral directors anywhere. They provide first class care, are dedicated, loyal and professional. They know I am a perfectionist and that if you broke me open you would find the words F. A. Albin & Sons written there. This business is a part of me. For example, if there is a problem with the exhaust, then I will be in the garage the same night trying to fix it. Another funeral director might wait until it falls off before doing anything. And if one of the limousines gets scratched, then, again, I will want it repaired immediately. I believe perfection is all about doing the small things well; the big things will look after themselves. I can, I know, be a very demanding boss, obsessive even, but my staff also know I am very fair and genuinely concerned for their welfare. And they have as much pride in the company as I do.

Women play an important role in the funeral industry today. I remember the time I went with Jackie, my office manager, to remove the body of a one-year-old baby who had died of Aids. The mother refused to give the child to me but eventually she passed the baby to Jackie, who has a special gift for working with bereaved families. I realised then what an important role women had within the funeral industry. They are the mothers of the world.

My dad used to say to me, 'Son you must always look the epitome of sartorial elegance in everything you wear.' And I believe my staff are the smartest you will find in any funeral firm. Their mourning suits were specially made by renowned tailor Simon Oakes. I have tried to get away from the colour black being the sole colour associated with death and funerals by, for example, introducing burgundy collars on our coats. The staff also wear a cravat to give their appearance that little extra touch. If you leave it to individuals some will turn up wearing brogues, others wearing slip-ons; some will turn up in double-breasted jackets, others in single-breasted pinstripe jackets. This is quite common amongst other funeral directors. Even when my staff are not on a funeral, but are in the funeral home or visiting a hospital, they all dress identically: the men wear black trousers and black polo neck shirts and the women wear white shirts, black jackets and skirts. What's more, apart from alcohol, I don't allow my staff to smoke, chew gum or wear jewellery when they are on a funeral. All staff agree to this when they join the firm.

I smile when I recall how Fred Albin used to take me to a clothiers just over Tower Bridge. He would go in and say, 'I've brought the staff for fitting out.' And then out would come all these old mourning suits smelling of moth balls. I used to call my trousers Billy Cottons because there was plenty of ball room in them. Holding in the back, Fred would smile and say, 'They fit you perfectly, boy.' And I'd think to myself, 'Yes but so did Coco the Clown's.'

Football managers have taught me more about business and management than so-called business gurus have. When Malcolm Allison took over Crystal Palace after his spell at Manchester City he found that the black and white players weren't mixing in the dressing room or off the pitch. So just before they were about to get on the coach for an away game he called all the players together and told them that from now on they were neither black nor white, they were all green. He then said he wanted the light green players to sit in the front of the coach and the dark green at the back. The reason why Manchester City had been so successful was because they played together. Initially, I thought what Allison said was silly, but then I realised that it was an excellent piece of psychology. Allison was realistic enough to know that he would never erase the differences amongst the players, but he could make the players aware of what they had in common.

I remember going to a West End restaurant once with some friends and meeting the ex-Liverpool and England footballer Phil Thompson. He told us a story of when he was a teenager at the club, trying to break into the first team. Ronnie Moran, the trainer, assured him that he would be named in the team the following week. But he wasn't. After this happened several times Thompson was annoyed and plucked up the courage to see Bill Shankly in his office. 'What's your name again?' asked Shankly when Thompson entered the office (he knew who he was, of course). 'Phil Thompson,' replied Thompson before asking why he wasn't in the first team. Shankly asked him what was the score on Saturday. 'We lost 2–0,' said Thompson. 'Who to?' came back Shankly. 'West Ham,' answered Thompson. 'That's right, West Ham,' replied Shankly. 'We lost to the worst team in the league. You would have learnt nothing from them. And I don't want to spoil your future, because you can go all the way and be Liverpool and England captain. You're that good.' Phil Thompson said he walked out of the office feeling ten feet high. It wasn't until later that he realised he still hadn't made the first team and was back where he started.

This is a perfect example of how you motivate staff and I use similar techniques myself. You have to give your staff psychological boosts. Another time, when I met Kevin Keegan once at a dinner, I asked him what was the greatest thing Bill Shankly had ever said to him. He told me about the time Liverpool were playing West Ham, again, and Shankly told him that he would run rings around Bobby

Moore because he had seen him in the tunnel and he was knackered after being out drinking all night. Keegan was fired up when he ran out on to the pitch. But Liverpool lost 2–1 and Moore was as impeccable as always. Afterwards, Shankly came up to him and said, 'That Bobby Moore, drunk last night. What a player!' What that meant was that Keegan hadn't done badly but he had played against one of the greatest players in the world. That was a superb piece of psychology. Bill Shankly may not have been a great businessman, but he knew how to get the best out of his players, as the trophy cabinet in the Liverpool boardroom proves.

My success at team building was acknowledged by Price Waterhouse in 1994 when they made me Managing Director of the Year, after one of my bank managers nominated me. It was a very proud moment, as was when I was made a Freeman of the City of London. I am now entitled to draw my sword in the City without being arrested and take sheep across Tower Bridge. In 2001 I won the Southwark Corporate Citizen of the Year Award. My standing in the community was also acknowledged when I was invited to be a magistrate. In moments of vanity, I sometimes think that it would be nice to be knighted. Sir Barry of Bermondsey has a certain ring about it, don't you think? But such accolades are for more worthy people.

Apart from finding the right staff, security is a key issue for any business. My funeral home is equipped with CCTV cameras and a private security company makes regular patrols through the night. Nevertheless, we have had a few incidents. When the funeral home was being built in 1976 I caught four teenagers in the grounds. I had been expecting them, as a few nights before they had broken in and caused several thousand pounds worth of damage to a recently cemented area. I had had enough. I captured them and marched them all down the road to Rotherhithe police station in order to have then formally warned about their behaviour.

On another occasion, I caught a youth trying to climb over the fence. I shouted at him to get down but he wouldn't, so I pulled him down. An hour later he returned with his father and they began swearing at me. It was clear they had both been drinking. I walked over to them and the father aimed a punch at me. I wasn't having this and caught him with a right hook. The son then jumped on me. It all ended with me breaking their umbrella in two and chasing them up the road. Walking back into the yard, I realised that they had smashed our sign and set off after them. As I caught them a police car turned up by chance and the two men were arrested. I never pressed charges. Things are often settled like that in Bermondsey.

Cars have always been my passion, ever since, at the age of fourteen, I first backed the old Rolls Royces into the garage in Southwark Park Road. In fact, I can probably trace it back to when I used to run around in homemade carts. And after passing my driving test, my dad bought me a Ford Popular, which I soon exchanged for a Morris 1000 Traveller. I really wanted a more fashionable and faster Ford Cortina 1600E, but Dad and Fred insisted that I drove a sensible car. Fred was a great wheeler and dealer and a bit of a specialist in cars, especially Rolls Royces. He once sold an old Rolls hearse at the end of its life span, only to hear later that it was sold for a fortune at Sotheby's.

Another time, he bought a Rolls with a mother of pearl dashboard and a machine gun turret on the back from a sheik in Saudi Arabia.

When I was thinking about a new fleet, I asked Fred Albin what he thought of Mercedes. The only cars used by funeral directors back then were Rolls Royces and Daimlers. 'Over priced and over bloody here,' he replied deadpan. 'You don't want them in Bermondsey because during the war they bombed our chip shop.'

To mark the purchase of my new fleet of three Daimler limousines and two Daimler hearses, all specially built for Albin's and with a burgundy trim, I held an open day at Culling Road in 1991, attended by the staff, friends, associates, local clergy and MP Simon Hughes. As I've said, I like to add little personal touches to my business to make it unique. When I bought my fleet of limousines I paid the DVLC in Swansea for ALB number plates. But you can only request specific registrations on new cars. I then went to Ireland to buy several AIB number plates from old hearses. A contact of mine over there had told me they were up for sale. I also obtained the registration AL8 1N, on which I have made the 8 look like a B. It's a little bit illegal, but who could call it a crime?

My twenty-strong fleet includes two 1932 sister Simpson and Slater Rolls Royce bodied hearses. I had tracked down the second one at Kendal's funeral directors in Dalston. Bringing it back to Albin's, where it had begun its life, was like bringing it home. I also own two luxury saloons, one convertible floral hearse, which is used in the summer to carry floral tributes in front of the horse-drawn hearse, a landau to accompany the horse-drawn hearse, two private ambulances, a Luton van for delivering coffins from our factory, a trailer, a four-wheel drive Jeep for towing the horse box, three vehicles for general use and an air-cooled interior vehicle for long distance removals. I also succeeded in purchasing the Queen Mother's Daimler. Let's just say it cost me quite a bit, but it was worth it. For it now means that people in Bermondsey can travel in the car the Queen Mother used to travel in. I like the idea of that. And so does Bermondsey.

Like any company, we have had problems with bad debts. One of the occasions when I never got paid for a funeral was when a young pro-Shah Iranian man was blown up by his own bomb in Kensington. His father gave me a cheque for the funeral. By the time I had discovered it had bounced he was back in Iran, in prison, I think. Years ago when this happened my dad would park the hearse outside the house of the bad payer and knock on the door for the money. This told all the neighbours that someone hadn't paid for a funeral. Those were the days when neighbours would sign up on a subscription list to help a poor widow pay for a funeral. Anyone who didn't contribute was considered the lowest of the low.

My approach has been lower key, chasing up a debt myself by writing to the person, phoning them up or, sometimes, going around to someone's house. I have also used debt-collecting agencies and taken people to court. Once, Jackie had to travel all the way to Plymouth to get a county court judgment against someone. But in cases like these we are losing money because of the legal costs. The law seems to be against the honest trader. On all the occasions when I have succeed in obtaining a county court judgment I have never recovered a penny, even though they are usually only asked to pay a small amount regularly.

That's not a lot to ask and we will always help anyone in real need.

Today, if someone is on a low income, the DSS will provide a Community Care Grant, which may cover the entire cost of the funeral or only leave the person with a couple of hundred pounds to pay, which we allow them to do in £5 or £10 per week instalments, if need be. I like to think I am very fair with people and will not make unreasonable demands on them if their income is low. All I ever ask is that they make regular payments and be honest.

F. A. Albin & Sons is one of around 3,500 funeral firms in the UK (precise figures are difficult to come by). However, the £1 billion-a-year industry has been undergoing major changes in the last twenty years. Along with the Co-op, SCI now conduct the funerals of a large percentage of the 680,000 deaths in the UK every year. While the name above the funeral home in your local high street might not have changed, behind the scenes the approach to funerals has.

I remember attending a meeting of Kenyon's shareholders (of which I was one) at the Portland Hotel in the West End. I had been listening with growing impatience as the chairman spoke enthusiastically about how good Kenyon's were. At the time, they were the official funeral directors to the Royal Family. He stressed that just because they weren't an independent family business it didn't mean that they didn't provide a good service.

Unable to hold my peace any longer, I stood up. 'I agree. Independent family firms do not have the monopoly on care.' I said, aware that all eyes were now fixed on me. 'But can you tell me how many of your shops opened on time today?' He looked a bit puzzled and eventually replied that they all did.

'So, you mean that out of all the receptionists at all your shops not one of them was sick and not one of them was late?' I continued. I went on to say that I had three outlets and I knew when my staff checked in and where they all were at any time. The chairman shifted awkwardly in his chair and looked at his colleagues alongside him on the podium. Neither of them seemed to know what to say.

'But if I was in your position, I wouldn't know either. That's just the nature of the animal.' I sat down to applause and murmurs around the conference room. The point I wanted to make was that because Kenyon's was so big the chairman could not have the same hands-on approach at ground level.

SCI are, as I have said, the world's largest firm of funeral directors. From their head office in Sutton Coldfield, West Midlands, they now run 530 funeral homes, including those previously owned by Kenyon's, twenty-two crematoria and five cemeteries. In an average year they conduct 80,000 funerals.

When SCI first arrived in Britain in 1994 they took on a lot of stuff they didn't want and didn't need. They bought out Hodgson plc and the Great Southern plc, two of the largest funeral companies in the UK at the time. This often meant that in some towns and cities they had shops opposite each other in the same street and were in competition with themselves. This was stupid, but unavoidable, if they were going to win the major share of the market.

I have very good relations with SCI and I meet regularly with Peter Hindley, SCI's head of their UK operations, usually over a meal in a restaurant. Peter is doing a fantastic job at SCI. At one time, SCI employed me as a consultant, as did Pompes Funebres Generales in Paris, and I advised them on many aspects of their business, such as their coffin manufacturing operation, terms and conditions for staff, their fleet of cars and whether they should buy a particular cemetery. I recognised that they needed to centralise their services rather than operate in a fragmented way, as they had been doing. From my travels in America I had learnt that centralisation was the key to effectively running a funeral business.

I'm not going to say that just because we are a small family business we have all the answers. There are some good managers working in SCI and the other larger companies. But you don't get the personal touch and flexibility that a firm like ours offers. The big funeral companies work much more to set methods like, say, Tesco or Currys. Often the person conducting a funeral for a company like SCI may not have met the family until the morning of the funeral, and won't know anything about them. This makes the job very difficult.

For example, when I opened up an office down the road in Deptford in 1994 there were already two funeral directors there: the Co-op at one end of the High Street and Chappel's at the other. Within five years both had closed. Needless to say, our business has gone up dramatically as a result, although it took me six years to recoup the £100,000 I had spent on the shop. The reason I succeeded and the Co-op and Chappel's failed was because we were able to be more hands on. Our staff are very dedicated because, like me, they want to provide the best service possible and they have helped people on low incomes claim their correct entitlements through the DSS. Elaine, my manager there, came in at 9 p.m. every night for two weeks so that a family could view their loved one in the chapel. The Co-op at the other end of the high street would close at 4 p.m. To be fair, if I owned the Co-op or Chappel's I would face the same problem.

The kind of personal touch that independent family funeral directors can provide is also illustrated by the case of a man in Bermondsey who comes to me every year on his birthday. Let's just say he's had a very unfortunate life, for various reasons. We have drafted his will, as we often do free of charge for people. He has asked me to be his executor, clear his flat and not notify his brother until after the funeral. This one visit a year makes him feel very comfortable about his affairs. I'm a bit like social services. He hasn't paid me a penny yet. He trusts me so much. The fact that his will is locked away in our safe at Culling Road puts his mind at rest. And I'm so proud of this. Big companies, such as the Co-op or SCI, wouldn't and couldn't take this approach, and because of their size they cannot afford to.

However, our downfall as a company is that we sometimes take on too many responsibilities, such as looking after people's documents. On one occasion an elderly woman came in to pay towards her pre-need funeral. However, we couldn't find her file.

'Oh, I can't trust you anymore,' she said jokingly as she reached the door.

I told her not to worry; we would find the file, which we did in the end. She had taken it home to show her sister and forgot to return it. But although she was only joking, those words hurt me a little, as I had done a lot for the lady over the years, and earned absolutely nothing. She was a typical, kind Bermondsey woman, although she grew up in Ireland, and I had always liked her. I had first met her when I brought her daughter back from Spain, where she had been killed in a car accident. Apart from collecting and embalming her daughter and conducting the funeral, I helped the lady claim compensation of several thousand pounds from the insurance company. Later, I did her will – which I have changed on numerous occasions when she has a change of heart – and a pre-need funeral. I also agreed to set up a trust for her son, so that, when she died, he would get a small annuity each month. Because of his drink problem she didn't want him receiving a lump sum. She has even come to me when she has had problems with her rent book. She's difficult, but I have a soft spot for her.

I have over 2,700 wills in storage and even keys to people's flats. The payment for me from all of this sort of work is the trust people place in me. I don't earn any money when I sort out someone's rent book or keep the keys to their flat. Fred Albin also did this, but in a much smaller way. If someone wants to send me a nice letter or something, that's reward enough.

During the Victorian era the planning for death often took place well in advance. For example, the actress Sarah Bernhardt kept her coffin in her boudoir. The wealthy would wear mourning costumes and hire professional mourners, while the deceased person would be carried to the cemetery in an elaborate horse-drawn hearse, decked with ostrich plumes and crepe. Those were the days when the wealthy would have a silk funeral. Bows made of silk would be attached to the wand and bands of silk tied around the hats of the funeral directors. The final gesture would be the erection of an often flamboyant memorial of the kind we can see today at cemeteries such as Highgate or Nunhead.

Less well-off people had cotton funerals and, if they wanted to avoid a pauper's funeral, would often join a local burial club or pay weekly premiums to one of the large insurance companies.

By and large, it is the older generation who pay for their funerals in advance. Those born in the 1960s have grown up in a culture that often refuses to acknowledge death as a reality. In fact, through so-called anti-ageing creams and plastic surgery for non medical reasons, it tries to postpone the inevitability of death.

During my travels around America I was struck by how well pre-need funerals, or funeral plans, worked. I told Fred Albin that it wouldn't be long before companies like Sun Alliance would offer funeral plans. The Great Southern, then one of the UK's largest firms of funeral directors, had already started selling pre-paid funeral plans through Age Concern. I concluded that the small funeral directors were getting left behind. With the support and encouragement of my good friend Paul Darnell, I drew up the Laurel pre-paid funeral plan, along the lines of the old friendly societies, whereby people paid as they went along and their funeral costs would be guaranteed to be paid.

What made my plan different from other ones was that if you moved to Australia or somewhere and you wanted to cancel your plan you would get your money back plus interest at the HSBC deposit account rate. The other plans only gave you your original investment back. Furthermore, the price is fixed. For example, if you give me £1,000 today and return in ten years' time to say that you have changed your mind, I will give you the £1,000 back along with the interest it has earned. Other funeral plans will only give you your original £1,000. The plan also provides flexibility to have as many cars as you want or other additional extras, such as a reception after the funeral.

Every year, the trustees invest all the money. I meet the cost of advertising through my business. The trust only pay me when I produce a letter from a family stating that the funeral has been carried out to their satisfaction. The surplus money provides a reserve to guarantee funerals in bad times. When someone takes out a funeral plan it means that I have guaranteed work in the future.

I once had a meeting with Marks and Spencer to discuss the possibility of them building in a pre-paid funeral plan into their package of staff benefits. Although they were very enthusiastic and carried out detailed research into the idea, nothing ever happened, as the company took a decision to reduce their staff welfare benefits. Nevertheless, I do believe that in the future companies will need to give serious thought to cradle-to-grave benefits to entice and keep staff.

The gratitude my staff and I receive from people for the way we have conducted a funeral is so important; just as important as money in some ways. When I look at how I have run my business I think I have managed to strike the right balance between making enough money and providing a first-class funeral. I am prepared to work as many hours as necessary, but I am not prepared to conduct three funerals in a day if I feel I can only do two really well. Some funeral directors are prepared to do this for reasons of profit. For me, it would go against my whole philosophy as a funeral director. I will not do a funeral badly. In other words, never take the goodness out of the job.

Unlike Howard Hodgson and SCI, I have never wanted to create a funeral empire, having believed that small is beautiful. Throughout my life I have always planted seeds and watched them grow, sometimes many years later. In business you have to be able to take a long-term view. Following my strategy of gradual growth and the reinvestment of profits, Albin's is now totally self-sufficient: we have our own well-trained staff, backed up by Martin Green's first-class support staff; we have a mortuary; we do our own embalming; we will soon run our own in-house college; we have our own Rolls Royce and Daimler hearses and horse-drawn hearse; we operate our own coffin-finishing and supply business; and, after a long battle with bureaucracy, we have our own cremation cemetery. I am very proud of this. I have created an Albin's image, what some would call branding.

In 2000 I purchased Hitchcock's funeral directors in the East End, having bought another company, Wilson & Wedge, in Mottingham a few years before. I did so because I wanted to save one of the few remaining old-style funeral businesses. Hitchcock's shop front on Barking Road hadn't changed in 100 years and the first entry recorded, in copper handwriting, in their book is dated 1898. When I went over to view it, it was like revisiting my childhood. The trapdoor to the cellar, the wardrobe lined with white calico to keep the dust off the clothes, the damp rooms upstairs, the chapel of rest out the back, the outside toilets, all of this was identical to Albin's former funeral home on Jamaica Road.

The Hitchcock's business included the funeral home, stables (where I hope to eventually stable my horses during the day), one limousine and a hearse. Russel, the owner of Hitchcock's, could probably have sold the business for a higher price to SCI, but he wanted to keep the family tradition alive and also stay and help us. That is why I am keeping the name Hitchcock for five years. After then, I may rename it Albin & Hitchcock's. I see the purchase of Hitchcock's as the final piece of the jigsaw and as something that will bring F. A. Albin & Sons up to its final capacity. With our shops in Bermondsey, Deptford, Mottingham and Barking Road, we have gone full circle, as at one time we had shops in Bermondsey, Lewisham, Downham and Leytonstone.

Interestingly, a couple of weeks after the purchase had been completed, Russel sent me a letter written by Fred Albin senior in 1952. In it, he expressed his condolences about the death of the father and then went on to say that he would be interested in buying the business. Maureen, one of my staff at our Bermondsey funeral home, remarked, 'If I didn't know, Barry, I would have sworn that you wrote it.' And she was right. The tone, language, lengthy sentences and formal style of the letter were exactly the way I write.

All along, I have tried, gradually, to bring the company back up to date in the twentieth century while keeping the charm of the nineteenth. After buying the business, I was keen to reinstate horse-drawn funerals, which Albin's had ceased to do in the 1940s. So, in the early 1990s I travelled to Ireland to buy a horse-drawn hearse, which had ended up in an agricultural museum. Made in Birmingham by Marsden's in 1864 for use in Ireland, it had carried the coffin of Douglas Hyde, the first Irish president. We brought it to London on a trailer, stripped it and rewooded it and Fred Albin did a marvellous job applying paint and gold leaf. As far as I am aware, it is the biggest and heaviest horse-drawn hearse in the country.

I also bought two fabulous seventeen-month-old black

Fresian horses that came from the same farm in Belgium that the firm had bought horses from in the early 1900s. In those days, as many as six horses could be driven by the hearse driver, but police regulations required a postillion, a man who rode on the near side at the front. Each horse had black ostrich feathers except for the one driven by the postillion, as this would have obscured his view.

As I told that gentleman who phoned from the prison, I named the horses Fred and George after Fred Albin and my dad. I stable them on a farm near Chelmsford in Essex and they are looked after by Nick Cook, a great horseman. The first funeral they did was that of Debbie, a lovely local girl who was killed when a friend's mini overturned in Rotherhithe. Because her death really touched me I attached a plate to the hearse to mark the event. Although I'm not what you would call a horsey type, my wish before I retire is to ride one of the horses at the head of the cortege.

As an aside, I remember an occasion when I was taking the coffin out of the back of the horse-drawn hearse when all of a sudden one of the horses passed wind. Embarrassed, I turned to the wife of the deceased and said, 'I'm terribly sorry.' 'Oh, that's all right, Mr Albin,' she replied. 'You've no need to apologise.'

Our mortuary is one of the most prestigious and modern in the UK, containing freezers, super freezers and a power shower for the staff. I have adapted my facilities at the funeral home for disabled people. For example, I have made the trestle tables lower so that if someone is in a wheelchair and they want to kiss the deceased person they can. I am also working on a braille version of our company brochure. As with any modern company, computers (I have a computer program that, fifteen minutes before I leave to conduct a funeral, plays Doris Day singing 'The Deadwood Stage'), the Internet, fax machines, mobile phones and telephone systems that do everything but talk to you have become essential business tools. At the end of the day it's a pair of hands that matter. The emphasis on technology has, I believe strongly, resulted in people losing sight of the human factor.

Although I made an error of judgement when I passed up the opportunity to buy Brookwood Cemetery, I am one of those people who has a flair for making a business successful, and I have always had a tremendous capacity for hard work.

When I was simply an employee of Albin's, I was also involved in a number of business ventures. I had been a director of a company selling soap powder, ghee – a sort of butter and second-hand Mercedes cars to Iran (the car trade ended when the Iranian courier, a friend of mine, was stripped naked, tied to a tree and robbed of a large sum of cash in the mountains of Afghanistan). I was also a director of Turner's Air Freight and had set up my own coffin-finishing and supply company. What's more, in order to save enough money to be able to buy F. A. Albin, I had driven wedding cars on Saturday mornings and embalmed for Taslim Ali at his funeral home in Whitechapel.

In recent years, I have put my business skills, experience and knowledge at the service of local non-league club Fisher Athletic, who made me their president. I also bought the 8,000 circulation *Southwark News*, in order to prevent what is probably London's only truly independent local newspaper from going bankrupt.

There's nothing wrong in having wealth. It's about how you use it. St Paul didn't say that money was the root of all evil, but that the love of money was the root of all evil. Over the last fifteen years I have reinvested most of the profits of my company. And I've done it wisely. I've never been a gambler – although when I was a boy I would try and pick out the winners at Saturday lunchtime and then at the end of the day see how many I got right.

Companies have a responsibility to their local community, I strongly believe. Where possible, I always prefer to spend my money where I live, as I did, for example, when I conducted my biggest funeral, that of Mr Jafari. I have very deep roots in Bermondsey and Rotherhithe. It has never occurred to me to live in Chelsea or Hampstead. I like to live amongst the people I serve.

I founded the Albin-Dyer Bermondsey and Rotherhithe Foundation, a charity for local people. And when my friend and parish priest Fr Alan McLean decided to erect a set of gates to prevent people parking without permission in the church car park, I donated a substantial sum. This was because on the mornings of funerals we had often had trouble finding spaces for mourners to park their cars. The situation had become intolerable. It is not unusual for me to have to gather my team and bump a parked car to the side of the road in order to make way for my hearse and limousines. The money I donated will also go towards creating better access to the church for disabled parishioners and parents with buggies.

Earnshaw's, my stockbrokers, once suggested I put Albin's on to the London Stock Exchange. While it looked an attractive way of raising extra finance, it also would have meant that I would have lost a lot of control of the business and would have left myself open to hostile bids. In effect, becoming a plc means that you have lost control of your company. If money was my sole concern, I would have taken Earnshaw's advice. But then again if money was my sole concern I would have sold up to Howard Hodgson or SCI.

The success of Albin's is down not just to the fact that I have built an excellent team but also to my two sons and my business contacts. I have always believed that you don't have to have studied at Eton or Oxford to be part of an old boys' network. I have a network of friends that goes back to the late 1960s when I studied for a business studies course at the old Regent Street Polytechnic (now the University of Westminster). What has kept us together over the ensuing years is football. We have played together most weeks ever since, and each year a group of us go off to Yorkshire for a weekend, where, amongst other things, we enjoy fish and chips at Harry Ramsden's in Guiseley. Without the Polytechnic I wouldn't be half the man I am. It matured me and introduced me to a variety of people, who went on to become draughtsmen, doctors, lawyers, bank managers and so on. We have helped each other out on countless occasions down the years.

Funeral directors in the UK are represented by the National Association of Funeral Directors (NAFD) and the national Society of Allied and Independent Funeral Directors (SAIF). The NAFD, which was set up in 1905, has around 1,500 members and is the most important organisation for the funeral industry.

SAIF was formed in 1989 as a response to the way in which large multinationals, such as the Great Southern and the Co-op, were, supposedly, putting profits before people. SAIF was set up to protect the interests of independent funeral directors and promote good practice. Today, around

700 funeral firms in the UK, representing 996 funeral homes, are members of SAIF. The average number of funerals per year for a SAIF member is 250. As I've said earlier, my average is around 1,000.

A funeral director has to work in a legal framework when it comes to burial, cremation and exhumation. But other than that, the industry is so far unregulated. However, both SAIF and the NAFD – I am a member of both – have codes of practice, which all members are expected to abide by. In an attempt to promote better standards, SAIF asked me to write a good practice guide. Produced by the Independent Funeral Directors' College, it covers everything from how to remove a body to how to correctly carry a coffin. I was more than happy to help write it because I believe that all funeral directors should strive to be the best.

But, as with any industry, there are times when clients are unhappy. In 2000 the Funeral Ombudsman Scheme dealt with just 172 complaints, which fell into two broad categories, services and costs. Most were about service, such as problems with ashes or graves, late running of funerals and the viewing of the deceased. While the Funeral Standards Council and SAIF are members of the scheme, NAFD are not. It has its own mechanism for dealing with complaints. Although the ombudsman scheme is voluntary, it has the power to impose fines. There was once a case where a minister went to the wrong cemetery for a funeral, even though the funeral director had given him the correct details in writing. What's more, during the service, the minister read out the wrong name of the deceased. The family complained to the funeral ombudsman, who found in their favour and fined the funeral director a large sum.

He decided that the funeral director had sub-contracted the funeral. However, I have never had to face a tribunal with the funeral ombudsman.

I've heard of a person who doubles as an undertaker and Catholic deacon. As a deacon, he takes Communion to the elderly in their homes and in residential and nursing homes and signs up people for pre-need funerals. This is unacceptable and – as Catholic priests I have spoken to agree – presents a conflict of interests. The diocese concerned is aware of this, but chooses to do nothing. The Church needs to draw up rules about which jobs are compatible with the ministry of deacon and which are not.

Anyone can legally operate as a funeral director. Some years ago a funeral director opened up in a vacant shop in Abbey Street, Bermondsey. He placed a handwritten sign in the window. Concerned by the arrival of someone who was clearly a bogus funeral director, I went to find out what he was up to. He was a very strange character, who hid behind his second-hand desk and repeated that he didn't want any trouble. It turned out he was a squatter and that he had pulled the same stunt in Tottenham, where the only funeral he had conducted was for a cat. He never even buried a cat in Bermondsey. After a few weeks, Southwark Council evicted him and he was never seen in the area again.

Both SAIF and NAFD carry out spot checks on funeral homes and even go through the motions of arranging a funeral, unbeknown to the funeral director. As a member of SAIF and NAFD, I have to provide a written estimate, offer help in claiming benefits from the DSS where appropriate, and assist in registering the death. Failure to comply with these guidelines could lead me to be refused either association's seal of approval.

While I welcome the spot checks by SAIF and NAFD, I like to go a stage further. Three or four times a year I make unannounced visits to my branches to make sure that everything is being run the way it should be and also to discuss any problems the staff might be experiencing. I also, in order to keep my staff on their toes, go undercover to observe my staff conducting a funeral. This involves finding a vantage point where I can't be seen. Trees, parked cars and tower blocks are some of my favourites. All my staff on a funeral are expected to follow my style but develop their own techniques. For example, the conductor must always take his hat off when the hearse passes by, but he can do it in his own way. I can tell from the way my staff behave if they have spotted me because they start doing things in an exaggerated way.

In her book *The American Way of Death*, first published in 1963, Jessica Mitford changed the way people thought about funerals by claiming that funeral directors were unscrupulous individuals. Some years later, she came to Britain to make a TV programme about funerals. I very much wanted to be part of it – as I disagreed vehemently with her views. But the TV company wouldn't allow me to be involved because they just wanted to project her opinions.

I remember her visiting London Caskets, one of the largest suppliers of caskets in the UK. The owner and the producer agreed the questions in advance. But when Mitford interviewed him she tried to make out that he was making a fortune out of funerals and kept pressing him to reveal the profit margin on the caskets they sold. The caskets sold by London Caskets are expensive, but they are imported from the USA. He's a good man and didn't deserve this. I would have loved to have got my hands on her at that point. Would she walk into a car showroom and ask how much they paid for a car? And what has she done but make money out of death through her book?

At one point, the managing director appeared very uncomfortable and turned to the director to ask if this part of the interview was being recorded. If you buy a package holiday you don't expect a breakdown of the cost of the air fare, food, taxis, accommodation and so on. So why did Mitford want to know how much each element of a funeral cost?

She chose to ignore the costs involved with funerals, claiming that the funeral director is just out to make a fat profit from people's misery, that they prey on the guilt of some bereaved people, and that embalming and caskets were costly and unnecessary. All of this was, she concluded, due to what she called the Americanisation of death. That the cost of funerals is too high is a charge often levelled at my profession, and unjustifiably so.

Mitford forgets that companies such as F. A. Albin & Sons provide a twenty-four-hour, seven-days-a-week, 365-days-a-year service. When the funeral home in Culling Road and our shops in Deptford and Mottingham are closed, calls are redirected to the homes of staff, who work a rota system. We can and do get called out at any hour of the day or night with sudden deaths. I have to maintain offices, a mortuary, a fleet of hearses and limousines, not to mention my staff.

My profit on a funeral, after tax, is around 6 per cent. Our lowest cost for a funeral is £900 and the highest around £5,000. The average cost of a funeral we conduct is £1,700. If I owned a sports shop, for instance, I would make about 200 per cent profit on a pair of trainers. There are funeral directors who would do a funeral for £600. Any fool can do a funeral for next to nothing. But in six months' time we would have half the number of people working for us and be half as good and with no real service.

And it shouldn't be forgotten that the seed from a funeral drops in many places. First of all it drops with the people in, say, Africa or Latin America, who cut down the trees and those who plant the new ones. Then there are the people who ship the wood over to the companies which produce coffins. Then there are the people who make the handles on the coffin, the shroud, the interior and the engraved name plate. We then have the people who own the cemetery and who work at the cemetery, the church, the florists, the car manufacturers, the oil companies, the petrol stations, the garages that repair the cars, the tyre manufacturers, the local council, and the gardeners. You can go on and on. Death provides life. Yes, I make a profit. But it's the hardest profit you could ever earn. For some reason, profit always seems to be a dirty word in Britain, and success frowned upon. Interestingly, back in the early days the cost of a funeral was about thirteen and a half times a Bermondsey docker's wage. Today it is three and a half times the average weekly wage. In other words, the cost of funerals has come down in real terms.

I have nothing against the kind of DIY funerals that Mitford came out in favour of. It's the same as many other things. If you wish, you can conduct the conveyancing of a property yourself without using a solicitor. You can carry out your own painting and decorating. But it is important to know what you are doing and the amount of time involved, and, if it goes wrong, you shouldn't expect to get advice from a funeral director for free. Would you go to a painter and expect him to lend you his ladder and brushes for nothing? What people pay for with a funeral is experience, knowledge, skill and to be cared for. True, it may work out cheaper to do it yourself, but a funeral director undertakes to take care of everything that is involved in a funeral: the deceased, the church, the flowers, the transport, the documentation and the cemetery and crematorium. In other words, we offer a package deal, like a travel agent does.

Very few people want to take on all the various arrangements and responsibilities that are involved in a funeral. A few years ago Britain's first and only 'funeral supermarket' opened down the road in Catford. These have become common in France. But I have to admit I don't like this off-the-shelf approach to funerals. Planning a funeral is not like planning your weekly shop at Tesco. Interestingly, the 'funeral supermarket' which opened in Catford, selling everything from urns to memorial stones (though shopping trolleys are not provided), has failed to attract customers and is now up for sale.

Funeral directors do not only hire limousines out for weddings and official functions but they often receive requests from film and TV companies, either to hire a hearse or limousines or to use the funeral home as a location. Whatever you think of funeral directors, we are very visual, what with mourning suits, top hats and hearses. Over the years, my vehicles and staff have featured in a number of films and programmes, including *The Bill* and *London's Burning*, both of which regularly film on the streets of south London. At one time, a film company hired my Rolls hearse to ferry an actress, Christina Ricci, to the West End film premiere of *The Addams Family*. She was dressed entirely in black, we closed the black curtains on the hearse and one of my sons and several of my team donned mourning suits to accompany her.

Sometimes, though, I have been annoyed by the inaccurate way the programme makers have depicted funerals. Part of the problem is that they rarely weight the coffins properly and also they use actors instead of real funeral directors. Once, a fellow funeral director did a horse-drawn funeral for *EastEnders*. He looked very smart and convincing walking ahead of the funeral. The scene was spoiled, however, by the two actors alongside him wearing ill-fitting suits and the use of Saab funeral cars instead of Daimlers, which would have been far more elegant for such a traditional funeral. When a funeral director friend of mine was once asked to do a staged funeral for *The Bill* he was more than happy to oblige and excitedly told everyone the date when the episode was to be broadcast. You can imagine his face when the evening of the programme came and he discovered that the storyline was about a crooked undertaker.

*Sins*, the BBC TV drama series in 2000, starring Pete Postlethwaite as a reformed criminal turned funeral director working in his uncle's family business, came closer than any other programme I have seen to understanding what it is like to be an undertaker. I don't know how he discovered the secrets of the funeral business, but he did and the programme was brilliant. There was a marvellous scene when the Pete Postlethwaite character walked into Uncle Ernie's workshop to find him making a coffin while drinking whisky and playing Pink Floyd music. Seeing the shock on the face of his nephew, he said, 'This is the music I really like. I found these tapes in my son's room when he died.

235

But every day I can't be what I would really like to be. I have to play a role every day; the role people need me and expect me to play. But who am I deep inside?' He added that one pinprick of joy overwhelmed everything else in life. He then admitted that he had never liked putting shoes on someone; shoes that had never been anywhere.

In the final episode, when Uncle Ernie, played by Frank Finlay, died – in the bed of a woman who ran a massage parlour and with whom he had been conducting a clandestine affair – he was given a marvellous funeral. His body was carried first in his own hearse, then on a barge down the canal, and finally in a horse-drawn hearse. I was in tears when the Pete Postlethwaite character realised that, like me, he had to continue the family business and pick up the historical mantle. And my hope is that my two sons, 25-year-old Simon and 22-year-old Jonathan, who are both turning into first-class funeral directors, caring, dedicated and trustworthy, will also pick up that same historical mantle, when the time comes. Yes, they will have to work hard to maintain the company's high standards, but I have no doubt that they will be very successful. I have to say that running Albin's has not been easy, but it's all been worth it. Carpe diem.

# 9

# FUNERALS AMERICAN STYLE

'If you were going to open a new funeral home on what basis would you do it?' asked a senior director in his deep-south accent, swivelling his chair. The walls of his office were decorated with saddles.

'Demographically and based on the age of the community,' I replied after a moment's thought. 'And service.'

'Exactly! Demographically and based on the age of the community. Why don't they think like that here?' he declared, banging the desk with his fist and choosing to ignore the most important factor, namely service.

He then took a map of Houston out of a drawer, spread it out on the desk and placed over the top of it a transparency with red shapes on it. 'These here red sections represent the areas with the highest number of over-fifties,' he said, running his finger over the transparency. 'And here are the old people's homes. This here area has the second highest number of over-fifties.' He might as easily have been a general planning a military campaign, so methodical was his approach. But then the Americans have always thought big, sometimes too big.

It was 1998 and I was at the swish headquarters of the world's biggest funeral directors, Service Corporation International (SCI), located in a skyscraper in the middle of Houston, Texas. Wanting to talk to me about adding Albin's to their growing list of funeral directors in the UK, they had flown me in on their private jet.

'You know, Barry, we're mighty keen to buy your business. It has a great tradition. Why, your firm's nearly as old as the United States, I'll be damned. But we'd also like to buy your experience.'

'I know, but I won't sell. Buying Albin's was my dream, and now I'm living out my dream. You have to understand that.'

He grinned. 'We'll see.'

'But I may be able to help your operation in the UK in other ways,' I said.

Travelling in a limousine, I was given a tour of a number of cemeteries and funeral homes run by SCI and also their impressive Commonwealth Institute of Funeral Service in Houston. Situated in pleasant parkland, the Common-wealth Institute not only has lecture theatres with the latest audio visual equipment, laboratories, mortuary, a library, a TV studio and an IT room, but also a mock-up of a funeral home and a funeral museum, containing a selection of immaculately restored hearses from the last 150 years together with eighteenth-century subscription lists and other memorabilia from F. A. Albin & Sons, gifted by me. I have always felt it would be great to see something similar in Britain.

In some ways you could say that, with their fast

turnaround approach to death, SCI are the McDonalds of the funeral industry. Located in eighteen countries in five continents, SCI operate 3,611 funeral homes, 569 cemeteries and 200 crematoria. But McDonalds are the most successful company in the world because they only sell McDonalds fast food. SCI, on the other hand, have diversified into insurance, property, cemeteries, crematoria, memorials and florists. This has been to their detriment. More critically, from my point of view, SCI put demographics and marketing strategies before the most important factor in a funeral, namely serving the bereaved family. As I said earlier, they do not have the personal touch of a small company such as F. A. Albin & Sons. Throughout our long history we have built up a relationship based on trust with the local community we serve.

SCI have come in for some sharp criticism over their sales techniques which, it has been alleged, manipulate the emotions of people in order to sell pre-paid funeral plans. They have also been accused of forcing up the cost of funerals in the UK and bringing them in line with those of the USA. This may have been true at the beginning, but this is not the case today. SCI's UK director, Peter Hindley, has done much to improve the way the company operates.

But SCI are only a part of the American funeral industry in a country that is 435 times the size of Great Britain. Scattered in towns and cities from Alabama to Wyoming are around 22,000 funeral homes, ranging from those with a makeshift hearse or a caravan as an office to those with a fleet of brand new Lincolns and the most modern facilities. Unlike in Britain, most funeral directors in America are not, generally, to be found in the high street but in quieter parts of town. And, again, unlike in Britain, they often have a service chapel attached to their funeral home, something that doesn't go down well with the religious authorities.

My initial introduction to the American funeral industry came in my late twenties and early thirties when I undertook a number of short courses at Campbell's Funeral Home College in Manhattan, New York. Campbell's are one of the most famous funeral directors in America and have buried many stars, including Judy Garland and John Lennon. Academically, I had never considered myself to be bright, but sitting there in the lecture theatre at Campbell's I felt supremely confident; I felt that no one there knew more about the funeral industry than me. Nevertheless, I learnt, amongst other things, some new embalming techniques and I was fascinated to learn that during the American Civil War Thomas Holmes, who many would say was the father of modern embalming, embalmed around 1,000 soldiers and put them in tunnels under the Missouri river before returning them to their families after the war.

It was when I became involved with Airline Mortuary Services (AMS) that I really got to know America and how the funeral industry operates there. When I met John Bumbaugh, their head of operations, at a conference in Eastbourne in 1988 I told him about my idea for streamlining the cost of shipping human remains (HUM), sometimes known as 'horizontal passengers'. I had learnt much from my work with Turner's. Back then, different countries charged different rates to transport human remains. And the United States had different rates for different parts of the country. AMS, through their mother company Continental Airlines, had a busy trade with 'snowbirds', mainly elderly Jewish people who would take off to Miami for the summer to avoid the harsh winter of New York. Some, however, died there and then had to be transported back home.

It occurred to me that it would be much easier, and less confusing, to have a fixed rate throughout the USA. And that way you would be able to tell the family exactly how much it would cost without depending on the weight of the coffin and without having to make phone calls to various airlines. When I explained my idea to John he thought it sounded very workable and invited me to visit AMS in Houston, Texas. I think he was also impressed by the fact that Albin's had recently been accepted on to the list of preferential funeral directors at the American Embassy in London and I had begun to transport deceased persons to the States. Up until then, the embassy had mainly been using Kenyon's, the Royal funeral directors at the time, but I convinced them that I could get better rates to the US than Kenyon's, so they added me to their list.

A few weeks later I flew out to Houston on an AMS travel pass, feeling quite excited at the prospect of working for AMS. The company was located on the eighth floor of a modern building in a busy street amidst the skyscrapers that are the hallmark of Houston, just a few miles across the city from the headquarters of SCI.

Having always tried to be a snappy dresser, I made a special effort for the Americans, pinning a flower to the lapel of my suit. I suppose I fitted their image of what an English businessman should look like, talking in the kind of English picked up from *The Times*. When someone said, 'Gee I love your accent,' I would reply with a smile, 'I don't have an accent; you have one.' They loved this.

Sitting in a lively Mexican bar in downtown Houston

one evening, I pointed out to John that the shipping of human remains from Europe to the US was not co-ordinated. I suggested keeping a supply of wooden air trays (similar to pallets) at key airports and channelling business there. This way, we would make some money and European funeral directors would find shipping remains to the US a lot easier.

Your average funeral director in Europe would only ship one or two human remains to the US each year, and they are unfamiliar with the procedures, rates, types of coffins required and airline timetables. John agreed that there was a golden business opportunity here, and with my experience with Turner's Air Freight Agency I had the necessary experience to take the job on.

I enjoyed my few days in Houston, a bustling, chaotic city, and I got on very well with Carol Beardon, the office manager at AMS, and we have been fantastic friends ever since. She opened many doors for me when I travelled around America.

The first time we met she took me to see her son play in the Little League, junior baseball. I had told her about my passion for football. The following year I saw her eldest son play at a packed all-seater stadium in the high profile college American Football game. It was, unlike football matches I had been to in Britain, a real family occasion, with cheerleaders, marching bands and hot dog sellers. It was fantastic. Of course, British football has now borrowed some of these ideas. I can't see Fisher Athletic ever taking on cheerleaders. But, then again, you never know. Bermondsey certainly has enough talent and pretty girls.

Six weeks later, I returned for further business discussions with AMS and a month later, to my delight, I was awarded the European agency. I immediately placed adverts in funeral industry journals and it wasn't long before Albin's had signed up funeral directors in the UK, Ireland, France, Italy and Spain. This meant that every time a funeral director transported back remains to the States through AMS Albin's would receive $25. In addition, we were also supplying a number of funeral firms with air trays or shells for transportation, as well as general advice; something I still do to this day.

The system worked like this. If a funeral director in Europe had a body to transport to a small town in the US, he would make a free phone call to AMS in Houston, who would arrange for the 'horizontal passenger' to be transported via Continental Airlines from, say, Charles De Gaulle Airport in Paris to Newark Airport near New York. The body would then be taken to a special holding area and then put on to an internal Continental Airlines flight to the local airport, tracked on the computer, from where a private ambulance would ferry it to a funeral director.

Once I had been awarded the European agency, I began making regular business trips to AMS. They provided me with a pass that entitled me to free travel. But if my seat was required by a fare-paying passenger then I had to give it up. On a number of occasions a stewardess would lean over and politely ask me to return to the departure lounge to wait for the next flight, and I would sheepishly make my way down the aisle to the exit, with all eyes watching me. I could read their expressions: what had he done? But on other occasions I would be upgraded to first class, which was great.

Having travelled so extensively in America, I have my own take on the country's airports. Cleveland is a permanent building site, Las Vegas, with its slot machines, more of a casino than an airport, while Bangor Main is a nightmare (very appropriate considering that horror writer Stephen King lives there). Pittsburgh might be where the two great rivers meet but at the airport the people certainly don't. It's too crowded. Washington DC was similar. I went there once – but my luggage never did. JFK was over-priced and over-rated. At Newark, a vast, sprawling place, people seemed to go to the airport to hang out in the sports bars rather than catch flights. Orlando is quite pleasant, but due to the zeal of immigration officers it should be named Queuesville. Houston is built like a Texan oil well, long and deep and impossible to find your way out of. Salt Lake City was clean, open and not too busy, but, given that it is the spiritual home of the Mormons, I found myself grappling with the moral dilemma of whether to have a brandy or not. At Boston there always seemed to be a strike and everyone seemed to be just passing through rather than stopping there. If you want the best eggs Benedict in America, then go to Flanagans restaurant at New Orleans. Tampa has to be the friendliest airport and Miami the most threatening. I once had a twenty-one-hour delay at Chicago because vital parts for the plane could not be found and I've had my luggage sent by mistake to both Barbados and Dallas.

My introduction to first-class travel was on a return flight from Newark to Gatwick. I was allocated – appropriately, you might think – the 'death seat' – a single seat in the nose of a jumbo. It's called this because it's the first seat off the ground at take-off and the first to hit the ground should the plane crash.

Continental Airlines required its representatives to wear

a suit and tie. This was no problem to me as I always wore a suit. But other members of staff would sometimes stand out like a sore thumb: top shirt button unfastened, tie in a hanging position, and sweating badly. To me first impressions are crucial and when I was on a long haul flight I would always change into a spare shirt fifteen minutes before landing. I learned that in the US they serve two kinds of food: fast and faster, and there are two kinds of hotel: with space and without space.

Despite the busy schedule, I always made sure that I took a couple of days out on each trip to unwind. This wasn't easy for me at first because I had always been a bit of a workaholic and found it difficult to relax. But Carol and John and I used to take short breaks in various parts of the States (on one unforgettable occasion I was attacked by a parrot in a hotel on Padre Island!). We were referred to by the airline staff as the 'ghost squad'.

One evening after a meal in my hotel in Newark, where I was spending a night before flying to Houston, I was getting into the bath when all of a sudden I was gripped by searing pain. I had never experienced anything like it in my life. Panicking, I rang Carole, who was in her room, and before long I was lying on a stretcher with an oxygen mask over my face and being lifted into the back of an ambulance.

The next thing I remember was being pushed quickly through the swing doors of a charity hospital and then left in a shabby, smelly corridor. The scene around me was chaotic. Doctors and nurses were rushing about and people were screaming and shouting, while two burly armed security guards were wrestling a youth to the floor by the coffee machine. I noticed the man on the trolley next to me was handcuffed. Another man was bleeding from what looked like gunshot wounds. My pain was worse than ever and I could feel everything becoming a blur. I called out for one of the nurses to help me, but she muttered something and carried on past me. I called to another nurse.

'Stay there!' she snapped back. 'Wait your turn.'

'But I'm in agony!' I cried. 'Why won't you help me?'

'Wait your turn. I've told you,' she repeated tersely and disappeared into a room.

For the first time in my life I felt that I was dying. The pain was so bad. I could see my life disappearing in front of me. Was this it? Having stared at death in so many faces on so many occasions – and missed being caught up in the siege of the Iranian Embassy by minutes – I felt I was now on the verge of my own death. I would become the body on the mortuary table; the most famous person in the world for a day. Standing at the graveside in so many cemeteries over the years, listening to the prayers being said and watching as handfuls of earth were scattered on the coffin, I had often wondered how I would confront the eternal mystery. There are those who might think that the funeral director has some secret knowledge about death and beyond and therefore he doesn't carry within him the terror of the unknown. But the fact is that funeral directors know no more about the mystery of death than anyone else.

After lying on the trolley for twelve hours, listening to people shouting and swearing, I was then hurriedly wheeled down the corridor through a set of swing doors and into a ward. A stressed-looking young doctor appeared at my side, briskly examined me, gave me an MRI scan and then told me I had a kidney stone problem but would be fine. He gave me an injection of morphine and I was sent on my way with a prescription for some tablets and the instruction to drink plenty of water and see a specialist. It was with great relief that I climbed into a cab outside the hospital entrance and headed back across the city to my hotel. On reflection, I was in more danger from the hospital than from my kidney stones.

Funeral industry exhibitions are very popular in the States and take place throughout the year in different cities. They are similar to something like the Ideal Home Exhibition, if you can manage to square death with looking for a new fitted kitchen. You could say they try to put the 'fun' into funerals. Usually held in large hotels or conference centres, you will find stands offering the latest coffins and caskets, urns, cosmetics for deceased persons, embalming instruments and fluids, suits, gowns, music CDs, computer software and hearses and limousines. You can even buy paint to spray on the earth after a burial to make it look like grass! Attending these exhibitions I learnt that the US Army, Air Force and Navy have their own mortuary and funeral professionals. These men were also fully trained officers. As with any such exhibition, you come away at the end of the day with a wad of business cards and a carrier bag bulging with brochures and leaflets, most of which go straight in the bin when you get home.

I was once manning an AMS stand at an exhibition in Oklahoma. I had taken a number of British urns made of Windsor oak over with me. In order to highlight the urns I had hung some Union Jacks on the stand. John Bumbaugh said to me that if I sold one he would buy 500. I did, in fact, sell one, to a strange-looking man who ran a funeral home out of a trailer in Houston. For some reason the image of this man stuck in my mind. I don't know why. Then a couple of years later I heard that the man had been arrested after body parts from local medical schools were found in and around his trailer. It turned out that medical schools used to pay him to bury or cremate bodies, but for some weird reason he cut up the bodies and kept them.

One of the funniest American funeral incidents I heard about was the cremation of a famous heart surgeon. On its way to the cremator the coffin passed through a broken heart of flowers. Then one of the mourners began laughing.

'Why are you laughing?' asked the minister.

'I was thinking of my own funeral,' replied the mourner.

'Well, what's so funny about that?'

'If I am given the same symbolic floral tribute it will be very embarrassing.'

'What do you mean?' asked the minister.

'I'm a gynaecologist,' answered the mourner.

Death seems less of a taboo in America than it is in Britain. Adverts on TV and radio, in magazines and on road signs extol the merits of various funeral homes, cemeteries and pre-paid funerals. Furthermore, in America they believe it is a great honour to be a bearer at a funeral, and families will often send out invitation cards and give gifts to the bearers. On the other hand, what surprised me the most in America was that there are separate funeral homes for blacks, Asians, Mexicans and other ethnic groups. In the UK running a funeral home along racial lines would be unacceptable but in the USA it seems to be viewed as an inevitability.

Every time I returned from the States I had a new idea to improve Albin's. My staff used to find this amusing. 'What is it this time?' they would laugh when I arrived bubbling with enthusiasm on a Monday morning. One year I returned with a canopy, to cover areas around the graveside to keep people dry. On another occasion, I brought back a coffin-lowering machine. I bought an organ that plays itself, chair covers with the name of F. A. Albin embroidered on them and pendant jewellery which people could buy and keep a lock of hair or ashes in.

Leafing through some documents one day about the Dyers, distant relations of my father, who ran a funeral business in Walthamstow, I was astonished to read that Arthur Dyer visited America in the 1920s and 'came back with many good ideas'.

What really struck me first when I began travelling around the States was the power that the funeral director – known as a mortician – has. Morticians are licensed by individual states and cannot work anywhere else without obtaining another licence. There are several guides to the American funeral business and they include sections on 'crematories', funeral products, national cemeteries, mortuary colleges, organisations – such as Flying Funeral Directors of America – air shipments and conventions. In addition, there are a number of magazines, such as *Funerals of the Famous, American Funeral Director, American Cemetery*.

It is common in America for mourners to meet before a funeral at the funeral home. This takes place in a viewing room with settees and tea and coffee. Some family and friends haven't seen the deceased person for many years. Meeting beforehand makes the actual funeral less of an ordeal. I think this is an excellent idea for helping to ease the pain of a funeral and I am currently building a sitting room with a connecting chapel at my funeral home.

In Britain you cannot do anything without the permission of various authorities. For example, you can't remove a body until the doctor has given permission, you can't embalm unless the coroner has decided an autopsy doesn't need to be carried out and before the funeral can go ahead the death has to be registered.

In America, the funeral director is allowed to embalm the body immediately. In some states funeral directors are licensed to register deaths, which they do in big logbooks. He can then issue death certificates, which are then taken to the local justice of the peace to be signed.

In my part of south-east London, on a Monday morning in the winter when fifty people might have died over the weekend in local hospitals all the families have to go to the same bereavement office, where they receive the deceased's possessions and the death certificate, and then on to the same registrar of deaths. Often at my funeral home I have seen a family walk in only to find other families they have seen earlier in the day at the bereavement office and registrar's already sitting there. 'Oh, hello. We're following you everywhere,' is the usual remark. It would make more sense for funeral directors to be allowed to register deaths, phone the coroner with the details and then every quarter file all the death certificates and cremation and burial certificates at the registrar general's record office.

Unlike in the UK, cremations are not popular with funeral directors in America. Cremations are seen as second-class funerals. Cardboard coffins are used and a memorial service held. Most of the time a cremation is seen as a disposal rather than a full funeral. American funeral directors don't favour cremation because it threatens their future.

This is now slowly changing, I gather, and some funeral homes have installed their own cremators. Twenty years or so ago cremations accounted for only about 11 per cent of funerals. Today, the figure has risen to 17 per cent, although in Los Angeles it is nearer 50 per cent.

I remember once visiting a large funeral home, which had parking for about thirty cars, and being amazed that the owner had conducted only forty-two funerals in the previous year. How on earth did they make it pay? But then I learnt that the average funeral bill was around $20,000 because of the price of the caskets and the variety of services and accessories offered.

The finest maker of caskets in America is Marsellus Caskets in Syracuse, New York State. Set up alongside the Erie Canal in 1872, by John Marsellus, they use only the finest woods and textiles and only employ the best craftsmen. That's why their range of caskets can cost many thousands of dollars. Amongst those who have been buried in their caskets are J. F. Kennedy and a number of other American presidents and numerous celebrities, including Jackie Onassis and Judy Garland. Like me, John Marsellus was a perfectionist, believing that the fulfilment of perfection was dependent upon the commitment of each and every worker. Whether you are buying a car, a suit, or a casket, if you want the best quality, then you have to pay for it.

The factory was large and old and looked like one of those 'satanic mills' Blake wrote about. John Marsellus Junior, a charming and gentle man, took me on a tour of the factory and introduced me to some of his staff. Despite having done the tour so many times, he was so enthusiastic that it might have easily been his first time. I can remember the wood stacked in a huge warehouse, the piles of casket handles, the smell of polish, the relaxed way that the staff worked. 'Hi, John,' they all called out as we passed by. 'Hi,

Peter,' he would reply cheerfully. He employed around 100 people and knew them all personally. I eventually won the contract to supply his caskets in the UK. He has since sold his business to SCI, which had become by far his largest client. When they made an offer it seemed like common sense to sell up. However, SCI have continued to maintain the high standards of the company.

But the biggest casket manufacturer in the world is the Batesville Casket Company, which has its headquarters in the town of the same name in Indiana. I am one of their five UK agents. Employing 3,500 people in five states and offering caskets in 500 styles and colours, including gold-plated, as well as coffins and urns, you could say that Batesville is the Nike of coffin manufacturing. I was amazed at the sheer size of it. It was so large that I was taken around it in a golf cart and it took half a day to see everything. It even had its own airstrip.

John Hillebrand, who founded the company in 1906 when he rescued a small coffin manufacturer from insolvency, told his son, John A. Hillebrand: 'Concentrate on serving your customers first. You will have the greatest chance of long-term success if you build on a philosophy of partnership and mutual trust with your customers, rather than turning a quick profit.' I couldn't agree more.

One of the most famous funeral firms in America is Gawlers, who have buried many American presidents. Their funeral home was a big mansion in Washington DC. Inside it was equally impressive, with chandeliers and oil paintings of US presidents everywhere you looked. Various pieces of memorabilia are on display, such as a handkerchief from J. F. Kennedy.

Just like in Britain, funeral directors go about their work

in different ways, not all of them to my satisfaction, I have to admit. I once met a funeral director called Fred, a big, tough-talking Texan who ran a funeral home near the Mexican border and who saw Mexicans as the lowest of the low. As he was showing me around his funeral home I tried to open the door to the chapel. He told me it was locked. Why was that I asked puzzled. 'To keep the staff from screwing,' he replied nonchalantly. My mouth dropped open when I heard this. Fred or my dad would have probably fainted at these sorts of goings-on in a funeral home.

Using a network of agents, Fred used to transport human remains across America for a flat rate and he wanted me to be his UK agent. I was once at a funeral exhibition with him when he went up to a man and said that he owed him money for some kind of work he had done. When the man denied this Fred answered, 'Hey, man, I might be as big as an elephant, but also I never forget, just like an elephant. And you owe me three hundred bucks, you son of a bitch, and I want it now, or I'm gonna kick you until you scream.' Fred, not a man to mince his words, got his money. But I have to say that's not the way I would pursue my debts.

On another occasion, after an exhibition had ended I was sitting with Fred in his office when two girls from Delta Airlines came in. In return for a free first class travel pass Fred had agreed to distribute their leaflets at the National Funeral Exhibition in Orlando with his own publicity material. He wasn't really interested in talking to people who came up to his stand. He would just hand them one of his plastic bags, which contained all they needed to know about his business. He worked on the basis that if you gave out 5,000 bags you could expect you would get ten customers.

The girls, naturally, wanted to know how the exhibition went. Fred told them it had gone brilliantly. Hundreds of people had come up to the stand, he went on, and they had all thought Delta Airlines' human remains service was terrific. He added that he was so busy he had run out of their leaflets. The girls looked very pleased and handed him an extra free travel pass, telling him that they would bring more leaflets for the next big funeral exhibition. 'Sure, sure,' he replied, putting the pass in his pocket. After they had left, he breathed a sigh of relief, grinned sheepishly, and pulled out a big box of Delta Airlines leaflets from under his desk and began throwing them into the bin in the corner of the office. He hadn't given one of them out. Needless to say, Fred and I never did do business.

It was while on my travels in America that I first came across something called cryonics. With its aim of freezing people at death and then, one day, bringing them back to life, it sounded bizarre and straight out of science fiction. Little did I know that I would end up becoming their European agent.

# 10

# CRYONICS: THE TECHNO FUNERAL

I rang the doorbell to a rather drab-looking building in a
poor area of Detroit and waited. Dressed in my best suit, I
felt out of place, and especially when I noticed a group of
dubious-looking youths in baseball caps across the road,
eying me suspiciously. I could already see the headline in
the *Southwark News*, 'Bermondsey Undertaker Mugged in
America.' I stood there for what seemed to be a long time
and then rang the bell again.

After a while, I finally heard the muffled sound of
footsteps and then the small hatch in the door opened. An
eye appeared and a deep voice said, 'Yes?'

This was bizarre, I thought, as images flitted through my
mind of Marty Feldman in *Young Frankenstein*. I said to the
eye, 'I'm Mr Albin from London.'

'Stand back from the door please.'

I heard the sound of bolts being undone and eventually
the door slowly creaked open. Standing there was a small,
round-shouldered man, clad in a white coat with a collar

255

rolled up to his neck and wearing thick-soled Doc Marten boots. He had a very serious-looking face and large ears. I couldn't help but think that he looked as if he had stepped off the film set of one of those old black and white horror films. 'Walk this way,' he said, leading me down a dark corridor, his feet dragging along the floor. I'd better not, I'll get arrested, I thought to myself.

It was the summer of 1993 and I was visiting the famous – and infamous – Cryonics Institute, founded by Dr Robert Ettinger, regarded as the father of the cryonics movement. In his two books from the 1960s, *The Prospect of Immortality* and *Man into Superman*, he argued that dying patients could be frozen until medical technology was advanced enough to deal with their illnesses. In 1967 he set up The Immortalist Society (which later became the Cryonics Institute), the year that James Bedford became the first person to be cryonically suspended. Unsurprisingly, his books and institute sparked off a massive debate, for he was claiming that he had discovered the key to eternal life.

Ettinger and other cryonicists believe that death is not the absolute end, but rather medical science's inability to keep a patient alive. His view of science is based on the fact that, for example, a person whose heart stopped beating in the 1930s was considered dead and no attempt was made to resuscitate them. Therefore the definition of death in the 1930s and the definition of death in 2001 is different. People will be thawed out and brought back to life, claim the cryonicists, when scientific progress has reached a certain point, whenever that is. To support their optimistic view of science, they will point to kidney and heart transplants, frozen embryos and, now, cloning and say that years ago these developments would have been thought impossible. In Russia, or so I am told, cryonic research has brought rats and hamsters back to life for a period of time. Whether this is for hours or for days, I am not sure.

I had first become interested in cryonics when I heard about it through my work for the Houston-based Airline Mortuary Services (AMS) and I subsequently attended a number of funeral exhibitions around the world. But, as I said earlier, I never for a minute imagined that I'd become the sole European licensed agent for the Cryonics Institute.

However, after giving a lecture about the difference between the American and British funeral industries at a conference in Baltimore, I was approached at the end by a tall, bearded man who congratulated me on my knowledge of the subject. It turned out he was a client of the Cryonics Institute in Detroit and he was looking for someone to take care of some of his friends in Europe, who, upon death, would need perfusion, a method similar to embalming, before they were flown to Detroit. He asked me if I was interested in doing the work, and, always looking to improve the range of services I offer to families, I said I was. He then asked me if I would answer a sheet of questions about methods of embalming. Feeling I was back at school, I found a quiet corner and began answering the questions, which were really quiet easy for someone with my experience of different techniques of embalming. When I returned the sheet to him, he read through my answers, nodding at each one. A couple of weeks later, a fax arrived at my office, inviting me to visit the Cryonics Institute in Detroit and sign a contract which would make me their European agent.

257

So here I was in America's midwest, following this man down the poorly lit corridor of a bizarre institute. All sorts of questions were running through my mind: What sort of place was this? What did I really think about cryonics? Would it really be possible to bring people back to life? After all, a hundred years ago a kidney transplant or test tube babies would have been unthinkable. What was I getting myself into?

When we passed the open door to a room full of large fibreglass capsules, I stopped in my tracks in amazement. Around eight feet high, they resembled vats in a brewery, I thought. The man halted and ambled back and led me into the room. 'These are the cryostats where we keep our patients,' he said with a wave of his hand. 'This is Mr Ettinger's first wife. Here is Mr Ettinger's mother-in-law.' Then, pointing to a capsule at the far end, he said, 'And this is Mr Ettinger's dog.'

'What are those two capsules for?' I asked my guide, pointing to two capsules in the corner of the room.

'Those are for Ettinger and Ettinger's new wife,' the little man croaked, looking up at me. The thought of Mr Ettinger ending up between his two wives and a mother-in-law struck me as very amusing. It would be quite a reunion.

As we continued the tour, I discovered that people who have been cryonically suspended are known as 'patients', not deceased persons. After arriving at the institute, they are eventually frozen to minus 196 degrees centigrade, the point when physical decay ceases, and placed upside down (so that if any problems develop, such as thawing, only the feet will be damaged) in a cryostat, or capsule, filled with smoking liquid nitrogen, a dangerous, toxic substance that

258

needs to be topped up every so often from stainless steel capsules on wheels. The cryostats are alarmed and their temperature is checked daily. Electricity generators are in place in case there is a power cut.

I was later taken to a local funeral home run by Sally Bazan, who was registered with the Cryonics Institute to remove and perfuse their deceased members. Here I had to attend an embalming to prove that I was competent. Although her funeral home was the same size as mine in Bermondsey, she only did around forty funerals a year but she was able to make a good living.

They must have been happy with my knowledge of embalming, for a week after I arrived back in London I received a letter confirming my appointment as the European agent for the Cryonics Institute. As I read it, I wondered if I would be able to do my first cryonics case correctly. I had been explained the procedures when I had visited the Cryonics Institute and I had subsequently read about the subject.

What's more, I had carried out tests at my funeral home, placing a mannequin in a polystyrene and metal-lined coffin which was then packed with ice and foam and stored in different temperatures. Items such as butter and frozen meat were placed inside the coffin, along with a thermometer, to see how long it took before they began to melt. My job is not to freeze the body but to cool it down and keep it at around zero degrees centigrade, a temperature at which it must be able to remain for around forty hours, which would be more than enough time to fly anyone from Europe to Detroit. But no matter how much preparation you do in life, things can still go wrong.

Other questions surfaced. How would I feel about it?

Would the body arrive in Detroit in the right condition? Had I made the right decision in taking on this European agency? It turned out to be three years before I was to find out.

One day in June 1996 the phone rang and a heavily accented voice at the other end said, 'This is Mr Muller. Is that Albin?' It wasn't uncommon for me to be called simply Albin. The staff at the Iranian Embassy, for example, always referred to me in that way.

'Yes, speaking. How can I help you, Mr Muller?' Mr Muller lived in Essen, Germany, and a few months before had visited me to sign his elderly mother up with the Cryonics Institute.

Small, with bulging eyes, thick rubbery-looking lips, he had seemed a little bit eccentric. Many people who enter a funeral home feel a mixture of awkwardness and discomfort, due to being in a place which in their minds they associate purely with death. But Mr Muller was like a child in a toyshop when he had visited the funeral home. He made me show him the mortuary, chapels of rest, and a selection of coffins and caskets.

Now on the phone, he said slowly, 'It's my mother.'

'I'm very sorry, Mr Muller. When did she die?'

'No! No. She not dead yet, but I like you to send someone out here to get things ready,' he said in broken English. Then adding solemnly, 'It won't be long, Albin.'

'Very well, Mr Muller,' I replied, somewhat surprised. Without thinking, I found myself answering, 'I'll send one of my experienced staff.'

'Good. Phone me when you have arranged the travel details,' he said and put the phone down.

As this was my first cryonics case, I figured that it was,

after all, probably wise to send one of my team to check things out. I asked Rose, one of my longest serving staff members, and someone whom I had known since school, to fly out on the Thursday, stay overnight in a hotel and return the next day. She was thrilled at the prospect of a spot of overseas travel and quite fascinated by cryonics.

On Friday afternoon Rose returned from her visit to Essen. As soon as she walked into the funeral home, I could tell from her face that something was wrong.

'How was it, Rose?'

'Oh, Barry, it was awful. It was like something out of *The Rocky Horror Picture Show*. Boy, am I glad to be back.'

'And I'm glad I didn't go,' chimed Jackie, my manager, coming out of her office with an enormous floral tribute, in the shape of a pint pot, for a recently deceased pub landlord.

We crowded around Rose to hear all the details. She said that Mr Muller was one of the weirdest people she had ever met, and that he'd kept insisting she stayed at his house, a creepy place if ever she saw one, she said. His mother, who was confined to bed, did indeed appear to be very ill. Rose admitted she was petrified when Mr Muller took her down into the cellar to show her the table and a bath where the perfusion would take place.

About three weeks later Mr Muller phoned me again. I thought his mother must have now passed away. He told me she hadn't but he wanted me to go over to Essen.

'But your mother might live for many months or even years yet,' I said. 'I run a business. I can't sit out in Germany waiting for her to die, Mr Muller. Rose has already been over to see you. Don't worry, when the time comes everything will be fine.'

'Albin, no, you must come,' he insisted, getting a little irate.

'As soon as your mother passes away contact me and I will be there as quickly as I can,' I replied, determined to stand my ground. There was absolutely no reason for me to go over there while his mother was still alive. He put the phone down and seemed to accept this, albeit reluctantly.

But I was wrong. Every day for the next month Mr Muller phoned the funeral home to try and persuade me to go to Essen. But, I repeatedly told him, there was no point until she had actually died.

Then one day Joanna, my receptionist, knocked on the door of my office. 'Barry, it's Mr Muller. He's very upset. Maybe his mother has passed away.'

'Okay, you'd better put him through.' I sighed. I was in the middle of organising the staff rota, always a tricky job at the best of times, so the last thing I wanted was Mr Muller going off on one of his tangents. But as a funeral director, I always remind my staff, you must always keep in the forefront of your mind that you are dealing with people at their most vulnerable. You can't afford to be short-tempered or impatient, although, at times, it can be difficult, as any funeral director will tell you.

'Mr Muller. What's the matter? Has your mother passed away?'

'No, she very ill, Albin,' he said hysterically and then started babbling away in a mixture of German and English.

'Okay I understand, Mr Muller. But what do you want me to do?'

'She won't get better. Listen please. Listen,' he answered, ignoring the question.

Then I heard a very strange sound. What could it be? Interference on the line? No. I realised he had put the telephone on her chest.

'Listen, Albin. She's alive isn't she? How does she sound? Listen.' And he placed the receiver on her chest again and all I could hear was the muffled sound of her breathing. This was bizarre. In all my years as a funeral director I had never taken a phone call like this.

'Mummy very bad. Listen, Albin,' he repeated excitedly. 'She still alive, ja? What you think?'

'Mr Muller, I'm not a doctor. I don't know. Now, think calmly and contact me if there is any change.'

A couple of weeks later Mr Muller phoned me one morning to say, yes, his mother had passed away. I wondered whether I should turn the tables and ask him to put the phone to her chest to prove that she was no longer breathing.

'How long will it take you to get here? One hour? Two hours?' he asked urgently. 'How long?'

'I'm in London, Mr Muller,' I reminded him. 'I can't just hop on a bus. I'll be there as quickly as I can,' I said, reminding him to keep his mother in a cool place and pack ice around her head.

Knowing that Mr Muller's mother might be close to death, I had made arrangements in advance. Through my international contacts in the funeral industry, I had found a local firm of funeral directors in Essen who had agreed to take the body of Mr Muller's mother to Dusseldorf Airport for transportation to Detroit. I had sent them a specially made casket, lined with polystyrene to help it retain the temperature of the ice. They had assured me they would keep the mortuary extra cool and have the necessary amount of packed ice available.

263

I had made travel plans in advance as well. Cliff, my embalmer, would be travelling with me and also my eldest son, Simon. I had found a small airfield in Essex where I could charter a light aircraft to Germany at short notice. The reason for speed is that to carry out cryonic suspension you have to cool down the body as quickly as possible in order to keep the brain cells from dying. Having phoned the airfield to tell them we were on our way, we put our protective suits, embalming equipment and a change of clothes in the car and headed off towards Essex.

As the four-seater plane took off down the short runway, I thought that I must get round to booking some flying lessons. I had always been fascinated by flying, partly, I think, due to my travels across the United States. The pilot was very friendly and talked me through all the controls.

'Well, Barry, this is it. Your first cryonics case,' said Cliff, who had admitted that he was a bit nervous flying in such a small plane.

The pilot looked interested. 'Cryonics? What's that?'

'It's a procedure where a body is frozen at death in the hope that scientific advances may be able to revive them in the future,' I replied, knowing exactly what kind of response this would elicit.

'Seriously?' replied the pilot with a mixture of fascination and repulsion. 'Sounds a bit weird to me. So what's your involvement, then?'

'I'm a funeral director.'

'An undertaker!'

And that was, more or less, the end of the conversation. I sometimes have this effect on people. They seem to think that even being in the presence of a funeral director might

bring their own death a bit nearer. I've walked into pubs in
Bermondsey and people have said half-jokingly, 'Don't come
near me. I don't want to see you for a few years.' I always
reply, 'It's not when you can see me that you need to be
worried about; but when I can see you and you can't see me.
Then you're in trouble!' If they persist in pulling my leg, I
often ask, 'Do you know what I see when I look around
here?' No, they say. 'Next year's accounts,' I reply with a
grin.

In theory, I reflected, the perfusion should be straight-
forward and really no different to an ordinary embalming. But my main aim was that the ice shouldn't melt
before the body arrived in Detroit. As I said, I had carried
out a number of tests packing coffins with ice and storing
them in different conditions. I had given the local
undertakers instructions to have ten large bags of ice
ready.

An hour later we were touching down at Essen Airport.
Mr Muller had said he would be there to meet us in the
terminal building. Cliff, Simon and I stood in the arrivals
area and waited. They were curious to finally meet this man
who had become a bit of a living legend amongst the staff at
the funeral home. But he was nowhere to be seen. The
airport was quite small and there were, apart from a large
group of schoolchildren and a posse of Japanese business-
men in identical suits, only a few people waiting around.
After about half an hour I decided that we should get a taxi
to his house, which was in a suburb in the north of the
town.

As we drove towards the centre of the town, a typical
industrial-looking place with large blocks of flats dotted
here and there, I was beginning to get apprehensive. After

all Mr Muller's phone calls and pleas for me to come over, it was a little unsettling that he hadn't turned up to meet us as arranged. The taxi turned into a long street of large, grey three-storey houses and stopped halfway along. There he was, dressed in an ill-fitting suit, coming out of his house.

'Mr Muller, how are you? We were expecting you to meet us at the airport,' I said, walking towards him. But, I couldn't believe it, he just walked right past me. 'Mr Muller!' I called after him. 'It's Barry. I'm here to take care of your mother.'

He stopped and slowly turned around. 'Ah yes, Albin. Er, go inside, Albin,' he said absentmindedly, motioning us towards the house. And then he continued off down the street.

Puzzled, Cliff, Simon and I walked up the path and through the open door into the house. Rose was right. It was a gloomy place, with a musty smell and full of heavy-looking furniture, hundreds of books piled to the ceiling, glass cases containing stuffed fish and birds and rather drab-looking prints of flowers and German rural scenes on the walls. As we sat in the living room and waited for Mr Muller's return I could well understand Rose's reluctance to spend the night here. I half expected to see Christopher Lee poke his head around the door.

'I've got a funny feeling about this,' I said to Cliff.

'So have I, Barry.'

After about half an hour Mr Muller casually strolled in. Without any explanation about where he had been or why he hadn't turned up at the airport, he impatiently ordered us to follow him. He opened a door and began descending the steep wooden steps into the darkness of the cellar.

266

'Where is she, Mr Muller?' I asked, looking at various bits of junk scattered around. It was damp and hung with cobwebs. A single electric light bulb provided the only light. I thought I saw a rat, but I wasn't sure.

'Over there,' gestured Mr Muller matter-of-factly.

I turned around and saw that he was pointing at a small food freezer. No, surely not, I thought to myself. He hasn't, has he? But he had. He opened the lid and stood back to make way for Cliff and I. We peered inside and, lo and behold, bent double inside was the body of a small, elderly woman. I was astonished.

Cliff and Simon gasped out loud. When I had instructed Mr Muller to pack the head of his mother in ice, I hadn't anticipated that he would end up popping her in a food freezer. At least there wasn't food inside it, I mused, recalling the mortician at St Olave's Hospital who used to keep his food alongside human remains in the freezer.

'Right, off you go then,' ordered Mr Muller, clapping his hands, as though this was the most normal thing in the world. And with that he went back upstairs.

We looked at each other for a minute in disbelief and then got on with the job. Donning our white protective suits we lifted the elderly lady out of the freezer and placed her on a table. I had asked Simon to massage the deceased with a special cream we use. This is done in order to soften the skin and prevent it from coming off.

My first task was, using a pair of surgical scissors, to open an artery and vein in the neck and make small incisions in each, so that the deceased was ready for perfusion.

Mr Muller then returned. What was this? Surely not. He was clutching a video camera. Now I had seen it all.

'Ignore me, Albin,' he muttered, fiddling with the camera.

If only I could, I thought, as I lifted the vein and slid in a vein tube, a long thin instrument, to open up the vein. I then attached a tube from the vein to a jar.

I put a tube from a pump into the artery. This makes the pump a substitute for the heart. The pump pushes saline, and then glycerine and rose water, into the arteries and washes the deoxygenated blood out through the vein drain. Another fluid, heparin, is used to clear any blood clots and thin the blood.

'Are you sure you want to be here, sir?' I asked.

'Oh, ja. Ja,' he replied enthusiastically.

When I appeared on the TV programme *This Morning* in 1994 alongside a family from Luton who have signed up with the Cryonics Institute, Richard Madeley suggested that pumping saline and glycerine into a deceased person was a bit like putting anti-freeze into a body. As I said at the time, that is a slightly basic way to put it, but in some ways the process is a bit like that.

Throughout my work, Mr Muller, breathing heavily, stood pointing the camera over my shoulder, asking me every couple of minutes what I was doing. When I told him, he would say, 'Ja. Is good,' and repeat my words back to me in the manner of providing a running commentary, a bit like *Match of the Day* commentator John Motson. I hoped he wasn't going to ask for an action replay. But I couldn't understand why he wanted to watch his mother being perfused. I wouldn't want to watch it being done to someone I loved.

Then suddenly he would remember that it was his mother lying there and burst into tears before returning to his role as commentator. 'Excellent, Albin. What are you doing now, Albin?' While trying to concentrate, Cliff, Simon and I had to fight back tears of laughter – this was even funnier – or sadder – than the time Dr Jones stuck the thermometer up the backside of the man who had been washed up at Blackfriars Pier.

The perfusion took about four hours and, surprisingly, wasn't that difficult. My homework had paid off. In fact, Cliff and I agreed that we had both carried out straight-forward embalmings that were more difficult. For me, two of the most difficult cases I have ever done were when I brought the body of rock star Alex Harvey back from Bruges and the time at Waltham Forest Mosque when – with relatives screaming hysterically in the room – I embalmed five members of a Pakistani family who had been killed in a house fire.

Mr Muller seemed very excited. 'More fluid. Ah, Mummy look wonderful, Albin. You've done good job. What do you think, eh? Very good! Very good. Mummy, she live forever. Ja Ja.'

'God only knows about that,' I responded.

Two men from the local funeral directors arrived within half an hour. Despite the somewhat unusual nature of the removal, they seemed to take it all in their stride, though I could see from the looks on their faces that they thought Mr Muller a rather strange character. They placed his mother in a body bag, lifted her on to a stretcher and carried her out to the van. Cliff, Simon and I said our goodbyes to Mr Muller, told him not to worry and got into the car the local funeral director had sent. His mother would be in her capsule in Detroit within forty-eight hours.

'Are you sure, Albin? The ice no shmelt?' asked Mr Muller with concern.

'No, Mr Muller. You have nothing to worry about. Now, I think we had better go.' Before we did, he made us stand there while he walked around us with his camera. I felt like some strange species of animal, a bit like one of those stuffed birds of his, in fact.

As we were about to move off in the van, Mr Muller came running out of the house. What could be the matter now I wondered, winding down the window. 'You know, Rose, she like Mummy,' he said, trying to recover his breath. 'Tell her she is welcome to stay here if ever she comes to Germany.' He was a kind man really.

'I will, Mr Muller,' I replied, trying to keep a straight face. 'I'm sure she will be most grateful for the offer.'

Once at the funeral home, a small place at the end of a row of shops in the town centre, Mr Muller's mother was taken into the mortuary. Here, she was placed in a specially made container with polystyrene and ice inside, which I had shipped out in advance. Our primary task was to cool her head down. This is because the quicker the head area is cooled down the more chance there is of the brain cells remaining intact. Fortunately, the local funeral directors had provided the ten bags of ice I had requested.

'Dad,' said Simon, who had been wonderful throughout the perfusion. 'Guess what.'

'What,' I replied, preoccupied with breaking the ice into small pieces with a hammer.

'Look over there.'

I looked up and, lo and behold, who was standing in the doorway but Mr Muller. 'Ah, Mr Muller. Fancy seeing you here.'

'How's it going, Albin?' he said, pointing his camera at me. 'I come to see Mummy packed in ice.'

'Fine, but I think it's better if you go home now. We have to work very quickly to get your mother on that flight tonight.'

'Mummy very cold now. Albin, he make her very safe in ice.'

'That's right, Mr Muller. Now we've got to keep working.' Despite his somewhat eccentric manner, there was something endearing about him. And he was a sincere man who only wanted what he thought was the best for his mother.

He nodded and backed away, still pointing his camera. Reaching the door, he said, 'Albin, Mummy live forever? Albin, well done.'

After packing the coffin with ice, it was hermetically sealed and I completed the usual documentation to say that the container didn't contain drugs, guns or suchlike. The coffin was then placed in a van and driven to the cargo section at Dortmund Airport for a flight that evening to New York. Once there, she would be transferred on to a flight to Detroit, where staff from the Cryonics Institute would be waiting. I then phoned the Cryonics Institute to give them the flight details.

Mr Muller's mother would have what is known as full-body suspension. Other cryonics organisations, such as Alcol, who at one time had a facility in Eastbourne, carry out head-only suspensions, arguing that it is the brain that needs to be kept for the future and that the rest of the body will eventually be able to be replaced by new parts through cloning. I would never get involved in head-only suspensions, as to me this smacks of Frankenstein or the

271

Steve Martin film *The Man With Two Brains*. I had to explain this to a man who turned up at my funeral home one day and casually asked if he could sign up for a head-only suspension.

A few weeks after my encounter with Mr Muller, a letter arrived one morning from the Cryonics Institute, congratulating me on successfully carrying out the perfusion and the transportation from Essen to Detroit. Everything had been fine. It's always nice to be told you have done a good job. Often, I feel, we are quicker to complain than to give praise. The final paragraph of the letter added that Mr Muller had turned up unannounced at the institute to see his mother. I had to smile to myself reading this and I could picture the scene as Mr Muller clambered up the ladder on the side of the capsule to look inside to make sure his mother was there. I would love to have been a fly on the wall when he discovered that all he could see when the lid of the capsule was removed was the mist from the liquid nitrogen. What's more, did he have his video camera with him? Oh, I bet he did.

Because cryonics sounds far-fetched, and straight out of science fiction, people are fascinated by it. I've lost count of the number of times I have given radio or TV interviews about being the only funeral director in Europe involved in cryonics. I'm sure that producers and researchers have logged me down in their contact books as 'Barry Albin, The Cryonic Man'.

The subject has been explored in popular culture, as in the film *Forever Young*, where the character played by Mel Gibson comes back to life after being frozen for a number of years. And Denis Potter's play *Cold Lazarus* featured a man whose brain was revived nearly four centuries after it was frozen. Cryonics even received the comical treatment in the *Austin Powers* film.

Woody Allen is said to be a cryonicist. He once reportedly said, 'I don't want to live on in my work or my films; I want to live on in my apartment.' I don't know if it's true that Michael Jackson has signed up, as some say, or whether Walt Disney has been cryonically suspended (I believe Mickey Mouse is though!). But there is a man in Italy who has signed up to have his cat suspended, and there is an English family who have all signed up. At school, the son is known as 'ice pop'. So far, no one in the UK has been cryonically suspended.

The price of a lifetime's care at the Cryonics Institute, the cheapest of several cryonics organisations in the US, doesn't come cheaply. Each of the institute's several hundred members pays $28,000 dollars (it's $35,000 for a 'last-minute' membership, but this is not guaranteed). Some people have, I believe, set up trusts in Lichtenstein so that they will have some money when they come back. There are others, I gather, who have left the institute large sums to protect its long-term future – and, as they see it, their own. The institute guarantees to keep you frozen until science is able to bring you back to life. Interestingly, the Cryonics Institute puts a percentage of its income into research into the causes of things such as cell damage and Alzheimer's. I have heard that during some of this research scientists believe they may have found a cure for Alzheimer's, although they are still at the stage of clinical trials.

Cryonics, of course, is man's battle to overcome death and gain eternal life or, at least, an extended life. Our deepest desire is not to die. Our deepest desire is not to die because death – the door to the unknown – frightens us. On the other side will either be eternal life, in some form, or oblivion. Most cultures and religions have a belief in eternity. The ancient Egyptians, for example, believed that when they embalmed someone after death they were preparing them for a journey to eternity. That was why they placed food, valuable jewellery and other personal effects in the coffin.

But, as Judy Finnegan pointed out during that *This Morning* interview, if the brave new world of cryonics ever does come about, you don't know what kind of a world you might return to. Imagine if you woke up and found yourself living in a Nazi-style dictatorship, for example. I for one wouldn't fancy that. Cryonicists, on the other hand, argue that it would be wonderful if great figures such as St Paul, Plato, Shakespeare or Beethoven had been cryonically suspended, then, one day, they might have been able to return to the world and continue to enrich it.

Some people however are, understandably, disturbed by cryonics. I remember an argument I once had with a Catholic priest. When he accused me of playing around with life and death, I pointed out that I was simply preparing the dead. I told him I believed that only God could give life and take it away and if you had faith, then why should cryonics be a problem? In fact, a Catholic priest, with permission from his bishop, consecrated one of the cryostats.

What is wrong, after all, with people wanting to be frozen and placed in a capsule containing liquid nitrogen? It doesn't hurt anyone and gives many people a great deal of comfort – even if it is, in my opinion, misguided. But if you have no faith and believe this is the only life, then you want to hang on to it. I believe in a better life to come, so I don't need to overstay my welcome in this one.

Some cryonicists argue that if a person is suffering from something such as cancer or Alzheimer's, and you kill them by a lethal injection, they can then be returned to life at a later date, in good health. I cannot share this view that cryonics offers a solution to all the suffering in the world. Nor would I want to play God – even though roadside advertising hoardings in Italy once carried my photo with the words: 'This man can help you live forever.' In my view, suffering will always be a part of the human condition and, what's more, we will only return to life at the Resurrection.'

So why am I involved in cryonics if I don't believe in it? And doesn't cryonics clash with my Catholic beliefs? Ever since I conducted my first funeral, of that West Indian child in Brixton, when I realised that what was important was what the family wanted, not the funeral rules made by F. A. Albin & Sons, I have always believed that one of the most important tasks for a funeral director is to provide people with choice: whether to be embalmed or not; when they can visit the chapel of rest; the choice of a particular coffin or casket; a Rolls Royce hearse or a horse-drawn hearse; the day and time of the funeral service; the hymns or songs that they wish to be sung; the kind of floral tributes; the cemetery or crematorium; the type of headstone and inscription, and so on. I am proud that F. A. Albin & Sons have more stars than any other funeral director listed in the US-published Blue Book, a sort of Egon Ronay guide to funeral directors.

And that's why I became involved in cryonics, because it gives people more choice about what happens to them after

death. You might think that I do it for the money. I don't.
I haven't made any money from cryonics, although the
publicity I have received has, I admit, raised the profile of
the firm. If a person wants to be cryonically suspended,
have a woodland burial, have their ashes scattered at sea or
over Tower Bridge, be mummified (there's an organisation
in Salt Lake City that offers this) or placed inside a cryostat,
attached to a satellite and sent into space, then that's fine
by me. I need to be able to offer every way of disposing of
the dead. My role as a funeral director is not to judge
people but to undertake to care for the dead and for the
living.

While belief in Heaven is declining, at least in the West,
interest in cryonics is growing. In February 2001 I had the
unique and fascinating experience of assisting in a cryonic
suspension. This came about when I flew out to Detroit with
distinguished broadcaster and writer Edward Stourton and a
team from the BBC2 documentary series *Correspondent*. The
programme makers had invited me to take part in an edition
dealing with issues of human rights, life and death.

Since my previous visit to the Cryonics Institute quite a
lot had changed. The institute now occupied a low-rise
modern brick building in an industrial park in Clifton
Township, Michigan, a few miles north-east of Detroit
(Clifton Township has the dubious distinction of being the
home of controversial rapper Marshall Mathers III alias
Eminem). In black lettering on wooden panelling above
the glass doors are the words Erfurt Runkel Building. The
name is taken from two founder members, who are now
among the thirty-seven deceased persons suspended in
cryostats.

As we walked along one of the corridors I glimpsed

framed photographs of the deceased lining the walls. Each one captured the person in the younger or mid-life days because that was how the institute hoped to restore them. One important part of the institute that hadn't changed was the keeper, although I noticed he had got rid of his rolled-up collar.

In addition, I learned from Mr Ettinger Junior, that there are seven dogs and nine cats suspended. The cost for a cat or animal of a similar size is $5,800. Larger animals cost around the same price as a human, $28,000. What's more, the institute claims to have the world's largest cryostat. A white, rectangular construction, it is seven feet long, four feet wide and six and a half feet deep, and contains fourteen people – including Mrs Muller.

Also at the institute are the bones and tissue of a young man who was murdered somewhere in the Congo, I believe, and then buried in the sand. His remains were eventually recovered by his father and brought to the institute, where he was suspended. The thinking runs that because there are samples of his DNA, the young man might be able to be restored to life.

While we were filming, there was a flurry of activity and I looked around to see the twenty-four-hour, white-coated cryonics medical team wheeling in a trolley containing an elderly woman. Would I like to assist in the suspension asked the keeper, adding that the lady had been flown in from her home in Los Angeles, where, as is common practice, the team had used CPR and then placed her on a heart and lung machine to maintain circulation and the health of the tissues. The lady had then been placed in a casket, which had been packed with ice by a local undertaker.

Slightly surprised, I answered that, yes, I would like to assist. Edward Stourton's eyes lit up at this unexpected development. I donned a white body suit and rubber gloves and entered the operating theatre, where the lady was now on a steel table under six surgical lights. Her gown had been removed and her private parts covered with cloth, and she was having six tubes from an electronic pump attached to her arteries.

Following instructions from the team leader, I began to massage her hands, feet and legs as one of the team pumped heparin in to open her arteries, just as I had done with Mr Muller's mother. Looking at the cameraman tracking every move, and the enthralled expression on Edward Stourton's face, I couldn't but help think of Mr Muller with his video camera. I half expected to hear, 'Mummy good! Mummy good! Albin what you think?'

The lady's body was now dehydrated and had turned a yellowy brown colour. This is normal. We lifted her up and carried her over to a brown cool-down box with four handles. One of the team lifted the lid and we lowered her in. Wire netting was then placed over her. Another team member then placed blocks of dried ice on top of the netting. Dried ice doesn't rise. It's temperature drops downwards. The final task was to place a thermometer in the box.

The lady would remain in the box for two weeks until the temperature had reached minus eighty degrees centigrade. The reason for this delay before suspension is completed is so that the cells of the body are not damaged. Once the body had reached the right temperature it would be taken out of the cool-down box, wrapped in a white sleeping bag, and carried on a trolley to one of the

278

cylindrical cryostats which are kept behind locked metal cages. Using mobile ladders either side of the cryostat, the team, wearing face masks, would open the smoking cryostat and lower the lady inside, usually upside down, where she would be frozen to minus 196 degrees centigrade. After this, the lady would be taken out and placed in another cryostat, which would become her final resting place – or a temporary one.

Although Edward Stourton found the whole thing bizarre, he didn't send it up. He found the idea of cryonics, and the claims of its supporters, fascinating.

Afterwards, he said to me, 'Well, Barry, is it for you?'

'No. Is it for you?'

He didn't need to answer. The expression on his face said it all.

As I've already said, and as I told an intrigued Edward Stourton during the making of the programme, I see cryonics as nothing more than another form of embalming. Both processes, in different ways, preserve the body after death. What's the difference between embalming someone and burying them in Camberwell New Cemetery or placing them in a cryostat in Detroit? Either way you are dead. If you are buried or cremated there is no chance of you being brought back to life, other than at the last day, of course. And not everyone believes in the Christian idea of the Resurrection. But if you are placed in a cryostat and cryonically suspended, that possibility exists, no matter how small, if science makes the kind of leaps that cryonicists believe it will. For cryonicists, this would be their 'resurrection'. Cryonics could be seen as the ultimate insurance policy.

Put another way, if you want a Victorian funeral, I can

supply it. If you want the most modern funeral - or, to coin a new phrase, a techno funeral - i.e. a cryonic suspension, then I can also supply that. And that's what cryonics is, a modern way of providing a resting place for the dead, at least at this time. A hundred years ago, cremation was unheard of because the Church believed that burning a body was sacrilegious, and fire was also depicted in terms of the fires of Hell. Today, two thirds of all funerals in the UK end up at the doors of a crematorium.

Who knows, in a hundred years from now cryonics might be just another option for laying the dead to rest. At the time of writing, I am in the middle of buying a cemetery in south-east London. If I am successful in this purchase, I plan to open a British branch of the Cryonics Institute behind its mausoleum. To me, this makes sense. It would be far easier to carry out cryonic suspensions in London for European clients rather than ship them all the way to America.

Do you remember what I said about counting those marbles? So, then, have you thought about your funeral? Would you like it on a Saturday morning? What music would you like played? Would you like the horses? An Italian coffin? Or an urn in my cremation cemetery? Or do you want to be cryonically suspended? I know when I die I don't want to be cryonically suspended (unless the cryonicists are proved right; then we will all have to revise our thinking about life and death). No. I want to be buried in my old Rolls hearse in the yard of my funeral home - perhaps with a periscope so that I can see what's going on.